Pat Rush began her writing ... living in the Netherlands at ... for British folk musicians, hel... folk festivals, and later produced a weekly programme of folk music for national radio. So most of her early writing was music-related. She contributed to various music publications and also wrote hundreds of publicity handouts for a variety of performers.

In 1981, she returned to England after ten years away, and soon began contributing reviews and features to *The Stage*. Her many hundreds of reviews covered everything from minimal music to music hall and dozens of fringe theatre productions, as well as a large helping of folk music, before she moved away from London in 1987.

She continued to make occasional contributions to *The Stage*, however, and wrote a number of features for other magazines. Then, in 1990, she was asked to edit the first issue of the quarterly *Hugglets Teddy Bear Magazine*. She has been its editor ever since – also writing features on bear shops, bear makers, writers of teddy bear books, painters of teddy bears, and a host of other bear-related subjects. She has also carried out extensive research into the history of various British soft toy manufacturers.

She has contributed to teddy bear magazines in America and Holland, and to a book of *Teddy Bear Stories for Grown-Ups*. She gives talks on teddy bears and has organized Teddy Bear Weekends for readers of *Hugglets Teddy Bear Magazine*.

She has been collecting bears herself for more than twenty years, specializing in English bears – although any bear with an appealing face could persuade her to take him home. She ceased counting them all long ago, but estimates that some four hundred furry friends now share her Kent home.

She continues to write on various other subjects, however, including many different kinds of music.

The
BEAR LOVER'S
Guide to Britain

Pat Rush

Illustrations by
Wendy Sue Wilkinson

PAN BOOKS
LONDON, SYDNEY AND AUCKLAND

First published 1994 by Pan Books

a division of Pan Macmillan Publishers Limited
Cavaye Place London SW10 9PG
and Basingstoke

Associated companies throughout the world

ISBN 0 330 33368 2

1 3 5 7 9 8 6 4 2

A CIP catalogue record for this book is available from
the British Library

Typeset by CentraCet Limited, Cambridge
Printed and bound in Great Britain by
Cox & Wyman Limited, Reading, Berkshire

Contents

TEDDY BEAR WITH
MILITARY BEARING
SQUEAKER IN BODY
C. 1940'S 1/261

Wendy Sue '94.

List of Illustrations

Foreword

Bear lovers are lucky. Not only have numerous shops, museums and other places of bearish interest been springing up in recent years, but many of them are also situated in Britain's most beautiful towns and villages.

This book is intended to help anyone who loves bears to make the most of holidays or outings in Britain. Many of the places featured are ideal destinations for day trips, or even a longer stay, with plenty for all the family as well as the teddy enthusiast. Some can be explored in minutes, others may take an hour or two, but are definitely not to be missed if you are in the area.

There are suggestions both for serious collectors and for those who simply love bears of any shape or form. For this book is not just about building up a valuable collection. It is all about *enjoying* bears, and about making the most of any that you yourself own.

Part One

WHAT TO LOOK FOR

B ears are everywhere these days. Wherever you live, or whichever part of the country you have chosen to visit, you should find something to enhance your collection. The problem is knowing where to look – *and* what to look for. The aim of this book is to show you.

It provides detailed information on a large number of shops and other sources of bears and bear-related items (also known as bearabilia). But of course it is impossible to list each one of the thousands of retailers whose stock includes something with a teddy bear slant. It cannot even hope to include all the specialist teddy bear shops, as new ones are appearing all the time. What I hope it will do, however, is to provide you with ideas, so that wherever you happen to be, you will know how to seek out all the places where bears may be lurking.

Toy shops, gift shops, department stores, stationers, book shops, antique shops, china shops, jewellers – even some clothing stores may have something of interest. Special teddy bear fairs are held all over the country. Antique fairs, postcard fairs, swap meets, car boot sales, auctions – all can yield interesting additions to a collection. But before you can choose which to visit, you need to know what you are looking for. In other words, you need to decide what you want from your collection. One thing is certain: with so many teddy bears around, in every shape and form, no collectors can possibly buy everything they see.

Building up a collection

A bove all, a collection is something which should be enjoyed by its owner. So the most important consideration is whether what you are buying is something that you really love.

Another deciding factor for most people will naturally be, 'Can I afford it?' It is not necessary to spend vast sums in order to build up an interesting collection. Sometimes an outlay of just a few pounds (or even a few pence), in the most unlikely of shops, can dramatically increase the appeal or even the value of your collection.

OLD BEARS

Naturally, there can be no guarantees that a certain kind of collection will increase in value. But if that is what you want from yours, you may decide to specialize in good quality old bears. In this case, you should always aim to buy the best that you can afford, choosing one good bear in preference to two in poorer condition.

Early bears by the German manufacturer Steiff are often the most sought-after – especially those in rare colours and excellent condition. The most coveted are those which still have the Steiff trademark of a button in their ear as proof of their identity. But even those with no such evidence of their origins can still fetch high prices.

Bears by other German manufacturers like Bing and Schuco are also very much in demand. But in recent years there has been a surge of interest in bears by the major British manufacturers like Farnell, Merrythought (see Ironbridge, p. 213), Chiltern and Chad Valley (see Wellington, p. 262).

Generally, bears of a popular make, in good condition and with positive proof of their identity, are the most collectable. But even a balding bear of unknown heritage can cost a tidy sum. There are, however, ways in which you can increase your chances of finding something highly collectable at a more affordable price.

Your most useful tool is a good knowledge of the bears made by the various manufacturers. Unlabelled bears usually sell for quite a bit less than bears carrying some form of identifying mark. If, however, you know your bears so well that you can positively identify one with no identification marks (or perhaps with just the tiniest scrap of a label remaining), you have a far greater chance of finding a bargain.

The more bears you see, the more familiar will you become with them, and the greater your ability to make a positive identification. So visit as many teddy bear fairs and good antique fairs as you can, and any bear shops selling old bears. Have a good look at the bears, especially any with positive identification, and gradually you will find that you begin to get a 'feel' for those bears made by a certain company.

It is not just a question of the length of the arms, the shape of the head, the size of the feet or the stitching on the paws and nose, all of which are useful indicators. There are other, less definable characteristics which can only be recognized by seeing and handling a large number of bears.

Visits to teddy bear museums are another useful way of building up your knowledge (there are several mentioned in this book). So, too, are auctions. Several London auction houses, for instance, hold regular sales of toys, which often include a good number of teddy bears (see London: Auctions, p. 57). You may have no hope of buying any of the bears, although prices sometimes cover a very wide range. But you can still go to the pre-sale viewing and have a good look at the bears due to go under the hammer. Many of them will have been identified for you by the auction house's staff, and details will be included in the sale catalogue.

There are a large number of informative teddy bear books now available, too, including identification guides for everyone from beginners to experienced collectors. You may find one or two in your local library. But if you are serious about building up a good collection of old bears, you will want to start a library of your own. Study the books and become familiar with the bears illustrated. Then, if you see one for sale, you'll have a head start when it comes to recognition.

Until then, if you want your bears to be of a known make, it is best to stick to those with some positive form of identification, or to buy from a knowledgeable dealer that you trust to make that identification for you. If you are after a bargain, however, you need to find a bear that *you* recognize as collectable but that the seller does not.

Occasionally, you may find one in a general antique or bric-à-brac shop, although such dealers are becoming increasingly aware of values. (In fact, many bears from such sources are over- rather than under-priced.) General auctions may also yield the odd bargain, although you may have to visit dozens before you find a single bear, or at least a bear that hasn't attracted the attention of too many other bidders.

The same is true of jumble sales and car boot sales. Seasoned car booters know you have to be early to beat the dealers and snatch up a bargain. And even if you're out at the crack of dawn, you could still spend Sunday after Sunday trekking round stalls without seeing a single interesting teddy. Sellers are now far too aware of their potential value.

Nevertheless, people still do make interesting finds — especially of more recent English bears which can also be highly collectable. So it certainly pays to know what is what.

If you are visiting an unknown town, always make a point of checking the local paper (there's bound to be a copy in the library if you don't want to buy one). Special events like antique fairs, collectors' meets, car boot sales, jumble sales and auctions will be advertised there.

Incidentally, if you are buying a bear from its original owner or a member of their family, do ask them if they know anything about its history – when and where it was bought, for instance, and who its original owner was. Such information – the bear's provenance – can add considerably to its interest and value. It is also worth asking if they have a picture of the bear when it was young, possibly with its young guardian. You could then frame it and display it alongside the bear itself.

Even dealers may occasionally be able to tell you the history of a bear you wish to buy – if only that it was found in an attic. In some cases, they may be able to put you in touch with the original owner.

MODERN COLLECTABLES

Not everyone, however, wants to collect old bears. Many people find that the ones they like are invariably beyond their price range. Others simply prefer more modern creations. For them, there really is something to suit virtually every pocket, although it is far less easy to say which will increase in value, and by how much.

Some of the most collectable modern bears are again those made by the German company Steiff. Each year they produce replicas of a number of old bears, using the original patterns, and furs that are as close to the originals as possible. Many are produced in limited editions, usually of a few thousand bears each, and every bear is numbered. In general, the lower the total number in the edition, the more collectable the bear.

The most popular replicas are snapped up quickly and can rapidly increase in value once the whole edition has been sold.

There are other, unlimited ranges as well, like the Historic Steiff Miniatures introduced in 1992. The Classic teddies are reproductions of early bears, in unlimited editions but again produced with collectors in mind. Then there is the standard range, which includes both traditional, jointed bears and softer, cuddly teddies (both jointed and unjointed). The former have more appeal for collectors.

Prices vary enormously, with limited edition bears costing more than Classic and standard range bears of a similar size. But it is the limited editions which are the most sought after by collectors. Most specialist bear shops will stock a selection, and you will find them in some good gift shops as well as at fairs for collectors. Sometimes, however, you will find an even greater selection in a good toy shop, and many department stores sell them, too.

In fact, some popular replicas do not even reach the shelves of the specialists, who often receive a large number of advance orders from enthusiasts. If an edition has been available for a while, you may have more luck in finding what you want at a non-specialist shop.

A large number of stockists are mentioned in this book, but again it is impossible to be totally comprehensive, so it pays to keep your eyes open. In particular, don't forget to check the gift departments as well as the toy departments of major stores, as that is sometimes where the more collectable bears can be found.

Even modern Steiff collectables can prove beyond the pockets of many collectors, however – especially the limited editions. But fortunately there are many other manufacturers producing bears for collectors, and the range of prices is wide.

British soft toy companies like Merrythought and Dean's, for instance, now produce special ranges for collectors in addition to their toys for children. Germany's Gebr. Hermann and sigikid do, too, and so do some American firms, like Gund.

Serious collectors usually prefer limited editions, and mohair is generally more popular than synthetic plushes. But, as with every collection, it is still important to buy bears you love rather than to try to guess which will be the best investment.

Again, you will find selections of collectable bears from various manufacturers in most specialist teddy bear shops, as well as in many gift shops and toy shops and at teddy bear fairs. You may even find some in certain clothing shops, who sometimes commission their own special bears, to be sold exclusively by them. Canterbury Bears, for instance, have made bears for shops like Liberty, the Scotch House, Laura Ashley and Simpson's of Piccadilly. Merrythought make a whole range for Burberrys. Some of these shops have branches in a number of different towns, so it is worth keeping an eye open for them.

Of course, most gift shops and toy shops, and even most specialist teddy bear shops, also stock large numbers of less expensive, soft and cuddly bears, intended as gifts for children and loved ones rather than for the collectors market. Most are manufactured in the Far East. In general, these make less interesting additions to a collection, simply because of the vast numbers that are made. Now, however, a number of companies are bringing out budget lines of appealing, traditional bears made specially with the less well-off collector in mind. Golden Gifts' Tails and Tales is one such range, the Boyds Collection is another.

Later on I'll also be suggesting some ways of turning even the most unpromising budget buys into an interesting collection.

ARTIST BEARS

A relatively new development that has aroused massive interest among serious collectors is the so-called artist bear. These bears are designed and made not by large manufacturers but by individual craftsmen and women, usually in their own homes.

Many such makers are responsible for every stage in the

production of the bears – designing the pattern, cutting out the pieces, machining the seams, stuffing, inserting joints, stitching mouths and noses, tying ribbons and everything else that is needed to create a saleable bear. Others employ helpers to assist with certain processes like machining and jointing. But all design their own bears and most insist that the head at least is completed entirely by them.

In America, artist bears have had a strong following for many years now, with artists creating ever more innovative designs. Now British makers are catching up fast, with many of the most popular fighting a never-ending battle to keep up with the demand.

One of the great attractions of these bears for collectors is the small numbers made in each design. Collectors like to have something unique, or as near unique as possible. Bear artists supply that. Most of their bears are made in very small limited editions of twenty-five or ten or perhaps just four or five. Some artists even go a stage further, and make unique, one-off bears as well. Such creations are invariably popular with collectors, who are always looking for something different.

Such small editions also mean that the artists are constantly bringing out new designs, and many go to great lengths to ensure that they are offering collectors something that no one else can offer. Some dye their own furs or seek out unusual fabrics from which to make their bears. (It is not unusual to see an old coat or tablecloth or even curtains being reincarnated as collectable bears.) Others experiment with new mechanisms for jointing bears – so that the head can be posed more appealingly, perhaps, or so that the bear can bend its arms and legs at elbows and knees.

New stuffing materials are used (many artist bears are stuffed with tiny plastic pellets, for instance). New shapes are tried. And, increasingly, all sorts of costumes and trimmings are employed to add character and interest. Sometimes a whole tableau will be created, perhaps using several bears and a large number of 'props'. These can take the form of anything from a special Christmas design to characters in a television series, or a colourful 'strawbeary' picker whose 'strawbearies' are bright red teddy bear heads.

Some of the most original designs will be found at special teddy bear fairs, where bears can often be bought direct from the artists themselves. But artist bears can also be found at most specialist teddy bear shops. In fact, many shops ask artists to design bears specially for them. These so-called 'shop exclusives' are nearly always in small editions. They generally sell out very quickly, however, so it is impossible to give any precise details in this book.

Naturally, the cost of such bears can vary enormously, depending on the amount of work involved and the popularity of the artist. But many shops try to include bears by good, new, local artists in their ranges. So if you keep your eyes open, you may be able to find a bargain before a promising new artist is discovered by other bear lovers.

SPECIALIZING

Whether you opt to collect old bears or new bears, manufactured bears, artist bears, or a combination of them all, you will certainly be spoilt for choice. But there is no doubt that some of the most interesting collections are those in which there is some degree of specialization. For it is this which gives your collection its individuality.

Of course, this doesn't mean that you should restrict all your collecting to one or two particular areas. There will always be bears that you simply must take home, for no other reason than that you love them. But if at least part of your collection adheres to a certain theme, this can certainly add extra interest.

The possibilities are endless. If money is no object, for

instance, you might want to concentrate on splendid old Steiffs in beautiful condition. But for most people this is not a realistic option.

For lovers of old bears, a less expensive – but by no means inexpensive – option could be to concentrate on bears by just one British manufacturer. Those by Farnell are greatly sought after, and bears by Merrythought, Chad Valley, Chiltern and Dean's are also very popular.

Some people restrict themselves to a special colour, like pink or blue, but with old bears this can mean a lot of searching.

Collectors of modern bears can also concentrate on a single manufacturer. But with so many bears being produced, there are now endless other possibilities as well.

Some collectors have a large number of bears from a single artist; others buy each one of their bears from a different artist. With so many different fabrics being used today, another possibility with artist bears is to gather a multitude of different colours, or to specialize in a single unbear-like colour. A large splash of red or pink can look absolutely stunning in a collection made up mainly of bears in typically bearish brown.

Novelty bears are another interesting area. Old mechanical bears, pouring themselves a drink or turning the pages of a book, now sell for hefty sums. But some present-day manufacturers have also come up with modern mechanical designs, and some artists are incorporating intriguing mechanisms into their work.

Musical bears have included dancing bears and bears whose heads turn while the music plays. There have been somersaulting bears, bears riding bicycles, and bears whose heads not only turn round but also nod up and down. New ideas are emerging all the time, and many more will no doubt appear as makers continue to develop new techniques.

Miniature bears are an option for those for whom space is at a premium. This has been a growing field in recent years, with several manufacturers producing small bears in a variety of designs. A number of bear artists are specializing in tiny creations, often exquisitely dressed, as well. The time taken to make these bears means, however, that prices can be almost as much as those for their larger brothers.

Larger *dressed* bears are also now very much in demand and could provide another kind of specialization. Television characters, sporting bears, or bears engaged in various crafts are just a few of the ideas that artists have come up with. All could provide a theme for a collection. As such bears take a good deal of time to make, however, prices are generally higher than those for bears with no clothes – especially if the artist actually makes the clothes rather than buying them off the peg.

A relatively recent development has been an increase in the availability of artist bears from other countries. As more and more countries fall under the spell of the teddy bear, specialist shops start to sell their bears. Splendid American creations have been on sale for some years, and it would be possible to build up a magnificent collection from these alone. But now certain shops are ordering their bears from a whole variety of sources, both in Europe and further afield.

A number of makers from Australia and New Zealand sell their work here, for instance. You may find artist bears from France, Holland, Belgium and Germany, too. I've seen Swedish bears, and also exquisite Japanese creations, including some bears in splendid miniature kimonos.

Often the designs are very different from those of British artists, with makers being influenced and inspired by fabrics available locally as well as those imported from British weavers. Cotton plush is popular with Dutch makers, for instance, while I've seen an Australian bear actually made from fish skin. (Although its surface was covered with scales, it fortunately smelt more of leather than fish!)

BUDGET COLLECTIONS

Of course, collections of old bears or artist bears do not come cheap and most, if not all, of the above options may be beyond the means of many bear lovers. But a lack of funds need not prevent you building up a good collection of your own. It may take a little more effort, and certainly a bit more ingenuity. But your collection will probably be all the more enjoyable for that.

I have mentioned before the possibility of finding interesting bears at jumble sales and car boot sales. You can still find inexpensive yet highly collectable bears in antique shops and at antique or teddy bear fairs if you have a good eye. You may, however, need to visit a good number before you find anything worthwhile.

Although it would be rare to find a really old bear, even in poor condition, selling at a fraction of its value, what you may find is something interesting from the fifties or sixties. Many people believe these are too new to have any value. Collectors know otherwise. Unjointed bears, too, can often be overlooked by collectors. But early ones made by well-known British companies can sometimes be found at really bargain prices, and are well worth buying.

Another way of adding interest to some very ordinary bears is to look for things that can be displayed with them. It is amazing what a difference that can make, and often an outlay of a pound or two (or even less) can dramatically enhance your collection. You will find plenty of examples in the sections which follow.

PICTURE THIS

Cuddly, fluffy teddies may be adorable, for instance, but they are not generally considered to be very collectable. However, many of these bears are pictured on greetings cards or postcards. It is worth keeping an eye open for cards featuring bears identical to those in your collection. Displaying the card alongside the bear gives him a whole new dimension.

Of course, this idea can also be applied to any other kind of bear. As you can obtain even highly collectable old teddy bear postcards for a fraction of the amount you would need to buy another bear, they are a splendid way of enhancing your collection when funds are low.

Suppose you love old bears, for instance, but they are way beyond your means. An attractive display of postcards showing beautiful old bears could be a pleasing compromise. You could choose either old cards, showing the bears as they used to be, or (for even less outlay) a selection of modern cards featuring the old bears as they are today.

You'll find old postcards at many antique fairs as well as special postcard fairs (local papers or collectors' magazines will give you details). Modern teddy bear postcards appear in all sorts of gift shops and stationers, as well as museum shops and the specialist teddy bear shops.

If your 'collection' of old bears is limited to just one or two, you can again use postcards to add to their impact. Some of the old drawings of bears by postcard artists like Donald McGill and Ellam can look particularly good alongside the old bears themselves.

But it is not only old bears that can be enhanced in this way. Suppose you have a collection of new or mainly new bears by a certain manufacturer. It is always worth looking out for greetings cards and postcards featuring that company's bears. They can really add impact to a collection.

Many artists are now producing postcards of some of their bears. So if your collection includes artist bears, look out for any artist-bear postcards, too. Artists will often have them on their stands at teddy bear fairs.

Illustrations from books and magazines can be used in a similar way. Say you respond to an advertisement offering a bear at a special price or in return for so many box tops or labels. Keep a copy of the advertisement and display it alongside the bear. Most of these bears are not of a kind that would normally be considered collectable. But it would be possible to build up a fascinating collection purely from such promotional bears, together with the relevant advertisements from magazines or packaging.

You can often find these bears at car boot sales and jumble sales, or in all sorts of retail shops, where they are offered free with a certain purchase. If you acquire one, see if you can get a copy of the advertisement as well.

In fact, as such offers are necessarily limited, some of these bears actually become quite collectable in their own right. So it is also worth keeping an eye open for photos of them in books published for collectors and enthusiasts. If you find one of your bears illustrated, you can make him a real focus of attention by keeping the open book alongside the bear itself.

Again, this is something that applies to all sorts of other bears as well. Look out for books and magazines containing photographs of bears that you also own – or even whole articles on a favourite manufacturer or artist. Then display the open book or magazine together with the relevant bears.

Many teddy bear shops sell teddy bear magazines, and some also have a selection of books for collectors. But you will also find some collectors guides in general bookshops. In fact, many turn up in bargain bookshops, so don't leave those out of your bear hunts. Sometimes you will find whole books of teddy bear postcards there as well.

If you collect bears from a particular manufacturer, there may be various other ways in which you can add to your collection even when you cannot afford (or find) a new bear. Look out for their advertisements in magazines. Keep an eye open, too, for advertisements for retailers featuring your chosen firm's bears. See if you can obtain any of the company's catalogues. You will sometimes find these in teddy bear shops or at teddy bear fairs.

OTHER BEAR-RELATED COLLECTABLES

Certain bear manufacturers produce other promotional material such as badges, pencils, T-shirts and mugs, which again can be useful additions to a collection. Some are given away free, others are offered for sale, but even then they are usually considerably less expensive than the bears themselves. Look out for them in teddy bear shops and at teddy bear fairs where manufacturers sometimes have their own stands.

You may also be able to find ceramic miniatures of bears that you would love to have in your own collection but cannot find or afford 'in the fur'. These can be displayed with your own bears or built up into a delightful collection in their own right.

There are numerous teddy bear ornaments on the market now, of varying qualities and at a whole range of prices. But even for those on a budget, it is possible to build up an interesting display. Try keeping to a certain theme – sporting bears, say, or artist bears, or something else which relates to one of your non-bearish interests. Or look for different versions of a favourite character bear. Winnie-the-Pooh ceramics, for instance, range from inexpensive representations of characters from the books to large and incredibly detailed tableaux costing several hundred pounds.

You will find ceramic teddy bears in a huge number of shops – teddy bear shops, gift shops and the gift departments of large stores, stationers, china shops, souvenir shops. Hand-crafted ones may be found in craft shops and at craft fairs. Secondhand ones crop up on bric-à-brac stalls and at car boot sales. Even the smallest village may have something to add to your collection.

All sorts of other teddy bear-related items – or 'bearabilia' – are on sale, too, and what you choose to collect will be decided both by your interests and your pocket.

Maybe you have a china collection as well as a collection of bears. China featuring teddy bears will link your two interests. Old teddy bear china is particularly sought-after by collectors. But as the demand is high and the supply is small, prices can be just as high as for the bears themselves.

You may find something in a shop selling antiques or bric-à-brac, or at an antique or teddy bear fair. But don't expect any bargains unless you are lucky enough to spot something at a car boot sale or jumble sale.

Modern china featuring teddy bears can, on the other hand, be found for anything from a few pounds upwards, depending on how fine the piece is. Keep your eyes open in shops selling cookware as well as in fine china shops and the china departments of large stores. As usual, the more exclusive a piece is, the more collectable it is likely to be. But even inexpensive items, well displayed, can look extremely good in a collection.

China is just one of many kinds of bearabilia that you might find on your travels, however. The list really is endless although, of course, it is often the older pieces which are the most collectable. Look out for bears in children's games or on jewellery, or turned into any number of useful implements. Old wooden carvings of real bears appear on all sorts of devices made in the Black Forest and Switzerland, for instance – from clothes brushes to ashtrays, inkwells to pincushions, to name just a few. Again, the prices often reflect the collectability of the items, but bargains can still occasionally be found.

Modern bearabilia is much more prevalent, but although much of it may be fun to own, it is often produced in far too large a quantity to be very collectable. More unusual items are, as always, generally the most interesting, so keep your eyes open when visiting craft shops and craft fairs. You may be able to pick up something just that bit different, perhaps made by a local craftsman.

Alternatively, you could try picking a single speciality – like egg cups or stationery or cushions – and then collect as many different versions as you can. What you choose will depend on both the space you have available and how much money you have to spend.

There are so many teddy bear-related items available at the moment that you could, if you wished, equip almost your whole house with them. I've seen bears on blinds, wallpaper, bedding, shower curtains, soap dishes, lamps, wastepaper baskets, clocks, plates, cutlery, rugs, biscuit tins, tea caddies, and much, much more.

Mass-produced ranges will not necessarily enhance a collection. But well-chosen items displayed alongside the bears themselves can often add interest. A naughty bear can really come to life with his paw in a teddy-decorated biscuit tin. Or try placing a small plate of teddy-shaped sweets in front of the plumpest bear in your collection. Once you start looking, you will find yourself adding to your collection in the most unlikely places.

ON DISPLAY

All sorts of non-bearish items can be used to enhance a teddy bear display as well, and it is worth bearing this in mind when visiting a strange town. It can add a whole new dimension to your bear hunts and ensure that you rarely come home empty-handed. There are bargains galore to be found if you know what to look for and where to find them.

The most obvious example is clothing for your bears. A few years ago, most collectors adhered to the 'bare is best' policy. But the past few years have seen a dramatic increase in the popularity of dressed bears. Some well-chosen togs can really bring out all the character in a bear.

An old bear, for instance, might look perfect in a beautiful white christening gown, or a flower-trimmed hat, or simply a delicate lace collar. Look through piles of old children's clothes and dolls' clothes. But remember that bears are a different shape from both children and dolls. They tend to have large necks, plump arms and legs, and rounded tums, so you need to keep this in mind when looking for suitable clothes.

If you are handy with a needle, you could of course look instead for some interesting old fabric from which to make the clothes yourself.

Some old-style modern bears can also look good in antique clothes. But many can look just as stunning in more modern designs, like colourful shirts and dungarees, cheerful romper suits, T-shirts and shorts, or pretty frocks. If you like dressed bears, keep your eyes open for possibilities in chain stores, on market stalls, in charity shops, and at car boot sales and jumble sales. Or, if you have more to spend, have a look in some of the smarter children's wear shops that you see. They will usually offer something a little bit different and, if you are dressing an expensive bear, it might be worth paying that bit extra to find something that is just right.

As small children tend to grow out of their clothes rather than wear them out you can often find wonderful secondhand bargains.

Bear-sized accessories are everywhere, too – often intended for children, but frequently just what you need for a larger bear. Look out for little bags for them to carry, small chairs for them to sit on, pretty cushions to lean them against, or toys and games for them to play with. Small tea sets are also useful for creating teddy bear picnics, and it is not even necessary to seek out one decorated with teddy bears, although these are especially attractive.

Of course, for older bears you will generally want to find older accessories. But these need not cost a fortune. You may find just what you need selling for only a pound or two in a bric-à-brac shop, or for even less at a car boot sale. And once you start looking you'll see interesting possibilities at every turn.

Larger items like prams, cots and wooden chests also make wonderful display aids if you again look for things that comple-ment the bears in your collection.

More modern bears can often be teamed up with more modern accessories. But traditional, hand-crafted bears generally look better with traditional, hand-crafted props. Look out for wooden toys, like trains and trucks, for your bears to play with, and traditional games made of natural materials. You'll find them in certain toy shops and on craft stalls, and in some gift shops as well.

For tiny teddies, try creating a display using doll's house miniatures. A number of bear shops sell these as well, and many toy fairs include both stands selling teddies and those selling doll's house furniture and accessories.

THE BEAR COLLECTOR'S LIBRARY

Teddy bear story books can also be useful display aids. An older bear could bury his head in a beautifully illustrated tale of a similar age, while a modern bear could take charge of more recent books. Several are now produced in miniature versions as well as full-size editions. Needless to say, these bear-sized books look especially good with the bears themselves.

Teddy bear books can also make a splendid collection in their own right. But when it comes to the story books, you will be competing with book collectors as well as bear collectors, so prices can be very high.

First editions of A. A. Milne's *Winnie-the-Pooh* and *The House at Pooh Corner* can go for hundreds of pounds if they are still in good condition, complete with dustwrapper. Even a less pristine copy can fetch as much as a nice old bear. But third or fourth reprints – identical to the first edition except for the date – are much more affordable, and are much more likely to turn up in secondhand bookshops.

In recent years there have been Winnie-the-Pooh pop-up books, colouring books and cook books as well as Latin translations and even an explanation of Taoism using the bear and his friends. But most are considered less collectable. A large number of miniature books containing Pooh stories have also been produced. Again, they are available in far too great a number to be collectors' items, but they are useful for teddy bear displays.

Early Rupert books are as eagerly collected as early editions of *Winnie-the-Pooh*. Again, rare editions in good condition sell for many hundreds of pounds. But the more recent annuals are much more affordable and can often be found in secondhand bookshops. Some turn up in car boot sales as well.

Constance Wickham's beautifully illustrated teddy bear stories are among the many other older teddy bear books that now fetch high prices. But there are more affordable tales by other writers – often with charming black and white illustrations.

Gwynedd Rae's Mary Plain books were inspired by a real bear cub seen in Berne's famous bear pits. First published in 1930, there were about a dozen books in all, and although first editions have become highly collectable, it is still possible to find more affordable reprints.

Other favourites with collectors are Margaret J. Baker's Shoe Shop Bears, James Roose-Evans' Odd and Elsewhere, Mrs H. C. Craddock's Big Teddy and Little Teddy, and stories by Elizabeth Gorell. There are also some delightful books about a Cockney bear called Albert, written by Alison Jezard. Some are still available in paperback, while others can sometimes be picked up secondhand without breaking the bank.

It is hard to tell which of the most recent teddy bear stories will eventually become collectors' items. But there are a number that clearly appeal to adults just as much as they do to children. Jane Hissey's tales of Old Bear and his friends are among the most popular. Robert Ingpen's *The Idle Bear* is another favourite, as are the stories of Martin Waddell and Barbara Firth. Several of these books are available in miniature versions too.

Many bookshops have a whole selection of teddy bear story books, but you will also find them in gift shops, as well as in the specialist teddy bear shops.

Various non-fiction teddy bear books have also appeared over the years and, as I said, collectors of old bears in particular will find it useful to build up a good library of volumes filled with illustrations of interesting bears. Many of these books are published in America, but they are often available from specialist shops here, and some can be ordered through your local bookshop as well. British books, on the other hand, are generally widely available, both from bookshops and from a number of teddy bear shops. (You will find reviews of the latest publications in the specialist teddy bear magazines.)

Many of today's non-fiction bear books are all about collecting. But earlier publications were often more of a celebration of the teddy bear. Some of these books are now keenly sought after by collectors.

Those by Peter Bull are among the most popular. The actor was probably the teddy bear's greatest champion, and many enthusiasts blame him for setting them off on the bear-collecting path. In 1969 his book *Bear With Me* appeared, and several other volumes followed – each one full of delightful tales of bear lovers and their bears.

If you are lucky, you may find a copy of one of them in a secondhand bookshop. But you will be lucky indeed to find one of the special boxed and signed versions of *The Teddy Bear Book*, which were produced in a limited edition by the House of Nisbet. I have seen copies selling for more than £50 – and that for a book published as recently as 1983.

Look out for Mary Hillier's *Teddy Bears: A Celebration*, too (published in 1985) and the original hardback Mills & Boon edition of Margaret Hutchings' *Teddy Bears and How To Make Them*. There have been many bear-making guides since, including a paperback version of the Margaret Hutchings book. But this early volume is now very much a collector's item.

More recently, there have been a number of colourful photo books by Americans Rosemary and Paul Volpp, and Dee and Tom Hockenberry, for instance. These can also sometimes be found in teddy bear shops (or ordered through book stores), and are beautiful simply to look at.

Photo-filled books by American Ted Menten have been more widely available here. (Some have even found their way into the bargain bookshops.) But for something really different, look out for his *Teddy's Bearzaar* – a wonderful parody of *Harper's Bazaar*, full of advice, features and delightful advertisements for all a bear could desire.

Michele Durkson Clise's books about her bear Ophelia (again

originally published in America) are also delightful to look at. At the time of writing, the earliest books were hard to find outside one or two specialist shops. But you might find a secondhand copy, as they were once quite widely available in Britain. A forerunner of the Ophelia series, entitled *My Circle of Bears*, is now particularly collectable.

The past few years have seen a flurry of books on the making of bears, too. There have been biographies of famous bears like Rupert, Paddington, Winnie-the-Pooh and Sooty. Books of teddy bear quotations, teddy bear cartoons, even books of 'hugs' are just a few of the others which have appeared. So bear-loving bookworms can build up quite a library.

START HUNTING

Whatever your special interest – be it old bears or new, collect-ables or cuddlies, books or bearabilia in its many forms – this book suggests plenty of sources for additions to your collection. There are shops with hundreds of bears on sale and shops with only a few, shops selling all sorts of bear-related items, and shops without a single bear in sight – yet still with something of interest to the bear collector.

You'll also find museums where you can simply enjoy all the old bears on display. Or, if you are a fan of Rupert or Pooh, you will discover where you can follow in their footsteps. There are factories and workshops where you can see bears being made – not just furry teds, but ceramic and chocolate ones, too. And there are even places where you can learn how honey is made.

Wherever you go, I wish you happy hunting. But above all, I hope this book will help you gain even more enjoyment from your love of bears, however many or few you may have in your collection.

Part Two
PLACES TO VISIT

LONDON

Shops

It would be impossible to name all the London shops which have something of interest to teddy bear lovers. Department stores, toy shops, gift shops and china shops are all generally worth a look, and even a number of fashion chains have offered promotional bears at some stage. At Christmas, of course, stocks increase enormously, and shops which would not normally sell many, if any, bears may suddenly start offering large quantities.

Those which follow should, however, have something of interest throughout the year, and you'll find more London sources for bears to buy in the sections on Markets (page 42), Museums (p. 50) and Auctions (page 57).

COVENT GARDEN

If you're visiting the Covent Garden antique market held every Monday or the craft market which takes over from Tuesday to Saturday, both of which generally include a specialist bear stall (see Markets section, page 42), it is worth taking the time to have a look round all the little specialist shops on the Piazza as well. They can be a particularly good source of gifts for fellow teddy lovers.

The **Reject China Shops**, for instance, often have teddy-related items like teapots. You might find teddy candles in the **Candle Shop** or a frilly teddy in the shop specializing in lace.

Tiny furniture suitable for displaying with tiny bears can be found at the **Dollshouse Shop**, and there are two toy shops, both of which include bears in their ranges.

Eric Snook's are mainly of the cuddly soft toy variety, although you may find a few Merrythoughts (from their Heritage Collection, for instance). **Benjamin Pollock's Toy Shop**, on the other hand, offers Steiffs (including certain limited editions) and some collectable miniatures, as well as various cuddly teddies and souvenir bears wearing the shop's name on their jumpers.

Back in Long Acre, opposite the Underground station, the **Covent Garden General Store** includes a branch of the English Teddy Bear Company, with its various ranges made specially for the company.

Some are cuddly, unjointed teddies. Others are more traditional, made from a variety of fabrics and in various sizes. They include some dressed bears, and various clothes are also generally on sale.

In addition, the company has its own mugs, tea towels and T-shirts, as well as some specially packaged biscuits and preserves.

Other places of interest nearby (apart from the market itself) include the Theatre Museum in Russell Street. The constantly changing exhibits cover many kinds of performing arts, from the circus and variety to opera and ballet, since around the time of Shakespeare.

The area's many theatre connections are also commemorated in St Paul's Church in Covent Garden itself, where dozens of actors and actresses (some better known than others) are remembered in rows of memorial plaques.

Also in Covent Garden is the London Transport Museum. It tells the history of transport in the capital, from the early ferries across the Thames to the modern Underground.

Just a short walk away are Trafalgar Square and the National Gallery, and the start of both the Mall and Whitehall.

KNIGHTSBRIDGE

For many people, Knightsbridge means **Harrods**, and the renowned department store certainly has plenty to attract the bear lover. Their massive soft toy department is a particular joy at Christmas, but all through the year there are cuddlies of every description as well as some interesting collector bears.

Their range generally includes large numbers of Steiffs and Merrythoughts, among them a whole variety of limited editions. Steiff have made some limited editions specially for the store, while Merrythought has produced numerous Harrods exclusives.

Merrythought have, in fact, made bears for Harrods for many decades (sometimes even having fur specially dyed for them). Today they provide the Doorman Bear, and there has been a constant succession of other 'specials', some of them limited editions.

The popular Attic Bear, for instance, first appeared as an exclusive Harrods version, signed by Merrythought Managing Director Oliver Holmes and with a large label telling how his daughter Hannah had found the original bear in an attic. A Dr Italian bear, on the other hand, wore a dramatic green velour cape and hat. There have been special versions of the much-loved Cheeky, as well as a number of distinctive Ironbridge Bears, and splendid, boxed limited editions not obtainable anywhere else.

Collectable bears by other manufacturers are also on sale here in the so-called Toy Kingdom, but there are bears as well in the Harrods Shops, where all sorts of Harrods gifts are to be found.

A traditional Edwardian-style bear is made for them by Canterbury Bears, for instance, and the delightful Edward Harrod Collection of sculptured miniatures has been specially created by Peter Fagan of Colour Box fame. The pieces range from a simple copy of Edward Harrod to a delightful picnic hamper and a splendid fish counter. A bear clutching a large Harrods shopping bag is a perennial favourite.

There have been special Harrods mugs, towels and stationery with a teddy bear theme, too, and a whole variety of other bearish gifts.

MORTLAKE

Out to the south-west of London, in Sheen Lane in Mortlake, is one of the capital's few sources of artist bears, **Theodore's Bear Emporium**. They have been at their present site since August 1992, but for two years before that, they operated from a tiny unit in Richmond's Duke's Yard.

The present premises, known as the Teddy Bear & Dolls House Shoppe, are right by Mortlake main-line station (a twenty-minute journey from Waterloo). There are parking spaces at the rear to make life easy for those arriving by car.

The building was originally intended for the exclusive benefit of Queen Victoria, to be used as her own private waiting room on her visits to nearby Richmond Park. It was in need of considerable renovation when Theodore's took over, but now offers comfortable accommodation for a large assortment of teddies.

Proprietor Karl Gibbons started off by selling mainly manufactured bears in his Richmond unit. But he soon discovered that what many collectors wanted was something more unusual, and that meant artist bears. With British artists struggling to keep up with the demand, he soon started to look to America, and in no time at all had arranged exclusive United Kingdom representation for a large number of American makers. More names are being added all the time, as he visits American fairs to look for interesting new creations.

Theodore's Bear Emporium also stocks bears by a number of

British artists. Some are well-established names. But, like most shop owners, Karl is always looking for good new makers as well – especially ones who are not yet overwhelmed with orders, and can therefore guarantee prompt delivery.

Some are commissioned to make limited editions specially for the shop. But, as editions are generally small, the range changes constantly. Theodore's likes to ensure that regular collectors will find something new on every visit. Bocs Teganau, Naomi Laight, Mother Hubbard, Bear With Me, Apple of My Eye and Waifs and Strays are just some of the makers whose work has been sold to date.

The shop holds special previews to give collectors a chance to meet some of the artists and see their bears before they go on general sale. And it has its own Theodore's Bear Club, with monthly evening meetings giving members a chance to get together with fellow collectors who love bears as much as they do.

Other events have included special receptions for some of the American bear artists represented by Theodore's Bear Emporium here. A number have then gone on to visit one of the major British bear fairs, and to give talks at British bear clubs.

Not all the bears on sale at Theodore's Bear Emporium are artist-made, however. Others are from major manufacturers like Steiff and Hermann, and include those companies' limited editions. Some sell out almost as soon as they reach the shelves, so if you are interested in a particular bear, it is best to check the availability before making a special journey to the shop.

Among the British makes on sale are Merrythought, Canterbury Bears and Big Softies. In addition, although the shop specializes in bears for collectors, they also have some of the popular character bears, like Pooh and Paddington, and there are some more cuddly offerings from companies like Ty.

A repair and restoration service offers help to sick and injured bears. And those looking for a present for a bear-loving friend can save themselves a difficult choice by opting for the shop's own gift vouchers instead.

As the shop's name indicates, however, it is not only a teddy bear specialist. Also on sale are doll's houses and doll's house miniatures, which are in the charge of enthusiast Julia Day. She sells modern collector dolls, too, and looks after the teddies when Karl is away.

When you have seen them all, both Richmond Park and Kew Gardens are within easy reach for those wanting to turn a visit into a complete day out.

SOUTH KENSINGTON

South Kensington is especially well known for its museums, with four of the most famous in the world all within a short distance of each other.

The Victoria and Albert Museum in Cromwell Road covers art and design through the ages, with collections which include costumes, paintings, ceramics, sculptures and furniture from many countries. The Natural History Museum, also in Cromwell Road, has exhibitions featuring everything from birds, insects, fish and mammals to minerals and meteorites. The displays at the Science Museum in Exhibition Road deal with all forms of science and technology, including medicine, while the Geological Museum (again in Exhibition Road) has splendid collections of gems and fossils.

Also in Exhibition Road is a tiny shop called **Kensington Bear**, crammed from floor to ceiling with bears of many descriptions and all sorts of bear-related items.

Since they naturally attract a large number of tourists, they have the usual popular gift lines, like the Andrew Brownsword bears which can also be found in many card shops. But they have many bears for collectors as well, including limited editions.

You'll find manufactured bears from companies like Steiff, Hermann, Merrythought, Dean's, Canterbury Bears and Big Softies. They stock Gabrielle Designs, too, and the Muffy Bears from the North American Bear Co., as well as some of the Lakeland Bears. But there are also some artist-made bears from a number of different British makers. Among them are various bears which are exclusive to the shop.

Stationery, mugs, magnets, teddy ornaments (by Colour Box, for instance), T-shirts, clothes for bears and greetings cards are some of the bear-related items to be found there, too.

WEST END

Most people visit the West End for its shops, and you will find plenty of bears there if you know where to look. For a start, several department stores have teddies in their toy and/or gift departments. These often include both the softly huggable variety and limited editions aimed specifically at the collectors market.

Selfridges in Oxford Street, for instance, has a particularly good selection. The store includes a large area devoted to toys of every kind, and among these are bears by many leading manufacturers like Steiff, Hermann and Merrythought. They stock limited editions from all these companies and, as it is a shop that some collectors overlook, it is often a good place for filling gaps in a collection.

Specialist teddy bear shops may sell out of the most popular lines before they even arrive. Selfridges, on the other hand, can carry much larger stocks, and may just have what you are after.

Of course, they have lots of less expensive bears as well, and you'll find more bearish items (like the Colour Box miniatures) in their gift department.

Also in Oxford Street, **D. H. Evans** tends to have items of teddy bear interest spread throughout various departments on several different floors. On my last visit, I found some of Merrythought's Heritage Collection, like the Policeman and Chelsea Pensioner, in the ground floor Tourist Shop, which also had a good selection of Colour Box miniatures. There were more of Colour Box's resin teddies up on the third floor, while the fifth floor toy department had a few traditional Merrythought and Steiff bears as well as some unjointed softies. Some of the Merrythoughts were of a type I have only ever seen in House of Fraser stores.

Next door, in **John Lewis**, the toy department offers a number of teddies, but those of most interest to collectors will probably be the bears made specially for the company by Merrythought.

Downstairs in the Gift Department, on the other hand, some limited editions by Steiff and Merrythought are among the collectables vying for attention. The same department also offers the Colour Box range of teddy bear miniatures, and you should find other teddy bear ornaments here as well.

A short way up nearby Regent Street is the shop which most bear-loving visitors to London have at the top of their itinerary, **Hamleys**. Said to be the finest toy shop in the world, a large part of its ground floor is given over to soft toys of every imaginable shape and form.

Needless to say, there are vast numbers of huggable bears and other animals, of numerous makes and in all sizes. But the shop also has a splendid range of collectables. There are large numbers of bears by Steiff, Hermann, Merrythought and Dean's, including good selections of limited editions as well as bears from the companies' regular ranges. They also stock the bear-related items made by these companies – like miniature tea sets, full-size mugs, jewellery or postcards. But of special note are the various bears made only for Hamleys.

These generally include a special limited edition by Steiff, others by Hermann and Dean's, and there are invariably some bears made exclusively for the shop by Merrythought as well.

Other ranges of interest to collectors are the Canterbury Bears, bears by Nisbet, and the North American Bear Co.'s Muffy, in a variety of different costumes.

Well-known characters like Paddington and Sooty are also in good supply, as well as various popular ranges of teddy bear ornaments.

There are more bears and bear-related items over the road at the **English Teddy Bear Company**. Some of the bears are made of mohair, others of less expensive plush, and there are both traditional jointed designs and the more huggable unjointed variety. All are made specially for the company. There are both dressed and undressed bears, and the shop also sells a number of items of teddy bear clothing for those who don't believe that bare is best. Waistcoats and bow ties are always popular.

Teddy bear mugs, badges and a number of different T-shirts are also exclusive to the shop, and they have even had biscuits, jam and marmalade packed especially for them.

Also in Regent Street are one or two shops which have something unique to offer but which could easily be overlooked by bear-loving visitors.

Liberty, for instance, have had a number of different bears created for them in recent years, with paw pads made from one of their famous prints. You should find the current bears among the gifts on the ground floor.

Then there is **Burberrys** which, in addition to its famous rainwear and other items of ladies' and gentlemen's clothing, also has its own very distinctive bears. Keen collectors will recognize the work of the Merrythought factory, but again the paw pads are special, this time made from one of the distinctive Burberrys® plaids. The bears come in three sizes, and there are two different furs.

The whole range is featured in a delightful little book, written and illustrated by popular artist Prue Theobalds. This, too, is on sale in the shop.

(If the Regent Street shop does not have the full range, you may also find some of the bears in the **Burberrys®** shop in nearby Haymarket, which has a larger children's section.)

Pooh lovers, on the other hand, will find plenty of Pooh Bears and some other Pooh-related items among all the Disney-ana in Regent Street's **Disney Store**.

Simpson's in Piccadilly is another shop with its own special bears, again with distinctive paw pads to mark them out as Simpson's teddies. Then, a short walk along Piccadilly, is another source of bears which could easily be missed.

Fortnum and Mason is probably best known for its ground-floor fine food department, but that is only a small fraction of what is on sale. Tucked away on the splendidly refurbished second floor, for instance, are the toys and, as would be expected from such a shop, they have just the type of high-quality, traditional bears that are popular with collectors.

Some are by Steiff, and include limited editions, and there are more limited editions among the bears from Merrythought and Dean's. There are also bears by Hermann, Canterbury and Big Softies, and the ever-popular Paddington.

It is worth having a look round the food department, too. You might just find something in an unusual teddy bear tin or pot, as many of the shop's foods are intended as gifts.

Back at Piccadilly Circus is the **Trocadero Centre**, which includes a number of shops and cafés. When it first opened, it also boasted one of the country's earliest specialist teddy bear shops. That is now long gone. A more recent arrival is **Teddyland** but, in spite of the name, the teddy bears are under attack from an assortment of other lines aimed unashamedly at the young tourist.

Nevertheless, it could hide the odd surprise. Among all the

cuddlies you may find some limited editions by Steiff or Merry-thought. Better still, as the shop is even more likely to be missed than all the department stores, you could find just what you are looking for if you have a single (recent) edition in mind.

For those who are more interested in a souvenir of London, there should again be some bears from the Merrythought Heritage Collection (like the Beafeater and Guardsman), and I've also seen some traditional bears in special Trocadero jumpers.

Among the centre's other attractions are the Guinness World of Records, which includes models of some of the people and animals cited in the famous book. The London Experience, on the other hand, traces the history of the capital.

WINCHMORE HILL

If you collect modern manufactured bears by the likes of Steiff, Hermann and Merrythought, one shop not to be missed is **Dolly Land** in North London's Winchmore Hill. It is almost in Middlesex, so if you are on public transport you will need to take the Piccadilly Line up to Wood Green, and then catch a 329 bus out to Winchmore Hill. It is quite a distance from the station, but the shop is not hard to find, as the bus travels right along Green Lanes, and the numbers of the shops and houses are clearly visible. Approaching from Wood Green, number 864 will be on your right, just after the road bends sharply to the right in front of the Green Dragon pub. The nearest bus stop is the one just before the pub.

At first glance the shop might not seem very special. There are shelves of limited editions and other traditional bears from Steiff, Hermann and Merrythought, with those that won't fit on the shelves hanging from hooks from the ceiling. But look again. In addition to this year's range, you'll find a whole load of bears from previous years, many of which have long been absent from other shops. On my last visit, I even spotted the original Richard Steiff replica which first appeared in 1983 and is now greatly coveted by collectors.

There are usually some Steiff bears made specially for the American market, too – again including some that have long since disappeared from most other shops. And Dolly Land's Greta Hollman has many more bears stored away than she can cram into her crowded shop. So if you cannot find what you want, it is worth asking, just in case.

Many bears by Hermann and Merrythought are also stocked, again including some editions that disappeared from other shops long ago. In addition, Greta has had bears made specially for her by both companies. The Merrythoughts have been copied from a design in one of the company's first catalogues. They have open mouths, and have been made in black, white or brown fur. The Hermann bears are also open mouthed, with two colour variations.

Dolly Land is a Steiff Club Store, so the shelves and cabinets also hold a number of Steiff animals. Then you will usually find a number of old bears, not to mention dolls old and new. These include an international selection of older costumed dolls as well as some modern creations by Steiff.

There is some doll's house furniture, too, and any remaining space is crammed with a variety of other goods ranging from old toys, games, jewellery and some china, to much more modern door handles and screwdrivers.

Greta's doll and teddy shop once housed a kitchenware and garden shop, while the premises next door were devoted to DIY. Greta bought both from the husband and wife who owned them, and it was some three years before the dolls and teddies took up residence in the old kitchen and garden section (Greta's son now sells die-cast models next door). The old kitchen and DIY stock is gradually being sold off, but some still remains. So the bears share the shelves with riveters, cloth dyes, cups and saucers and sachets of windscreen washer additive.

It is the kind of shop where every time you look you see something else. And if you don't see what you want, don't forget to ask – you never know what Greta may have tucked away.

ADDRESSES

Burberrys, 165 Regent Street, W1; tel. 071 734 4060

Covent Garden General Store, 109–115 Long Acre, WC2; tel. 071 240 0031

Dolly Land, 862–864 Green Lanes, Winchmore Hill, N21; tel. 081 360 1053

English Teddy Bear Company, 153 Regent Street, W1; tel. 071 287 3273

D. H. Evans, 318 Oxford Street, W1; tel. 071 629 8800

Fortnum & Mason, 181 Piccadilly, W1; tel. 071 734 8040

Hamleys, 188–196 Regent Street, W1; tel. 071 734 3161

Harrods Ltd, Brompton Road, SW1; tel. 071 225 5848

Kensington Bear, 16 Exhibition Road, South Kensington, SW7; tel. 071 823 9295

John Lewis, 278–306 Oxford Street, W1; tel. 071 629 7711

Benjamin Pollock's Toy Shop, 44 The Market, Covent Garden, WC2; tel. 071 379 7866

Selfridges, 400 Oxford Street, W1; tel. 071 629 1234

Teddyland, Unit 12A, Trocadero Centre, Piccadilly, W1; tel. 071 734 1927

Theodore's Bear Emporium, The Teddy Bear & Dolls House Shoppe, The Old Waiting Room, Station Approach, Sheen Lane, SW14; tel. 081 876 2996

Tourist Information Centre, Victoria Station Forecourt, SW1, and Liverpool Street Underground station, EC2 (personal callers only)

London Tourist Board, 26 Grosvenor Gardens, London SW1W
0DY (written enquiries only)

Markets

You could find an interesting old bear at any antique market.
In addition, handmade bears and bear-related items crop up
at many craft markets and, of course, general markets may offer a
fluffy teddy or two. But there are three London markets with
something more for the teddy bear lover: Camden Passage,
Covent Garden and Portobello Road.

CAMDEN PASSAGE

Camden Passage is a relatively new market, and is not actually in
Camden at all, but in Islington, just a short walk from the Angel
Underground station. The street was originally called Cumber-
land Row, but in the late nineteenth century the name was
changed in honour of the first Earl of Camden, whose land it had
been.

Up until the 1950s, it contained ordinary houses and some
typical local shops, but in 1958 the first antique shop was opened.
Two years later, the market came into being. Now it is crammed
with antique shops and arcades, with an open market known as
the Georgian Village at its northern end, and all sorts of antiques
and bric-à-brac laid out on tables and even on rugs along both
sides of the street.

The market opens on Wednesday mornings and all day
Saturday, although shops will start to close halfway through the
afternoon on a quiet day. On Wednesdays, business starts early,
with dealers making up many of the customers. On Saturday,

however, things are much more leisurely, with many of the shops not opening their doors until at least 10.00 a.m.

It is a very gentle market – a perfect place for a leisurely stroll on a sunny day, followed by an excellent lunch at one of the smart restaurants or busy pubs.

Bear lovers will, however, head straight for **Pam Hebbs**' tiny shop at 5 The Annexe, not far from the northern end. Pam has been in Camden Passage since 1978. Initially she sold general antiques and dolls' accessories with the occasional doll. But it wasn't long before someone brought her some teddies, and they quickly became her speciality at a time when no one else was showing any interest in them.

She has moved two or three times over the years, but she took over her present little shop in about 1987, and it has become a real honey-pot for collectors. The shop is so tiny that just a couple of browsers constitutes a crowd. But on Saturday mornings it turns into something of a social club for bear lovers, with collectors popping in to see what is new, or just to have a chat.

Pam's favourite bears are still the old ones, so you should find a good number to choose from. On my last visit I saw splendid Farnells and Chad Valleys in beautiful condition, as well as some slightly more worn but equally appealing offerings.

Not all the bears are old, however. Pam has always tended to be ahead of the field, perhaps because she ignores trends and simply buys what she likes. So she was offering American artist bears long before they became as sought-after in Britain as they are today. Several American artists sell their bears exclusively through her in Britain, and others create editions specially for her.

There are bears by several English artists, too – again usually with some made specially for the shop. And Pam also stocks the Steiff limited editions, although many barely reach the shelves before they are sold.

Bears can sometimes be found on old china or old gadgets,

and Pam herself has a splendid collection of such pieces. From time to time some will find their way into the shop. She also still has a few lovely old accessories, like tiny shoes and purses, although not in the same quantities as she once did.

Another interest is old Christmas decorations, and she also loves old animal soft toys, like those by Steiff, so you should find some of those as well.

Bears also turn up elsewhere in the market, so it is worth taking the time to wander round – exploring all the outside stalls as well as the shops and arcades. One stall just south of Pam Hebbs' shop, for instance, generally has a number of teddy bears and other soft toys, while to the north, just round the corner, you will find **Jeannette** at No. 1 The Annexe. Dolls were, and still are, her great passion, but then she started falling in love with bears as well. Now there are usually several in the shop (mainly English ones when I last visited).

Outside are the market stalls of the Georgian Village, where you may again find a bear or two, and any of the other stalls in Camden Passage could hold something of interest.

You'll find all sorts of things that can enhance a teddy bear display, for instance – from little bear-sized cups and saucers to a bear-sized cinema organ, perhaps, and all sorts of old toys and games (some of them featuring teddy bears).

A piece of old lace or some old jewellery may be just the right accessories for one of your bears, or you might find a beautiful antique dress or other garment. Look out for David Barrington, in the Angel Arcade, who sells both dolls and dolls' clothes. Many dolls' clothes are the wrong shape for bears, but you can sometimes find a suitably roomy design which fits the bill perfectly.

COVENT GARDEN

The Covent Garden market of today is very different from that of a hundred years ago. The old market buildings are still there, now carefully restored. But the boxes of fruit and vegetables have gone – removed to New Covent Garden down in Nine Elms. Today the market is full of smart specialist shops, trendy cafés and tourists, and the stalls in the old Apple Market now sell crafts and antiques.

Monday is the day of the antique market, and that is the day you will find **Heather's Teddy's** under the glass roof of the Apple Market, surrounded by stalls selling a variety of antiques and bric-à-brac.

Heather has a genuine love of teddies, and her stall is invariably crammed with appealing faces. The bears cover a wide range of ages, from the earliest onwards, with valuable German bears by companies like Steiff and Bing as well as British makes like Farnell, Merrythought, Chad Valley, Dean's, Chiltern and Pedigree. There are always a good number of lovable but unidentifiable bears, too, ranging from the pristine to the well-loved.

Prices cover a similarly wide range, with even fairly recent English bears now fetching high prices, and with old Steiffs fetching amounts several times higher. But even if you cannot afford to buy, the attractively laid out stand can still be viewed and enjoyed, and perhaps a favourite bear cuddled for a few precious minutes.

You may find a few animals as well as the bears, and perhaps an occasional doll. But Heather's great love is teddies, especially teddies with character, and that is her speciality.

While you are there, it is worth taking time to look round the other stalls for any interesting accessories to display with your bears. In addition to the stalls in the Apple Market, you will find more out in the open air, behind the Opera House.

From Tuesday to Saturday, you will find a different kind of market, with a wide range of craftspeople setting up their stalls. The creations on offer are naturally very varied, but on Wednesdays and Thursdays (and on most Tuesdays, Fridays and Saturdays, too), you will find another teddy specialist in the Apple Market – **Bedford Bears**.

Eddie Richard-Owen began designing his own bears in the days when teddy bear artists were few and far between. Now his creations include traditional mohair bears, made with collectors in mind, as well as a 'standard' range, again of traditional jointed bears but this time in modacrylic furs. Eddie, his partner and just three or four outworkers sew all the Bedford Bears between them.

A popular line is the Ann-y-mates hand puppets, produced in various furs. With a little practice, they take on a life of their own, and their filled bodies also mean that they can be cuddled like a normal teddy.

New bears are regularly added to the range, but a perennially popular line is the Bedford Blues©, reminiscent of the many blue bears which appeared during the immediate post-war period. In fact, they are replicas of Eddie's own first bear, and the colour of the fur has been carefully matched to that used originally.

The Bedford Bears sell all over the world. But some designs are made specially for Covent Garden and are available nowhere else. Those on offer change constantly, however, so that regular customers will keep on finding something different.

There are more bears in some of the Covent Garden shops – both on the Piazza itself and in the immediate vicinity (see London – Shops, page 29). And, if you cannot decide which to choose, there are plenty of bustling cafés and pubs where you can sit and ponder the pros and cons.

There is plenty of free entertainment, too, ranging from Chinese folk music to break-dancing, mime artists to magicians. A popular pitch is outside St Paul's Church, the actors' church. Inside are dozens of memorial plaques to stars of stage and screen, among them the likes of Noël Coward and Charlie Chaplin.

PORTOBELLO ROAD

Possibly the best-known antique market in the world, Portobello Road positively seethes with people each Saturday, when you'll find stalls and shops selling everything from fine antiques to inexpensive bric-à-brac, and even tourist souvenirs.

Much less gentle than Camden Passage, it is a perennial favourite with young people. Many are simply out for an afternoon promenade, and they saunter past the stalls with barely a glance. But a good number of first homes are embellished with Portobello finds, and the mêlée conceals some serious collectors as well.

In the early nineteenth century, the area was one of the city's least salubrious – home to a number of pig breeders. The first house appeared in 1850 and after some years it was joined by many more.

The market first appeared in the 1880s, but it was not until the late 1950s that the fruit and vegetables began to give way to antiques. By the 1960s the market had become a popular

Saturday haunt for young Londoners and for visitors from all over the world.

Now, there are literally hundreds of stalls, as well as the permanent shops and arcades that line the street for over a mile northwards from Chepstow Villas at the Notting Hill Gate end until the antiques and bric-à-brac give way to more general merchandise, including food.

It is worth exploring as many of the arcades as you can, and rummaging through a large number of stalls. You never know what you may find. In general, though, bears tend to be few and far between, with the exception of **Heather's Teddy's** Saturday spot outside the World Famous Arcade at number 177 (opposite the Midland Bank).

The range of bears is similar to that Heather takes to Covent Garden (page 45), although some bears taken along on a Monday may be left behind on the Saturday to give others an 'outing'. In general, however, there will be both German and English bears, from the very old to the not so old, and from the tiny to the complete armful. Some will be pristine and still bearing their original labels. Others may be well worn and of totally unknown make, but with an appeal all their own.

Heather spends much of her week travelling to see bears that have been offered to her, or visiting auctions. So the range changes constantly. And, as at Covent Garden, you may find one or two other animals or the odd doll, or some character toy like an old Mickey Mouse.

Look out for the odd bear elsewhere in the market, too – perhaps among the antique dolls and toys in the **Antique Market** at number 101 (its distinctive sign is in the shape of a large teapot). Other stalls may have teddy bear ornaments, some of them quite modern. Or, if you are looking for accessories or 'props' to liven up a teddy bear display, you could find something just about anywhere in the crowded street. Toys, clothes, jewellery, bear-sized cups and saucers, little bags, a child's chair . . .

the list is endless, although you may have to look hard to find any real bargains.

At the **Spectus Gallery** in nearby Westbourne Grove (about halfway down Portobello Road) you will also find some modern collectables – mainly limited editions from Steiff, Merrythought and Dean's, although you may discover a few other (new) bears as well.

You could find bears at any other craft or antique market in the capital. At **Alfie's Antique Market** in Church Street, NW8, for instance, the Granny's Goodies stand has both old and new bears, including Steiff and Merrythought and artist bears. There are also some other bear-related items, including books.

Bermondsey antique market is held each Friday, and attracts dealers from all over the country. Trading is usually underway by 5.00 a.m. or even earlier, and you'll need to be fast to grab a bargain – and to be able to recognize a bargain when you see one. Fake bears are by no means unusual these days.

ADDRESSES

Bedford Bears, Covent Garden Craft Market, WC2 (various days). Postal address: 8 High Street, Dunton, Beds, SG18 8RN; tel. 0767 318443

Granny's Goodies, Stand S001, Alfie's Antique Market, 13–25 Church Street, NW8; 071 706 4699 (Tuesdays–Saturdays, 13.00–17.00)

Heather's Teddy's, Stand 28, Apple Market, Covent Garden, WC2 (Mondays); World Famous Arcade, 177 Portobello Road, W11 (Saturdays); tel. 081 204 0106 (home)

Pam Hebbs, 5 The Annexe, Camden Passage, Islington, N11; tel. 081 361 3739 (home); open Wednesday 7.30–15.00, Saturday 10.00–16.00, and at other times by appointment

Jeannette, No. 1 The Annexe, Georgian Village, Camden Passage, Islington, N1; tel. 081 958 6101 (home)

Spectus Gallery (Kathy Gilbert), 298 Westbourne Grove, W11; tel. 0753 543258 (home; open Saturdays)

Museums

L ondon has no specialist bear museum, and none of its other museums has a vast collection of bears. But there are still some that teddy bear collectors will enjoy visiting, not just to see their teddies but also to see other toys made by well-known bear manufacturers like Chad Valley and Schuco.

BETHNAL GREEN MUSEUM OF CHILDHOOD

A few stops from the West End, on the Central Line, is Bethnal Green, whose Museum of Childhood houses one of the biggest collections of childhood memorabilia in the world. It is actually part of the renowned Victoria and Albert Museum of art, craft and design, but here the focus is on the art, craft and design of toys.

Unlike many other such museums, the cases at Bethnal Green contain not only interesting exhibits but also a wealth of information about the manufacturers and their products. Together they present a wonderful insight into childhood through the ages.

Bear lovers, of course, will head first for the soft toy section, where some of the earliest bears and other animals are by Steiff and Schuco. Schuco was a trademark of the German company Schreyer & Co. (who were well known for their mechanical toys as well as their teddy bears). They created various novelty teddy bears and other animals, and are especially well remembered for the so-called Yes/No mechanism, a device by which movement of the tail enabled the head to be turned from side to side or nodded up and down.

There are other, unidentified, early bears on display, and a charming collection of teddies and animals which all came from the same family. Dating from around 1906, they have with them a collection of photographs and water-colours of the toys.

Later (post-1930) bears by well-known English manufacturers like Chad Valley, Chiltern and Merrythought can also be seen, and there are other soft toys by major British companies. The doleful Dalmatian Dismal Desmond, for instance, was a huge success for Dean's in the twenties. Among the other animals on display are some made by Shropshire doll and toy maker Norah Wellings.

More recent exhibits include character soft toys like Super Ted and Paddington, and there is also a display of materials used in the making of soft toys.

The soft toy section makes up only a very small part of the whole museum, however. Far larger is the display of dolls,

Wendy Sue '94.

which date right back to the seventeenth century. There is a splendid collection of dolls dressed by successive generations of the same family, for instance, and a beautiful doll and layette bought for the Princess Mary around 1899.

There are dolls of paper and of wood, composition and wax dolls, dolls made from porcelain, bisque, hard plastic and soft vinyl. Some walk and talk. Some come from as far afield as Japan, India, Africa, Trinidad and Brazil. Others are from the Steiff factory in Germany, or from Chad Valley and Norah Wellings in Shropshire.

There are many splendid doll's houses in the museum, too, not to mention all kinds of puppets, circus toys, boats, cars, space toys, lead soldiers, games and puzzles. Included are many games and toys made by Chad Valley, who started making teddy bears during the First World War.

The museum shop sells various toys, including some inexpensive teddy bears, and there are various teddy bear cards among the many postcards of museum exhibits.

LONDON TOY & MODEL MUSEUM

The London Toy & Model Museum, housed in a listed building not far from Paddington Station, has attracted tens of thousands of visitors each year with its huge collection of toys and models of every description.

Optical toys, slot machines, a model fairground, cars, model railways, lead soldiers, farm animals, construction kits, dolls and doll's houses and, of course, teddy bears have kept young and old enthralled for hours. But with so much to fit into a limited space, the displays have sometimes suffered, with exhibits simply crammed into cabinets and little or no information about them included.

Now, new owners have planned a total refurbishment of the

museum, at a cost of several million pounds. A whole team of designers has drawn up a scheme for a series of themed rooms, with each theme related to the items on display.

A forest, for instance, is planned as the setting for the new soft toy display. The proposed centre-piece is to be in the form of a teddy bears' picnic, with a push-button activating the history of the teddy bear. As the story is told, spotlights will pick out the relevant items in the display.

There are plans to incorporate a model based on the famous Clifford Berryman cartoon showing President Theodore (Teddy) Roosevelt refusing to shoot a bear. It was this incident in 1902, and the cartoon of it, which led to the making of the first American teddy bears, and which also gave rise to the name 'Teddy's bears'.

Famous bears like Paddington, Rupert and Super Ted are also expected to be included in the display – with Super Ted actually flying above the picnic.

Large soft toys and clockwork animals are to be kept in a separate bank of display compartments. A Noah's Ark is planned, with a rotating display of animals and figures, and a 'jungle display' of toy animals is scheduled, too.

The project is not expected to be completed until at least mid-1995, and at the time of writing they had made no decision as to exactly which bears would be on view when the work is finished. But it was anticipated that Peter Bull's famous collection would be among the exhibits.

The bear-loving actor was responsible for introducing thousands to the wonderful world of the teddy bear through his books and personal appearances. Many sent him bears to add to his own collection. Most of these were left to the museum in his will, although not the most famous members of his 'hug'. The faithful Theodore, for instance, now lives with Peter's friend Enid Irving, who collaborated with him on his final book and illustrated his series of Bully Bear stories. Delicatessen, who starred as Aloysius in the television series *Brideshead Revisited*, has found a new home in America.

The other bears and a large collection of bearabilia have, however, provided a rather poignant reminder of the way in which things have changed since Peter's death in 1984. Peter's love of bears had nothing at all to do with how much they were worth (often a major preoccupation today).

The museum's proximity to Paddington Station has also naturally meant that a display of Paddington books, bears and other merchandise has formed one of the exhibits for many years. Again, there are no details as to how much will be on view in the new-look museum.

POLLOCK'S TOY MUSEUM

It is nearly forty years since this museum first opened. In those days it was housed in an attic room near Covent Garden, but it soon expanded into other rooms, and twenty-five years ago was moved to larger premises in Scala Street (close to Goodge Street Underground station in Tottenham Court Road).

The building is actually two small eighteenth-century houses, and is made up of many small rooms joined by narrow staircases. This, and the creaky old floors, provide just the right atmosphere for such a nostalgic collection.

Again, bears form just a small part of the displays, but they include some very old examples. Eric, for instance, dates from 1905, and Teddy was made in Germany in 1906. One bear has had a wax doll as his constant companion for more than eighty years. Another of similar age still has a picture of himself with his owner, when both were very young.

Of slightly later vintage is one of the famous Schuco Yes/No bears, made by the German company Schreyer & Co. around 1920. His head can be turned or made to nod up and down by moving his tail. Another bear dates from around the time of the First World War, and still has the army and police uniforms made by his owner, who was then aged between seven and eleven. A musical teddy was made in the early thirties and there are some later bears as well.

One of these will be found with the museum's puppet collection, which includes Sooty, Sweep and Soo glove puppets donated by Harry Corbett. They were apparently used by him in performances in the 1950s.

There are other soft toys in the museum, too, including a cat on a tricycle, made by Dean's, and one of that company's popular Dismal Desmond Dalmatians. He first appeared in the 1920s, and has recently been reintroduced into the company's range. The museum's example, however, is one of the originals.

One of Dean's baby dolls is also on display, and there are several of the distinctive soft dolls designed by Norah Wellings in the 1930s, after she left Chad Valley to set up in business on her own. They include one of her famous South Sea Islanders, and one of the many nightdress cases she created.

There are other dolls in the museum, too. The oldest crossed the Rockies in a covered wagon. But that is by no means the earliest toy on show. That honour goes to an Egyptian clay mouse, with a moving wooden mouth and tail, which dates back to around 2000 BC.

There are a large number of toys from other countries. One display is devoted entirely to toys from India. Another includes the work of the Canadian Eskimos. Toys have been gathered from Mexico, South America, Africa, Central and Eastern Europe, China and Japan. The Japanese collection even includes three bears, which were the totem animal of the Ainu people.

Other traditional toys like whipping tops, skipping ropes and skittles have also been collected from all over the world. The first jig-saw puzzles were created in England in the eighteenth century, and some of these can be seen, too.

Also on view are board games, optical toys (like magic lanterns), comics, toy soldiers, doll's houses, construction kits and space toys which go right back to before that first venture into space by Yuri Gagarin. There is even a whole room devoted to Toy Theatres, to which Benjamin Pollock devoted much of his life.

He died in 1937, twenty years before the museum carrying his name was opened. But his theatres and their associated plays can still be bought from the museum shop. So, too, can various collectable bears. There are Steiffs (including some limited editions) and Merrythoughts, as well as various individually made bears – among them bears by Naomi Laight. The greetings cards and postcards include some featuring bears, too, and there are books about bears as well.

Also on sale are doll's house miniatures and all kinds of traditional toys. So if you like to make interesting displays with your bears, you may find some unusual 'props' here.

ADDRESSES

(*Opening times can change and should therefore be checked before travelling*)

Bethnal Green Museum of Childhood, Cambridge Heath Road, E2; tel. 081 981 1711 (closed Fridays and Sunday mornings)

London Toy & Model Museum, 21/23 Craven Hill, W2; tel. 071 262 9450 (scheduled to be closed for refurbishment until at least mid-1995)

Pollock's Toy Museum, 1 Scala Street, W1; tel. 071 636 3452 (closed Sundays and Bank Holidays)

Auctions

I am sure that many readers of this book wouldn't dream of going to a teddy bear auction. If you've read about some of the record prices being fetched, you will probably have discounted the possibility of ever being able to bid for a bear yourself. Or maybe you're afraid that you'll get caught up in all the excitement and end up bidding for something you cannot possibly afford. Worse, maybe you'll scratch your nose and find that you've accidentally bought an expensive Steiff.

If you love old bears, however, it really is worth timing a visit to London to coincide with one of the major sales, even if your current bear budget is practically non-existent.

The bears are usually on view at the auction house for a day or two beforehand and, if it is an afternoon sale, on the morning of the sale itself. It costs nothing to go along and have a look. A telephone call to each of the auction houses will give you the dates of forthcoming sales and the days and times at which lots can be viewed. When you arrive, you simply ask at the reception desk where the teddy bears can be seen.

Sometimes the bears will simply be lying on shelves, and can be picked up and inspected at will. In the case of more precious lots, however, they may be out of reach and you will have to ask for a closer look. But you could find yourself cuddling a bear that fetches thousands of pounds on the sale day itself.

Unless you are planning to buy, you may decide not to attend the auction itself. If you are planning to buy, though, you will find that the bears usually form only part of the sale. If you ask, the auction house will give you some idea of when they are expected to come up. Otherwise, you may find yourself fidgeting your way through an interminable number of lots of other toys. Auction room seats can be extremely hard.

Even if your bear budget is low, you shouldn't necessarily assume that you will not be able to afford any of those on sale. Admittedly, the bidding can be fast and furious for rare Steiffs in excellent condition, and **Sotheby's** in Bond Street only accept items expected to fetch several hundred pounds or more. (Or they put a number together, so that the combined value of the lot reaches their minimum.) But elsewhere you could find that some items have estimated selling prices that are very much more reasonable – although that does not necessarily mean that the final selling price will be that low.

The hammer has, however, been known to fall on an even lower bid. Colour Box Ted Captain Arthur Crown, for instance, came up for sale at an auction at **Christie's**, South Kensington. He was a sorry sight, barely even recognizable as a bear. The auctioneer started his bidding at about £50 and proceeded to go *downwards* when there were no takers. Finally he was asking for bids of just £10, the lowest he had gone during the sale, and yet still no none was interested. Finally, a voice from the front called out, 'I'll give you a fiver,' and the hammer fell.

New owners, Frances and Peter Fagan, took their acquisition back to the Scottish Borders, provided him with lots of new stuffing, a saucy eye patch and a smart uniform, and his miniature became one of the most popular in the Colour Box range (see Lauder, page 327).

As for being afraid to bid accidentally, it really is not that easy. Auctioneers are very skilled at knowing whether a bid is intentional or not, and if they are not sure they will ask. As one auction house pointed out, they haven't made any mistaken sales in nearly three hundred years.

Getting caught up in all the excitement is, of course, something else. But bidding is often by means of a numbered paddle or card, which you obtain by registering in advance. If you want to watch but have no intention of buying, you won't register and therefore won't have a paddle or card.

If you *do* want to buy, however, but don't want to get carried away, you can always enter a written bid in advance. But at the very least, make a firm decision beforehand as to exactly how much you are willing to pay (bearing in mind commission and VAT). Write it down to remind you, and then *stop* when you reach your limit.

In London, four auction houses holding sales of teddy bears are *Bonhams Chelsea*, *Christie's South Kensington*, *Phillips Bayswater* and *Sotheby's* in Bond Street. They also carry out valuations, if you want to find out how much a teddy in your collection is worth. (There is a charge, however, if you want a written valuation for insurance purposes.)

BONHAMS CHELSEA

Bonhams have been including teddy bears in their doll and toy sales for many years now. Prices vary, with interesting Steiffs fetching several thousand pounds. But they also have less expensive bears. Those expected to fetch under £100 are usually combined into multiple lots, however.

There are usually four sales a year which include bears.

CHRISTIE'S SOUTH KENSINGTON

Christie's first introduced teddy bears into their sales in the early eighties. But two weeks before Christmas 1985 they went one step further and held the first sale devoted exclusively to teddy bears and soft toys. A total of 182 lots included bears of every shape, size and description, with the highest estimates just £400 and most lots expected to fetch £100 or less. The following day, *The Daily Telegraph* carried a report that a 'hump-backed teddy' made in 1910 had sold for £700, and pictured a Steiff in a striped dressing-gown which had cost its new owner £550.

Less than four years later, a bear sold there for no less than £12,100. His name was Alfonzo, and he was an extremely rare red bear, made by Steiff around 1908. Even more interesting, however, was the bear's story, for he was once owned by a Russian princess.

Princess Xenia was on holiday at Buckingham Palace when the outbreak of the First World War prevented her from returning home. She was still in England when the Russian Revolution began. Her father, the Grand Duke Mikhailovich, was assassinated, and the bear he had given the Princess remained a much-treasured memento which she kept with her all her life.

He can now be seen at 'Teddy Bears' of Witney (page 144).

Not all the bears at Christie's are expensive Steiffs, however. Large numbers of English bears have passed through their hands over the years, although they, too, are becoming more expensive. Nevertheless, the prices fetched cover a very wide range, and naturally vary very much from sale to sale.

PHILLIPS

Phillips, too, introduced their first teddies in the early eighties, and on 12 December 1985 – the day before Christie's special teddy sale – the *Daily Mail* reported that an American shop owner had paid £1,000 for a Steiff at a Phillips auction. In all, he had snapped up around a third of the fifty lots on offer, writing a cheque for a total of more than £4,000.

Five years later, a single black Steiff fetched double that amount. Like Alfonzo, he can now be seen at 'Teddy Bears' of Witney (page 144). In December 1993, a similar bear, this time in blue mohair, sold at Christies' South Kensington for £49,500. He had been made as a sample for Harrods around 1908.

The first Phillips sale of teddy bears was held in New Bond Street. These days, the sales are at Phillips Bayswater. Again, the bears sell for widely varying prices according to their rarity and condition. It is not all expensive Steiffs and coveted English Farnells.

SOTHEBY'S

Sotheby's was the auction house where, in 1989, a record £55,000 was paid for a beautiful Steiff teddy bear, bought by American Paul Volpp as a present for his wife Rosemary on their forty-second wedding anniversary.

Rosemary and Paul are well-known collectors, whose bears have been featured in many books and magazine articles. It was, however, purely by chance that they popped into Sotheby's during a visit to London and saw the 1926 Steiff. For Rosemary it was love at first sight, and Paul was determined to surprise her with the bear.

He knew that the previous record price for a bear was

£12,100, paid at Christie's for Alfonzo. Even allowing for the fact that the Sotheby's bear was extra special, he was not expecting the price to go much beyond £16,000 or £17,000. So when he asked a friend in England to attend the auction for him, he put no limit on the price he would pay. He was in for quite a shock. The sale made headline news on both sides of the Atlantic.

Since then, Happy (as she became known) has been much fêted and photographed, and has carved out a career helping to raise money for children's charities. In addition, her original makers, Steiff, have produced modern replicas in three sizes, which have joined collections all over the world.

At the time of writing, no bear sold since has reached that price, although a rare black Steiff, made in 1912 and in pristine condition, fetched £24,200 at Sotheby's in 1990.

Like that bought at Phillips a few months later (and now in Witney), he had originally been made specially for the British market. So Steiff produced a replica specially for the United Kingdom in 1991. The original now lives with an American collector. (Coincidentally, both new owners of these early black bears named their new acquisitions Othello.)

Sotheby's had first introduced teddy bears into their sales in about 1983. All the bears in that sale came from one owner, and none were known to be made by Steiff, whose bears have now long commanded the highest prices at auction. At that 1983 sale, no bear fetched over £400.

Gradually, more and more bears started to appear at Sotheby's, and top prices crept steadily higher. By 1987, an £8,800 bear sold there was making headline news, and two years later there was Happy.

Nevertheless, record-breaking prices are the exception rather than the rule. Sale prices at Sotheby's can be anything from a few hundred to several thousand pounds, and even identical bears can fetch vastly different amounts on different sale days.

ADDRESSES

Bonhams Chelsea, 65–69 Lots Road, SW10; tel. 071 351 7111

Christie's South Kensington, 85 Old Brompton Road, SW7; tel. 071 321 3277

Phillips Bayswater, 10 Salem Road, Bayswater, W2; tel. 071 229 9090

Sotheby's, 34–35 New Bond Street, W1; tel. 071 493 8080

SOUTH AND
SOUTH-EAST

Arundel

It is the Castle, dating back to the end of the eleventh century, which attracts many visitors to Arundel in Sussex. In summer, the town is full of life. In winter, when the Castle is closed, the town sleeps, with many shops and other attractions opening only at weekends (or not at all).

Arundel Teddy Bears is an exception. It opens Monday to Saturday throughout the year, and in summer it can often be visited on a Sunday afternoon as well.

The shop naturally attracts its fair share of visitors. But it has opted not to sell the wide range of gift items found in many other specialist shops in tourist areas. As space is limited, and as there are bear-related items in some of Arundel's many gift shops, owners Doreen and John Smith decided to specialize almost entirely in the bears themselves. They discovered that it was what most people wanted from them.

They do, however, still stock the Colour Box miniatures, and they have Steiff animals as well as their teddy bears, having become one of the company's Club Stores.

Their range of Steiff bears is wide, and includes the Classics as well as many limited editions. They also have some of the softer Steiff teddies, for those who want something more suitable for a child.

They have Merrythought bears, too, for those seeking something of British manufacture – again with a good selection of the company's limited editions. But those are the only other manufactured bears you can expect to find. Doreen and John decided that two manufacturers were enough for a shop of their size, and they have made a point of not selling any bears made in the Far East at all.

Instead, all the remaining shelves are filled with a variety of artist bears, from tiny miniatures to the toddler-sized, and in just about every conceivable colour.

Doreen and John have found that many of their collectors start with a traditional Steiff bear, but later begin to notice the artist bears because some of them are so different in design. In the beginning, customers may insist that they would never buy a dressed bear or a bear in an unusual colour. But in time, many change their minds, and the shop tries to cater for them all.

Knowing how much collectors like to have something different, Doreen and John try to offer a good range of artist bears that have been made specially for them. Usually, the editions will be very small as well – perhaps just three or four bears – so that the range is changing constantly.

Many British artists have made exclusives for the shop – top names like Mister Bear, Gregory Bear and Lillibet, for instance. But there has also been a special limited edition from Holland's Sunny Bears, and many more from North American makers.

In fact, Arundel Teddy Bears is the only British outlet for some American artists, while others make limited editions specially for the shop. But Doreen and John are still always on the look-out for good new makers – from both sides of the Atlantic – to keep them supplied with new and unusual creations.

Doreen makes bears herself, too, under the name Woodland Bears. They are especially popular with visitors because of their local connection. She actually started making them some years before they opened the shop. But it was some time before she began using mohair for her creations, and thus found more of a market among collectors.

Originally, she had thought that she could make her bears in between serving customers in the shop. But others have had similar ideas and, like them, she soon found that she could not sew and talk to collectors at the same time. In the summer, in particular, the shop can become frantically busy, often needing both Doreen's and John's attention. So now Doreen stays at home as much as possible during the winter months, to make her bears, while husband John takes charge of the shop. At busy times, however, she can also be found behind the counter – cramming her bear-making into any spare moments that remain.

Usually, she will make just two or three bears in a particular design before moving on to try something new. So again they help the shop to keep offering something different all the time.

One thing you are unlikely to find at Arundel Teddy Bears, however, is any old bear for sale. Doreen and John love them so much that they invariably find themselves unable to part with any that come their way. On the other hand, you may find a few at **Arundel Bridge Antiques**, a general antiques centre on the High Street. Other antique shops in the town could occasionally have something of interest, too.

The town has a large number of such shops for its size. In fact, by far the majority of its shops are aimed at the visitor rather than the resident. You won't find the large chains here. What you may find, however, is all sorts of interesting props and accessories to display alongside your bears.

Many of the shops open at irregular hours, though, especially in the winter when some open only at weekends. And even in the summer, you may find that Monday is best avoided, as some shop owners apparently use that day for their buying trips.

Shops are concentrated on the High Street, but don't miss those in Tarrant Street as well. Among them are some modern craft shops which may also have something of bearish interest.

Open Country in Quay House, down by the river, also has some teddy-related gifts, including ceramic miniatures, as well as souvenir Arundel teddies and generally a Paddington or two. And don't miss **The Venerable Bead and Basket Shop** at 47 High Street. Their range includes tiny and not so tiny baskets in various styles – some of them just right for smaller teddies.

Bear lovers will also not want to miss the **Arundel Toy & Military Museum**, right beside Arundel Teddy Bears. Its hours of opening vary, so it may be best to phone beforehand to check – especially in the winter, when it is closed during the week except by appointment. But it has a number of teddy bears among its exhibits.

Durban Ted was, as his name suggests, made in Durban, and came from a family who brought him with them from South Africa. There is a French bear with unusual green nose and feet. But tucked away in a corner is also a little English Merrythought, the childhood bear of the owner's wife.

Other bears are dotted throughout the various rooms. Some are in pristine condition. Some have clearly known better – and furrier – days, and many are of unknown heritage. But a Chad Valley bear is clearly identified by the button in his ear, and many collectors will recognize the Merrythought Cheeky Bear.

There is a lovely mechanical bear, too, of the type that pours a 'drink' from a bottle, and the keen-eyed will no doubt spot a bear or two among the collection of eggcups and on some of the children's china.

There are a number of other soft toys in the museum, including one of Dean's famous Lupino Lane dolls, an early Mickey Mouse, and Felix the Cat, not to mention various gollies. But the other exhibits range from trains and cars, lead figures, games, ships in bottles and a doll's house or two to a large collection of crested china, including planes, boats, cars, tanks, mugs and boots.

There are toy soldiers galore as well, while the militaria also includes regimental badges, a variety of helmets, medals, letters and photographs.

If you want to discover more about Arundel itself, the Heritage Museum traces its distant and recent history. But it is the Castle which attracts the largest number of visitors. Its many treasures include some personal possessions of Mary, Queen of Scots, as well as fine paintings and furniture. Set in more than a thousand acres of parkland, it has been the seat of the Dukes of Norfolk for more than five hundred years. (You will find the entrance to both the Castle and grounds in Mill Road, at the bottom of the High Street.)

The town also boasts some splendid churches. The Anglican church of St Nicholas is unique in that it actually has a Roman Catholic chapel under the same roof. But the town also has a Roman Catholic cathedral, designed by J. A. Hansom, better known for his invention of the hansom cab. Built as a church in the 1870s, it became a Cathedral in 1965. The building was, however, never fully completed after it was decided that the structure may not be able to support the planned 280-foot spire.

ADDRESSES

Arundel Bridge Antiques, 6 High Street; tel. 0903 884164
Arundel Teddy Bears, 21 High Street; tel. 0903 884458
Arundel Toy & Military Museum, 23 High Street; tel. 0903 882908/883101
Tourist Information Centre, 61 High Street; tel. 0903 882268

Brighton

Once it was a small fishing and farming village. Today they call it London by the Sea, the largest seaside resort in Britain.

All the usual seaside attractions are there – funfairs, boat trips, a Sea Life Centre, beach-side railway (actually the oldest electric railway in Britain), discos, nightclubs, not to mention nearly two hundred restaurants. But there is elegant architecture, too, and it has been said that the town has more listed buildings than any other in Britain.

It also has a splendid variety of shops – not just the well-known High Street stores, which are concentrated in the Churchill Square area of the town, but every imaginable kind of specialist shop. As a result, the town attracts visitors from all over the world, not just in summer but right through the year. Teddy bear lovers among them will find that Brighton is full of delights.

The area known as the Lanes will be the first stop for most of them. This maze of small passageways was the heart of old Brighton which, until 1800, was totally contained within the area bordered by North Street, West Street and East Street. Now the Lanes are crammed with small shops and cafés, and a cosmopolitan crowd of browsers throngs the narrow paths, especially on sunny summer days.

They are attracted by all the antique shops, jewellers, tiny boutiques and, of course, the gift shops galore, many of which have bears in some shape or form. You could find bears on anything from costume jewellery to cushions, not to mention all the ceramic teddies and the soft and fluffy creations that are always popular gifts.

Collectors, however, will be drawn irresistibly to the specialist **Bears and Friends**, at 41 Meeting House Lane. The shop first opened in 1989, but at that time it was situated twenty-five yards away, at No. 32. Then, in August 1993, the owners moved to their present premises. This not only gave them far more space for their huge range of bears and bear-related offerings, but also allowed them the chance to fulfil their dream of creating their own museum.

Before the new shop could be opened, however, a good deal of work needed to be done, and there were a few surprises in store. Before they bought the building, it had housed an antique market, divided up into numerous individual stalls. It was only when they started pulling them all down that they realized there was more to the building than they had originally believed.

Weeks of digging revealed not only a large basement absolutely full of rubble and rubbish, but an old chalk tunnel that no one was aware of. They also came across plenty of evidence of the shop's former uses. Bones and horns were a reminder that it had been a butcher's shop in the early nineteenth century. Later, it had held a manufacturer of window blinds, some of which had also been left behind. Hundreds of walnut shells were the legacy of a high-class fruiterer.

Today, however, it is bears which cram the shelves. For a start, the shop is a Steiff Club Store, so there are naturally plenty of that company's creations. They sell all the limited editions as well as many bears from the regular ranges. But some of the most popular collectors bears disappear very quickly.

Other manufacturers represented include Hermann, Merrythought and Dean's, again including the limited editions. But there are cuddly bears from some of those companies, too, as well as others made in the Far East. As the shop naturally attracts a large number of tourists, they try to cater for as many tastes as possible.

Alongside the Paddington Bears and Winnie-the-Poohs, you will also find an ever-changing selection of artist bears, including offerings from some of the country's top makers. Bears and

Friends generally has bears from well over fifty different British and American artists, many of whom also make exclusive limited editions for the shop.

As the editions are always small, the range never stays the same from one week to the next. But among the British makers who have created one or more limited editions specially for them are Bocs Teganau, Teddystyle, Mother Hubbard, Gregory Bear, Little Treasures, Susan Jane, Willow Bears, and miniaturists Anita Oliver and Nicola Perkins (Tree Top Bears). There are many American artist bears as well, so the range is invariably both colourful and innovative.

For those who prefer something less modern, however, there is usually a good number of older bears on sale, too, from a wide variety of makers.

Old bears and artist bears can turn out to be very expensive, of course. But those with less to spend have not been overlooked. The range of teddy bear ornaments is unusually wide, for instance, and can range from inexpensive resin miniatures to intricate sculptures costing several hundred pounds. There is usually a good range of pictures, including inexpensive prints as well as original oils and limited-edition etchings. There are clothes for the bears, and you will also find little pocket-money items, like magnets.

A speciality, however, is teddy bear jewellery, which includes everything from gold and silver to what they call 'fabulous fakes'.

They try to keep a good supply of old and reproduction prams, high chairs and the like in stock, too – always an asset when displaying bears. And there is a delightful range of cottage-style painted furniture, which includes bear-sized chairs, benches and tables.

A repair service is offered for teddies which have seen better days and, as if that wasn't enough, the Bears and Friends Museum should now be open, with an interesting collection of old bears on permanent view. They include many English bears as well as

German Steiffs and Hermanns, and a whole range of splendid bear-related items gathered over a number of years. The large Chiltern Bear which became the shop's logo is also to be found there.

Tourists pour into Bears and Friends all day long. But just around the corner, in Prince Albert Street, **Sue Pearson's shop** is a haven of tranquillity for the teddy enthusiast. Don't be put off by the need to ring the bell to gain entrance. All genuine enthusiasts receive a warm welcome, and the absence of a crowd means that you can take a leisurely look at the bears, which include both old and new.

Sue has been buying and selling old bears for many years now. She started collecting dolls and teddies as a child, and later started selling them from a market stall before progressing to a gallery and then, in the mid-eighties, her own shop. Gradually, the bears have been taking over from the dolls, however, and in recent years some newer creations have been creeping in alongside the old.

You should nevertheless still find plenty of splendid early teddies – including beautiful German Steiffs and English Farnells in excellent condition. Other English makes like Merrythought, Chad Valley and Chiltern can usually be found as well, in addition to bears from lesser-known companies or of uncertain heritage.

Sue's many years as a collector and dealer have meant that she is a fund of knowledge on bears and their makers, and she is happy to give advice to novice collectors afraid of making an expensive mistake. She also offers free valuations and appraisals to owners of old bears – a service that has proved popular both in her shop and at the many specialist fairs she attends.

In addition, the shop has a long-established Teddy Bear Hospital, where bears can be admitted for expert cleaning and repairs. In fact, the old bears on sale are also first given a careful clean, often to stunning effect.

All sorts of antique accessories are on sale, too, and any of them could look perfect with some of your own bears. You may find a beautiful old pram or chair, or perhaps some small item with a teddy bear decoration. It all depends what Sue has discovered on her bear-buying trips.

Some of those trips take her to America, and her new, artist-made bears invariably include some of the delightful creations she has found there. Others are the work of British makers and the range is changing all the time.

Sue is the only British stockist for some of her artists, while others make exclusive editions specially for the shop. Jo Greeno is just one of the top British artists to have designed bears especially for her. Others include the long-established Bo-Bear Designs and the popular Shultz Bears.

Sue Pearson also still sells old dolls, doll's houses and doll's house miniatures, and the 'hospital' admits dolls as well as bears.

There are still more collectable bears in this part of Brighton, in the traditional toy shop **Mr Punch**, in Market Street. His range of Steiff bears includes both limited editions and the popular Classic bears, and he stocks bears by Merrythought and Dean's.

There are more Merrythoughts and Steiffs among the soft toys in **Hannington's** department store in North Street, and they generally include some Steiff limited editions.

Many other shops in the town have gift items with a bearish theme. You'll find a variety of ceramic miniatures and of cute and cuddly teddies, but you could also find any number of more unusual creations in some of the specialist craft shops.

Another specialist shop has a rather different attraction for collectors. **The Mulberry Bush** is a few minutes' walk from the Lanes, in George Street (reached by walking eastwards along North Street, crossing over Old Steine and continuing a short way along St James's Street until you reach George Street on your left). You won't usually find many bears there. But alongside all the doll's houses and doll's house miniatures they stock a huge number of books on all sorts of toys including, of course, teddy bears.

Collectors' guides are their speciality. If a book for bear collectors is in print – and often when it isn't – you should find it in the Mulberry Bush.

Many of the books on their shelves are American publications, sometimes obtained through British distributors and sometimes imported direct from America when no British distribution has been arranged. Some are identification guides, full of pictures of interesting old (and sometimes new) bears, and with details of any unusual features that might help collectors pinpoint the makers of bears in their own collections. Others give advice on making bears, or clothes for bears, or on the history of bear making. But there are also albums of beautiful photos that are simply there to be enjoyed.

If you love bears and love books, this is definitely a shop not to be missed.

On the other hand, you could also find an attractive teddy bear story-book in one of Brighton's antiquarian bookshops. And some of the many antique shops could yield something bear-related, or an interesting accessory for one of your bears. If you love to browse round bric-à-brac stalls, however, then the best day for a visit to Brighton is probably Saturday, when the North Laine area around Upper Gardner Street is filled with all sorts of market and craft stalls.

During the rest of the week the North Laine area is home to all sorts of interesting small shops selling everything from antiques to Belgian chocolates, and from period clothes to the latest designer fashions. So it is worth a visit at any time. But on Saturday the shops are joined by stalls of every kind, and you never know what you might find there.

There are more antique shops in Upper North Street, and on Sunday mornings the station car park is turned over to all kinds of stalls, many selling all sorts of bric-à-brac.

Visitors to Brighton often spend their whole day simply browsing and, perhaps, buying. But there are, of course, many other things to see while you are in the town – in addition to the sea.

Most famous is the magnificent Royal Pavilion, the seaside home of the flamboyant Prince Regent (later George IV). Once simply a farmhouse, the building was steadily enlarged and embellished and is now one of the most exotic in the country.

Regency Square is one of many fine examples of Regency architecture. But Brighton is also full of so-called twittens and cat-creeps – narrow lanes and flights of steps leading from one street to another and offering a totally different impression of the town.

The town has its share of galleries and museums, too. But the most interesting for bear lovers will be the **Sussex Toy and Model Museum**, situated right underneath Brighton station. Naturally, its collection includes some splendid model trains. But there are also buses, cars, boats, aeroplanes, toy soldiers, dolls, Bayko and Meccano construction kits, and a handful of teddy bears.

It also includes a really splendid collection of toys related to the postal service, with everything from cars, vans and mail trains to post office sets, a toy telephone exchange and pillar boxes of every shape and many sizes.

ADDRESSES

Bears & Friends, 41 Meeting House Lane; tel. 0273 208940

The Mulberry Bush, 9 George Street; tel. 0273 600471/493781

Sue Pearson, 13½ Prince Albert Street; tel. 0273 329247

Mr Punch, 7 Market Street; tel. 0273 326049

Sussex Toy and Model Museum, Trafalgar Street (under Brighton railway station); tel. 0273 749494

Tourist Information Centre, 10 Bartholomew Square; tel. 0273 323755

Burley

The New Forest village of Burley, in Hampshire, is the home of **Goldilocks**, where they try to stock a wide range of bears to suit every pocket. You should find anything up to a hundred teddies, with prices ranging from little over £1 to about £100. Steiff, Hermann and Merrythought are all to be found there, as well as the more local Bransgore and Dorset bears.

The shop also has a wide variety of greetings cards and stationery – some of which naturally feature teddy bears – and there are various figurines as well.

Many visitors to the New Forest find their way to Burley throughout the year, so you will find many other small gift shops in the village. Some could have teddy-related items on sale.

ADDRESSES

Goldilocks, 4 The Mall, Ringwood Road; tel. 0425 403558
Lyndhurst & New Forest Tourist Information, Main Car Park, Lyndhurst; tel. 0703 282269

Canterbury

Canterbury has so many teddy bear connections that bear lovers really are spoilt for choice. Teddies are everywhere – in gift shops, specialist shops, department stores. A few minutes' drive from the town, a teddy bear factory welcomes visitors (provided they make an appointment). And Rupert fans can follow the Rupert Trail while taking in the Canterbury sights.

BEARS FOR SALE

The pedestrianized shopping area centred on St Peter's Street, High Street and St George's Street is home to many of the town's gift shops. The area seethes with browsers, winter and summer, and the atmosphere is often enlivened by street musicians and entertainers. There are splendid medieval buildings at every turn, encouraging the visitor to look and linger.

Needless to say, teddy bears often feature strongly among the gifts in shops like the splendidly nostalgic **Saunders**. There are two Saunders shops, one on either side of St Peter's Street. That at No. 50 opened in June 1899, in part of the historic Three Kings Tavern, where King Charles II once stayed. The other shop, directly opposite at No. 12, was formerly an inn by the name of Dogs Head in the Pot. It dates back to medieval times and was at one time owned by monks.

Between them, the shops generally have a particularly good range of bear-related gifts, like Colour Box miniatures, Winnie-the-Pooh and Rupert merchandise, Paddington Bears and Jane Hissey's books and stationery featuring the much-loved Old Bear and his friends. They also have a large number of reproductions of old metal advertising plaques, and these usually include a bear or two.

There is nothing but bears and bearish things at the nearby **English Teddy Bear**

Company, where everything they sell is made specially for them. You will find bears dressed and undressed, jointed and unjointed – some made from mohair and others from the less expensive synthetic plushes.

Some of the clothes are sold separately, too – little waistcoats, for instance, and bow ties. And there are English Teddy Bear Co. T-shirts in various sizes – intended for humans, but the smaller sizes may fit some of your bears.

They also have their own mugs and badges, and other specialities have included their own biscuits and preserves.

Upstairs, a tearoom serves various blends of tea (including honey tea) in mammoth pots, and they offer afternoon teas disguised as teddy bears' picnics.

There are many more gift shops tucked away in the small side streets running off the main pedestrian thoroughfare – down towards the Cathedral, for instance. And there are more bears in **Ricemans** department store in St George's Lane. In addition to plenty of cuddly toys, they have a good number of Canterbury Bears, as well as some Merrythoughts and Steiffs – but no limited editions when I visited.

As is often the case, however, the best sources of limited editions are a short way away from the main shopping centres and the busiest tourist tracks.

Turn down Guildhall Street (by Debenhams), and continue on into Palace Street, and you will come to the delightful **Magpie's Nest**, with its mixture of dolls, bears and miniatures.

Owner Diane Cleavely tries to carry a good number of bears not available anywhere else in Canterbury. She has Steiff bears as well, including the limited editions, and bears from British manufacturers like Dean's and Merrythought. But there is also a variety of artist bears.

Some are British made, like those by Dormouse Designs and some Pam Howells bears made exclusively for the Magpie's Nest.

There will generally be some bears by other British artists, too, but the range changes all the time as Diane keeps looking for bears that no one else in the vicinity is offering.

As she is American herself, it is hardly surprising that she is also constantly on the look-out for interesting bears by American artists that no one else in Britain has discovered. In fact, her shop was one of the first in the country to start selling American artist bears.

These days, Pat Murphy's Murphy Bears are sold only through the Magpie's Nest in the United Kingdom. Other shop exclusives include some lovely little dressed and accessorized teddies by Jody Battaglia selling at far more reasonable prices than many American imports.

As the shop also sells a good number of doll's house miniatures, it is no surprise to find that they have some miniature bears made exclusively for them as well. But for those with less money to spend, they have some appealing but less expensive teddies (the Tails and Tales range, for instance, and the popular Ty bears).

There are also various teddy ornaments, like the Cherished Teddies and the Small World range, as well as the tiny pewter teddies popular with many collectors. Other bear-related items include rubber stamps and a good number of greetings cards.

Dolls and the doll's house miniatures, gollies and a variety of pretty gifts fill the remaining shelves in a real Aladdin's cave of a shop that is well worth seeking out.

Walk on a little further – bearing right into The Borough and continuing on into Northgate – and you'll find another shop catering to the needs of the collector, **Teddy's Emporium**.

Owners Lesley and Mark Garbutt have been enthusiastic collectors ever since Mark's mother gave Lesley some money one birthday and she used it to buy an old bear. Then, as so often happens, their own growing collection gave them the idea of opening a shop to sell bears to other collectors. As they love to talk bears with fellow enthusiasts, it is a place that collectors often find it hard to leave.

Particularly welcome is the way in which Teddy's Emporium and the Magpie's Nest try to complement each other, rather than aggressively competing with the same range of bears. Naturally, Teddy's Emporium also stock the Steiff limited editions, and they generally have a large number of Merrythought bears (including the limited editions) as well as some bears by Dean's. But again they try to offer plenty of bears available nowhere else in the town, and try to ensure that artist bears in particular are not duplicated.

In fact, Lesley has been having a good deal of success making her own distinctive Mr Chump and Friends to sell in the shop.

They sell other artist bears, too, as well as the work of British companies like Big Softies and Nisbet, and there is usually a good selection of the local Canterbury Bears as well. The latter include a limited edition made specially for Teddy's Emporium.

You may find some old bears or other soft toys there as well. But there are also plenty of inexpensive new bears – and, of course, the Paddington Bears so popular with tourists. So are Winnie-the-Pooh and his friends, and there are various inexpensive bear-related items like brooches and postcards.

Lesley and Mark are also building up their stock of accessories for bears, having discovered just how much they appeal to collectors. They range from tiny terracotta flowerpots to bear-sized basket chairs to old display cases and other items of furniture, popular with collectors who want to show their old bears in a suitable setting.

There are also many general antique shops in Canterbury, and some of these can be useful hunting grounds for collectors looking for 'props' and accessories to bring a collection to life. Try the nearby **Coach House Antique Centre** in Duck Lane (off St Radigunds), or the **Canterbury Rastro** back in the High

Street (No. 44a, opposite Debenhams). Then there is **Curios** at 68 Stour Street (on the other side of the High Street).

If, on the other hand, your hobby is sewing, don't miss the **Handicraft Shop** at 47 Northgate, just a couple of doors away from Teddy's Emporium. Their wide range of embroidery kits and tapestries invariably include some featuring teddies, and bears sometimes appear on quilting fabrics, cushion panels and so on. They even have fabric paints for drawing your own teddies or, if you want to make a bear, you'll find fur fabric, eyes and other bear-making essentials, as well as some complete kits.

RUPERT'S CANTERBURY

Of rather different bearish interest is the **Canterbury Heritage Museum** on Stour Street. Full of relics from the City's past, it is also home to a special display on one of Canterbury's most famous sons, Rupert.

Rupert was the creation of artist and illustrator Mary Tourtel, born Mary Caldwell on 28 January 1874 at 52 Palace Street (not far from the Magpie's Nest). She came from a very artistic family. Her father Samuel Caldwell and one of her brothers (also called Samuel) both restored stained glass for the Cathedral. The work of another brother, Edmund, was shown at the Royal Academy, and he also illustrated children's books, in addition to becoming a well-known animal painter in Africa.

Mary eventually became known for her animals paintings, too. She trained at the Sidney Cooper Gallery of Art, receiving lessons from Thomas Sidney Cooper, a renowned painter of cattle. A rare water-colour from those days – showing the Cathedral cloisters – can be seen in the Heritage Museum.

Later, she married Herbert Tourtel, night editor of the *Daily Express*. When the paper was looking for a character to rival the *Daily Mail*'s successful Teddy Tail, it was only natural that she should be asked to come up with an idea. Especially as she had already written and illustrated some books for children.

She created Rupert. He was rather different from the Rupert seen today, however, with a jumper that was blue, not red, and with grey checked trousers and scarf instead of the distinctive yellow he now wears. His head was also much more like that of a real bear.

The first story appeared one Monday morning, on 8 November 1920 – tucked away at the bottom of the paper's women's page. It was just a single panel – in black and white, of course – showing Rupert about to set off on a shopping trip. Underneath were some of the now familiar rhyming couplets which tell the Rupert stories.

The story ran for a total of thirty-six episodes.

Mary also created several other enduring characters, which appeared in her stories from the earliest days. Algy Pug, for instance, had actually appeared in a story written by her before the first Rupert strip. Bill Badger was also an early arrival, as was Edward Trunk.

Mary continued to produce the Rupert stories for many years, and they were soon being reproduced in books as well as in the newspaper. (The first of these books is among those on display at the Heritage Museum.) Only when her eyesight began to fail was the drawing of the strips taken over by Alfred Bestall, in 1935.

The Heritage Museum shows the work of both Mary Tourtel and Alfred Bestall (who also created the first of the famous Rupert annuals). There is a life-sized model of Mary at work, as well as information and photographs of both artists, and the production of more recent stories is also covered.

Examples of the many Rupert books and annuals are on display – including the very first annual from 1936. And there are also samples of the huge range of Rupert merchandise which has been produced over the years – from Easter eggs to mugs, carrier bags to cassettes, and a record of Rupert fan Paul McCartney singing 'We All Stand Together' with the Frog Chorus.

The delightful video of Rupert and the Frog Song can also be seen.

There are many other places with Rupert connections in the town, and Canterbury's **Visitor Information Centre** in St Margaret's Street sells a booklet showing where to find them.

A plaque marks the house where Mary Tourtel was born, for instance, and the Sidney Cooper Centre in St Peter's Street was once the Sidney Cooper Gallery of Art, where Mary studied. (Now it is home to an antiques and crafts market each Saturday.) Some of her teacher's work is on view at the Royal Museum and Art Gallery in the High Street, while stained glass produced by her father and brother can still be seen in the Cathedral.

Baker's Temperance Hotel, where Mary spent her final years, is also still standing – although it is now known as Chaucer's Hotel. (It is also a good place to stop for lunch.)

Mary died on 15 March 1948, at the age of seventy-four. Her final resting place is on the raised terrace on the north side of St Martin's churchyard.

Of course, while following the Rupert Trail, you'll have a chance to see many of Canterbury's other famous sights. The Cathedral, for instance, is one of the most magnificent buildings in Western Europe, built between 1071 and 1500. After Archbishop Thomas à Becket was murdered there in 1170, Canterbury became second only to Jerusalem and Rome in its importance as a place of pilgrimage.

Ancient buildings still line the city's streets. Conquest House in Palace Street is, for instance, reputed to be where Becket's murderers spent the previous night. The famous Weavers House in St Peter's Street was one of many built by Flemish and Huguenot weavers – sixteenth-century refugees from religious persecution. On the outskirts of the city are the remains of a Norman Castle, while the West Gate (built around 1380) still guards the western end of St Peter's Street.

Many of the city's shops are housed in beautiful old buildings, and the Canterbury Heritage Museum occupies one of the finest of them all – the fourteenth-century Poor Priests' Hospital, once a home for retired clergy.

CANTERBURY BEARS

Bear lovers, however, may prefer to head for Littlebourne, just outside Canterbury, and the home of **Canterbury Bears**.

John and Maude Blackburn started making their traditional style teddy bears long before the collectors market took off in Britain. Now their bears can be found all over the world. But they never forget who their final purchasers are. Bear lovers are welcome to visit their workshop, provided that they ring first to arrange a convenient time.

It was in 1979 that they made their very first bear, after meeting a man who wanted a traditional jointed bear as a present for his eighty-year-old grandmother. He couldn't find one, so John (a product designer) was asked if he could come up with a suitable design. Then Maude and John made up a couple of the bears themselves, because they couldn't find anyone else to do it for them.

There was no way they could have foreseen the impact that the project would have on their lives. People wanted to know who had made the bears and, when the Blackburns confessed, they soon found themselves being asked for more. Before they knew it, they had set up a workshop in their own house, although it was some years before Maude herself joined the business full time.

John would design the bears and cut them out, and they

employed outworkers for jobs like machining and stuffing. Maude took care of the business side of things, as well as continuing with her former job.

Originally they made other soft toys as well as the bears. But they soon decided that teddy bears were their forte, and within a year or so they were making nothing else. Before long they were making their first tour of America, where enthusiasts grabbed the bears right out of their arms. Orders from Australia and New Zealand quickly followed.

Then their bears were certified by the Design Council, and went on show at London's Design Centre.

After a year, daughter Kerstin joined her father in the company. Later, Maude and son Mark came to work there, too, and in 1984 they finally moved out of their now over-crowded house into The Old Coach House in Littlebourne.

Much of the making of the bears is still done by outworkers. But when an urgent order needs to be completed, everyone pitches in to ensure that the bears are delivered on time. On a typical day, you might see a couple of helpers machining heads, bodies and limbs. Others will be brushing out the fur, tying ribbons or embroidering the noses, and John himself might be busy inscribing his and Maude's names on the feet of a special signed limited edition being sent to an American bear shop.

Many of the bears are sent to America, and John and Maude make regular tours there, visiting shops and fairs and signing thousands of bears for collectors. Each year, they also produce a special range for the American company Gund. A few of these bears are now made available to British collectors.

A huge number of other new designs appear each year, to be sold all over the world. Some are aimed specifically at collectors, but children are not forgotten either, with many of the company's bears going to toy shops like Hamleys.

Hamleys are just one of the many clients who have ordered exclusive Canterbury Bears designs. Harrods, Simpson of Piccadilly, Liberty, The Scotch House and Laura Ashley are a few of the others. Other exclusives have gone to Granada Studios, the Royal Academy of Arts and the Tower of London, to name just a few.

These days, Maude is designing bears too, and many of the special corporate bears are actually her creations.

Visitors have the chance to see not only a large number of bears in the current Canterbury Bears range but also samples of many others that are no longer in production. There is a copy of the special silk bear given to President Clinton, and featuring the presidential seal. And if your timing is right, you should see some of the bears being made exclusively for individual shops in various countries.

Tours of the workshop also take visitors through the whole bear-making process. They are shown the bolts of fabric, learn how the cutting blades are made and how they are laid out on the fabric to ensure the minimum wastage. They are told how bags of bear parts, including leather or suede for the pads (and any labels to be sewn in), are sent to the outworkers for machining. And they learn how, back in the factory, a machine is used to turn the limbs the right way out.

They see how the eyes are fixed into the heads, how joints are inserted (again with the help of a machine), and how the bears are blow-filled with siliconized Dacron before being sent back to outworkers for the final sewing.

Finally, they are shown how the bears are brushed, their bows and any accessories added, and how they are rigorously checked to ensure that they satisfy the company's strict quality standards.

Detailed records track the bears through every stage, and a carefully contrived system ensures absolutely accurate numbering of each bear in a limited edition and any accompanying boxes.

What will strike most visitors, however, is how so many

bears can be created by such a small band of full-time staff –
helped by their invisible band of outworkers.

ADDRESSES

Canterbury Bears, The Old Coach House, Court Hill, Little-
bourne; tel. 0227 728238
Canterbury Heritage Museum, Stour Street; tel. 0227 452747
English Teddy Bear Company, 4 St Peter's Street; tel. 0227
784640
The Handicraft Shop, 47 Northgate; tel. 0227 451188
The Magpie's Nest, 14 Palace Street; tel. 0227 764883
Ricemans, 6 St George's Lane; tel. 0227 766866
Saunders, 12 & 50 St Peter's Street; tel. 0227 760815
Teddy's Emporium, 50 Northgate; tel. 0227 769987
Visitor Information Centre, 34 St Margaret's Street; tel. 0227
766567

Carshalton

The pretty but little-visited Carshalton Village is not the kind
of place where you would expect to find a good selection of
collectable bears. But the family-run **Yesteryear's Charm** in
Carshalton has become well known among collectors as far afield
as America and Japan.

It is actually a quality gift shop, selling beautiful china, crystal
and figurines as well as a large number of collectable dolls. But
the bears have a whole room to themselves – the kind of old-
fashioned room that suits them so well.

You will not find inexpensive souvenir bears or children's
toys here. It is very much a shop for the collector. They aim to

have over two hundred bears on display at any one time, with every single one different. Even if they have two bears of the same design in stock, the second will be put out on the shelves only after the first has been sold. So the range is always wide, and choosing can be very difficult.

For a long time, the only manufactured bears they sold were those made by Steiff, including their limited editions. Eventually they added some Merrythought and Dean's limited editions, but the majority of their bears are still artist-made.

At the time of writing, they have the work of more than twenty top British artists on display, with sixteen of them producing one-off bears and exclusive limited editions available only at this shop. Naomi Laight, Mister Bear, Teddystyle, Pamela Ann Designs, Mother Hubbard, Bumblewood, Gregory Bear, Little Treasures, Hartrick, Bocs Teganau, Little Charmers and Forget-Me-Not Bears are just some of those to have made bears specially for Yesteryear's Charm to date.

The editions are never large, to ensure a constantly changing selection.

They try to have a good number of interesting old bears on sale, too, although these days that is becoming less easy. And you will certainly see a variety of bear-related gifts, ranging from cards and magnets to Irish Dresden figurines. They also have ceramic teddy sculptures of various makes and tiny pewter teddies, as well as a constantly changing range of other gifts like pictures, photo frames and bookends.

Some of the bears on show are seated in prams or pushchairs, or on rocking horses, and these are also on sale.

Most of the other shops in Carshalton Village are typical village stores, with the exception of a couple of antique shops which could just yield something of interest for a display.

Two ponds – one of the sources of the River Wandle – are among the village's other attractions, and you will also find a twelfth-century church, which has been greatly enlarged over the centuries.

ADDRESSES

Yesteryear's Charm, 30 Beacon Grove; tel. 081 773 4441
Tourist Information Centre, 72 High Street, Guildford; tel. 0483 444007

Cliftonville

When Janet Sackett took over the **Body Language** shop at Cliftonville in July 1990, it was her chance to turn a personal dream into a reality. For Janet is a genuine bear lover and dearly wanted to sell them. As soon as the boutique and gift shop was hers, she opened up her teddy bear corner.

Space is limited, but she usually manages to offer between sixty and a hundred bears, and has been steadily building up a firm following of regular customers as well as attracting many summer visitors.

She has bears by several major manufacturers. The Steiffs include the Classic range and the limited editions made specially for the United Kingdom. There are bears by Merrythought, Canterbury, Little Folk and Bransgore. But there are cuddly teddies, too, from Russ Berrie.

Artist bears will also be found there, with Bocs Teganau, Only Natural, Barbara-Ann, Dormouse and Mother Hubbard among the names stocked to date. In addition, the range of bear-related items includes greetings cards, postcards, bookmarks, gift tags, jewellery, rubber stamps, Winnie-the-Pooh items, Cherished Teddies, Colour Box miniatures, items from the Oscar and Bertie range, and framed prints. There are many non-bearish gifts, too, as well as clothes in a pretty shop with attractive window displays which invariably help to draw in customers.

Cliftonville itself is a seaside resort, and all the usual seaside attractions can be found in nearby Margate, whose places of interest include a fully operational windmill which is open on certain days during the summer months. The Lifeboat Station and Margate Caves are two other summer attractions, while Ramsgate (page 122) is also close by, with the East Kent Maritime Museum and Sally Line ferries to France.

ADDRESSES

Body Language, 125a Northdown Road; tel. 0843 299570
Tourist Information Centre, 22 High Street, Margate; tel. 0843
  220241

Ditchling

The unspoilt Sussex village of Ditchling is a real delight. Its beautiful old buildings include a thirteenth-century church built from local flints, and various timber-framed houses from the sixteenth century. But its history can be traced back much further.

There are written records from as early as 765, and it is known that the manor was owned by both Alfred the Great and Edward the Confessor. Later, William the Conqueror gave it to his son-in-law William de Warenne.

Today, it has a village green complete with duck pond, for quiet moments on warm sunny days. Or, if the weather is inclement, there is a museum telling the village's history, as well as a number of shops to explore. One of the latter contains a good number of teddies.

Kieron James opened his **St Dominic's Gallery** in the late eighties, intending to sell mainly traditional wooden toys. He still has some, but now bears are trying hard to take over. They include some bears suitable for children, but also a sizeable number aimed at collectors.

There are bears by Steiff, Hermann, Merrythought and Dean's, including some of each company's limited editions as well as the Steiff Classics and a good number of their miniatures. Big Softies have proved popular, too, and there are bears by Nisbet and Little Folk, as well as the cuddly Ty teddies and some by Russ Berrie. But you will also find a certain number of artist bears, by makers like Bo-Bear Designs and Barbara-Ann Bears.

There are bear-related items, too, including Colour Box miniatures, some pictures, greetings cards, postcards and a few books.

Bear-sized chairs (some of them rockers) are available in various sizes. The wooden toys and chalk boards make equally good 'props' for teddy bear displays, and the shop also sells some doll's houses and doll's house miniatures.

The village boasts several antique shops, too, although I found neither teddy bears nor interesting bear accessories there. I did, however, see a few bear-related items in Virginia Hogge Designs, the 'bespoke stationery' shop, just a stone's throw from St Dominic's Gallery.

ADDRESSES

Kieron James Designs, St Dominic's Gallery, 4 South Street; tel. 0273 846411

Tourist Information Centre, 187 High Street, Lewes; tel. 0273 483448

Dorking

Dorking in Surrey is well known for its antiques. There is an unusually large number of antique shops in the town, not to mention the antique centres which bring together various dealers, often with different specialities.

Many are concentrated in West Street and it is here, too, that you will find a large number of teddy bears – in the **Old Stockhouse** at number 60.

The shop is part of the oldest building in Dorking, a jettied row of houses dating back to around 1600, and reputed to have its own ghost. It is thought to have been the home of Pilgrim Father William Mullins, before he sailed on the *Mayflower* with his wife and daughter. Today, its low ceilings and exposed beams provide just the right atmosphere for a shop specializing in quality bears and dolls.

It is actually a general gift shop, selling much more than bears and dolls. But Eleanor and Peter Hutton have been stocking bears ever since they first opened twenty years ago, and can now boast quite a selection.

They generally include a few older ones, but most are modern – chosen very much with collectors in mind.

Among the manufacturers whose bears can be found there are Germany's Steiff and Hermann and Britain's Merrythought, Dean's, Nisbet and Canterbury. But there are also many artist bears, including various shop exclusives. Naturally, the range is changing constantly, but among the leading British artists whose work they have sold are Mother Hubbard, Mister Bear, Little Treasures, Pamela Ann Designs and Bearwood Bears.

They sell popular characters like Pooh and Paddington, too, and you will also find some bear-related items. But they tend not to have as many small bits and pieces as some other shops. You are more likely to find collectables, like the fine enamelled boxes made by Crummles and tiny pewter teddies. They do have some ceramic miniatures, however, and a selection of greetings cards.

The dolls include such leading names as Annette Himstedt and Käthe Kruse, and they also stock dolls by Steiff, in addition to their teddy bears.

Many of the West Street antique shops go for similarly high quality pieces, and these are unlikely to offer any inexpensive accessories for those who like to create interesting displays with their bears. But keen hunters may find the odd bargain – perhaps in one of the antique centres which offer a wide range of merchandise.

The town's non-bearish attractions include a fine nineteenth-century church, while more interesting old buildings are tucked away in the back streets. But it is the surrounding countryside that has the greatest appeal for many visitors.

Leith Hill to the south-west of the town is the highest point in south-east England. Its eighteenth-century tower, open to visitors during the summer months, affords a magnificent view of no fewer than twelve counties. It is said that the tower was built to increase the height of the hill enough for it to be classified as a mountain.

ADDRESSES

The Old Stockhouse, 60 West Street; tel. 0306 882783
Tourist Information Centre, 72 High Street, Guildford; tel. 0483 444007

Eton

Just a stone's throw from Windsor (page 141), over Windsor Bridge, is another place of considerable interest to bear lovers.

Eton is, of course, the home of the famous school whose past pupils have included twenty prime ministers. Founded in 1440 to give seventy poor boys the benefit of a grammar school education, Eton College now has over a thousand fee-paying pupils in addition to its seventy scholars.

Still in use is a classroom first used in 1443, and the chapel also dates from the fifteenth century.

Walking to the College from Windsor, you pass along Eton High Street, and it is here that the interest for bear lovers lies. Not only are there many antique and gift shops worth a browse, perhaps for a bear-related gift or an interesting accessory, but there is also one of the **Asquiths** teddy bear shops.

The original Asquiths, in Windsor itself, was opened in 1984. That in Eton was opened in 1988, and is on an altogether greater scale. It is crammed full of bears of all descriptions. Those of German manufacture include Steiffs and Hermanns, including both companies' limited editions. Merrythought limited editions and a Merrythought shop exclusive called Lofty are also on the shelves. But by far the majority of the bears carry Asquiths' own label.

The shop's owner Joan Bland creates the original designs and the many exclusive collectors bears are then hand-sewn in a Yorkshire workshop. But huge numbers of less expensive bears are made up in the Far East. They include the dressed Master Bear, in his gown and mortarboard, a City Bear in a bowler hat and a Henley Bear in a straw boater (as Asquiths also have a third shop in Henley-on-Thames, page 104).

Also exclusive to the Asquiths shops are intriguing Crystal

Talisman Bears in various colours, which combine crystal power with the principles of colour therapy.

The shop has a good mix of collectable bears and cuddly teddies, but it is also well known for its wide and ever-changing range of bear-related merchandise. Bear-sized satchels and bags, boaters, jumpers, honey-pots, chairs and other accessories are tucked alongside towels, bookmarks, magnets, greetings cards, books and bear brushes. There are also special Asquiths T-shirts, sweatshirts, mugs and so on.

People are drawn into the shop like bees to one of their honey-pots, and it is a rare bear lover indeed who can manage to walk out again without either a bear or some bearish accessory.

ADDRESSES

Asquiths, 33 High Street; tel. 0753 831200
Tourist Information Centre, Central Station, Thames Street, Windsor; tel. 0753 852010

Farnham

The Georgian town of Farnham has a long history. Situated in the south-west of Surrey, ten miles from Guildford, it was given its name by the Saxons (it means fern meadow). But the Romans were there before them, and there are even signs that the area was already inhabited in the Stone Age.

Today, a visitor's guide lists no fewer than twenty-two places of historic interest, yet you could see them all in little more than an hour (on foot), allowing plenty of time for browsing round the various shops.

It is not a major tourist resort, so you won't find streets crammed with gift shops. But the antique centre in South Street will be of special interest to bear lovers. About a dozen dealers have stalls there, selling a wide range of antiques and collectables. One, **Childhood Memories**, specializes in toys.

Dolls and doll's house miniatures are two of their specialities, but they also have a large number of teddy bears – at the time of writing, over a hundred in stock at any one time. And that does not include all the bears undergoing cleaning and restoration. So you should find a whole variety of makes and ages, with plenty of appealing faces tugging hard at your heartstrings.

They have some teddy bear greetings cards and clothes as well, and there is always a chance that you will find something bear-related on one of the other stalls. So it is certainly worth taking a look round them as well.

In addition, if you are visiting on the first Saturday in the month, don't miss the **Maltings Market** in Bridge Square. It usually includes a large number of stalls selling antiques and bric-à-brac, and you never know what you might discover, especially if you are on the look-out for interesting props and accessories.

Other places of interest in the town include the Castle and the Parish Church of St Andrew, both of which date back to Norman times, although most of the present church is from the fifteenth century. Then there is the Maltings, an eighteenth-century tannery which was rebuilt and turned into a brewery early in the nineteenth century. It became a maltings in the 1850s, but is now a thriving arts and community centre. Nearby is Tanyard House, built around 1500 and once occupied by the man who ran the eighteenth-century tannery.

A row of almshouses dates from 1619 – built for 'poor, honest, old and impotent persons'. The timber-framed Spinning Wheel is even older, and the town also contains some fine examples of Georgian architecture.

ADDRESSES

Childhood Memories, 27 South Street; tel. 025 125 3704
The Maltings Market, Bridge Square; enquiries 0252 726234
Tourist Information Centre, Vernon House, 28 West Street; tel.
  0252 715109

Guildford

Guildford is one of those towns where inside knowledge really pays when it comes to bears. They are there, all right, and in reasonably large numbers. But it would be quite easy to spend all afternoon in the busy shopping centre and still miss all the places of bearish interest.

The **Bear Garden**, for instance, is tucked away in Jeffries Passage, a narrow shop-filled alley running between North Street and the High Street. Seek it out, however, and you will find an ever-widening range of bears, from collectable limited editions to some inexpensive teddies made in the Far East.

They stock a large number of Steiff bears. Some of the limited editions can sell out quite quickly, but they also have the Classics and some of the regular ranges, like the Original Bears and the miniatures. You should find cuddly Petsys, too, as well as a selection of animals.

Hermann are also generally well represented, and there should be a good number of Merrythought and Dean's bears, again including limited editions.

Among the Canterbury Bears are those made for the American company Gund, while the Big Softies include a special Guildford Bear, complete with the Guildford crest.

Now the range of artist bears is gradually increasing, with bears from Bocs Teganau and local artist Simone King among the first to be stocked. When I visited, there were also a number of Australian-made bears for sale, and some limited-edition shop exclusives were in the pipeline, from both manufacturers and artists.

Lovers of more cuddly teddies have not been overlooked either, with bears from Ty among those on sale. And you should find popular character bears like Winnie-the-Pooh and Paddington, as well as various budget-priced bears from the Boyds Collection.

Bear-related items include Colour Box miniatures, greetings cards, pictures and books, and there are plans to expand this area as well.

You will find more collectables elsewhere in Guildford – like on the top floor of the **Army & Navy** department store, which has entrances in both North Street and the High Street. I found a few bears from the Steiff regular ranges alongside some of Merrythought's Heritage Collection, and cuddly teddies from companies like the Manhattan Toy Company Ltd.

There were more Manhattan bears at **Gay Corran** in Tunsgate Square (off Tunsgate), as well as bears by Little Folk and Bransgore. But if you like to display your bears with accessories or 'props', take a look at **Kiwi Connection**, too. Their speciality is things made of wood, and that includes the kind of wooden toys that look just right with many traditional bears. (The Kiwi Connection can also be found at 157 High Street.)

If old bears are your preference, however, you will want to seek out **Elaine Chandler** at 9 Martyr Road. She usually has a good number of older teddies in an antique shop which may also yield some interesting accessories for your bears. Turn into Haydon Place from North Street, and then right into Martyr Road.

If you stop off at **Guildford's Antique Centre** back in Haydon Place, you should find a few more teddies and soft toys there, in the care of Jennifer Carter. The centre brings together several different dealers, and again you could find something in the way of accessories here.

When you have had your fill of shopping, however, you will find plenty more to see in this county town. The High Street itself is part of a Conservation Area and includes a variety of architectural styles from many different periods. The Tudor Guildhall is one much-photographed landmark, with its seventeenth-century frontage and splendid gilt clock. The Angel Hotel, on the other hand, was one of Guildford's famous coaching inns, while Abbot's Hospital was built as a home for the elderly between 1619 and 1622.

The town's oldest building is the Saxon tower of St Mary's Church in Quarry Street, not far from the keep of a Norman castle, which is all that is left of Surrey's only royal castle. Of far more recent date is Guildford's cathedral, consecrated as recently as 1961.

ADDRESSES

Army & Navy, 105–111 High Street; tel. 0483 68171
The Bear Garden, 10 Jeffries Passage; tel. 0483 302581
Elaine Chandler, 9 Martyr Road; tel. 0483 505457
Gay Corran, 6c Tunsgate Square; tel. 0483 65111
Guildford's Antique Centre, 22 Haydon Place; tel. 0483 67817
Tourist Information Centre, 72 High Street; tel. 0483 444007

Hartfield

There can be few bears as well loved as Winnie-the-Pooh. He first appeared in print in 1924, in a collection of verses called *When We Were Very Young*, written by successful playwright and novelist A. A. Milne. The bear wasn't called Winnie-the-Pooh then. He was simply Mr Edward Bear, or Teddy. But that didn't stop him from becoming a firm favourite with the book's readers.

So much so that two years later, on 14 October 1926, he was rewarded with a book of his own. It was called simply *Winnie-the-Pooh*, and the author's introduction to the book explains how Edward Bear acquired his new name – after a black swan called Pooh and a black bear called Winnie.

Again, the book was an enormous success, although initially it was not, it must be said, as great a seller as the book of poems. Nevertheless, a second volume, *The House at Pooh Corner*, followed two years later.

Now, sixty years on, the books are still enjoyed by each new generation of children. But the stout little bear has an equally enthusiastic following among adults. Some have treasured their copies of the books since childhood while others have come to them far later in life.

It is adults as much as children who throng to the Sussex village of Hartfield to follow in the footsteps of Christopher Robin and his bear.

In 1925, A. A. Milne had bought Cotchford Farm on the edge of Ashdown Forest, some thirty-five miles to the south-east of London, and about ten miles from East Grinstead. Although he still had a house in Chelsea, the family travelled to Sussex as often as possible. The surrounding countryside would feature strongly in the two Winnie-the-Pooh books.

Maire McQueeney of **20th Century Walks** organizes occasional excursions to the Forest for Pooh enthusiasts, with walks punctuated by references to the books. But she has also published a detailed Pooh's Forest Map, so that independent walkers can discover for themselves some of the spots which appear in the books. There are buses from East Grinstead to Hartfield itself for those without their own transport, but it is a poor service. So Maire is hoping to run all-inclusive excursions from East Grinstead from 1994.

First stop for many people is the shop which has been known as **Pooh Corner** since 1977. Dating from the time of Queen Anne, some three hundred years ago, the building was once the sweet shop where Christopher Robin used to go with his nanny 'Alice' to buy his favourite bull's-eyes.

You can still usually find bull's-eyes in the shop, along with other sweets, ice-creams and soft drinks. But its greatest attraction for Winnie-the-Pooh followers is its unusually wide range of 'Pooh-phanalia'.

Back in 1977, when the shop first opened, the range of Pooh merchandise was far more limited than it is today, and a shop specializing in Pooh and his friends must have seemed a very risky venture. Now, numerous different items are available, with more and more companies bringing out new products each year – many of them at pocket-money prices. You will find a wide choice at Pooh Corner.

They also sell their own exclusive postcards of the famous 'Poohsticks Bridge', restored in 1979. For those who want to play the game themselves, an inexpensive pamphlet shows how to reach the bridge, but unless you are a keen walker you will need a car to get you there, as it is about two miles away. In addition, the path to the bridge from the car park is very rutted, and it can be very muddy for much of the year, so you will need suitable shoes.

If you want to play Poohsticks yourself, you will be hard put to find any nearby, and will need to take your own sticks with you. The shop has some for sale if you have forgotten to bring any.

The game was described in *The House at Pooh Corner*, with Pooh himself as the inventor. When someone shouts 'Go', each player drops a stick into the river from the upstream side of the bridge. Everyone then rushes to the other side of the bridge, calling out excitedly 'Come on, stick', or words to that effect, while waiting for the sticks to emerge. The first stick to appear from under the bridge is the winner.

Of course, one stick can look very much like another once it is in the water, so keen players will mark theirs in some way before throwing them into the water.

So many fans have visited the bridge over the years that the banks of the river have had to be reinforced there. But there is still a timelessness about the spot, and it is all too easy to imagine Christopher Robin himself playing there.

Another place popular with visitors was described at the end of the same book. Christopher Robin and his bear found themselves in an enchanted place called Galleons Lap. Its real name is Gills Lap, and it is here that a memorial plaque commemorates both the writer A. A. Milne and the illustrator E. H. Shepard.

It is an ideal spot for picnics, but lunches are also offered by some beautiful old pubs in Hartfield itself. In summer, however, they can become extremely crowded, so you may prefer to travel a little further afield.

If you travel northwards, you will pass Cotchford Farm, where Milne himself lived. It is not, however, open to the public, but is a private house, hidden away at the end of a steep drive.

ADDRESSES

Pooh Corner and Piglet's Ice-Cream Parlour, High Street; tel. 0892 770453

20th Century Walks, 22 Warleigh Road, Brighton BN1 4NT; tel. 0273 607910

Hastings

Like most seaside towns, Hastings in Sussex has its share of gift shops, any of which could have something with a teddy bear theme. The George Street area can be a particularly good hunting-ground, with both gift shops and antique shops to explore.

You may find some older bears at **Heuduk Antiques** in George Street itself, and there are more bears at **Children's Treasures** nearby. There, they try to find older bears to sell, but you should also find some by modern manufacturers (especially the limited editions). They aim to have around forty or fifty bears at any one time. In addition, you will find a range of bear-related items, among them greetings cards by local artist Prue Theobalds and various accessories for bears, as well as pewter miniatures.

They also sell various doll and teddy-making components, and doll's house miniatures.

There is much more to see in Hastings, however. The old net sheds down on the fishing harbour are a well-known landmark, and nearby are a Fisherman's Museum (in a converted chapel) and a Sea-Life Centre. St Clement's Caves now tell the fascinating story of the local smugglers, and the ruins of the first stone Norman Castle to be built in England have been turned into another popular tourist attraction.

ADDRESSES

Heuduk Antiques, 52 George Street; tel. 0424 434373
Children's Treasures, 17 George Street; tel. 0424 444117
Tourist Information Centre, 4 Robertson Terrace; tel. 0424 718888

Henley-on-Thames

Henley-on-Thames is best known for its Royal Regatta, but in recent years it has also become an important shopping centre. One shop has special appeal for bear lovers – **Asquiths** in New Street.

Asquiths opened their first teddy bear shop, in Windsor, in 1984. Three years later, they opened another, in Friday Street in Henley. But it was far too small for them, and when the lease expired they decided it was time for something bigger.

The shop in New Street opened in June 1991, just two weeks after the purchase of the sixteenth-century building was completed.

Since then, there have been some changes inside the Grade 2 listed building, most noticeably the opening of a restaurant and tearoom. They are now famous for their Sunday breakfasts and home-cooked lunches, not to mention champagne breakfasts during the week of the Regatta, and delicious home-baked teddy bear biscuits to accompany the teas and coffees.

No doubt many such beverages are drunk by collectors trying to make up their minds just which bear or bears will accompany them home. The shop is crammed with a large assortment, generally including a large number of bears by Steiff, Hermann and British manufacturers like Merrythought as well as special Asquiths bears, designed by the shop's owner Joan Bland.

Among the latter are splendid bears for collectors, made in Yorkshire to many different designs. But there are also less expensive exclusives, produced in the Far East. A Henley Bear in his striped blazer and Henley boater is especially popular, while other designs include a City Bear in bowler hat and Master Bear in gown and mortarboard.

The shop also has an exclusive range of Crystal Talisman

Bears, produced in a number of beautiful colours. Principles of colour therapy have been used in their creation, combined with the reputed power of crystals to create something distinctly different.

Also different from those found in other shops are many of the bear accessories on sale. They include specially made jumpers, little satchels and other bear-sized bags, and the boaters worn by the Henley Bears. For humans there are special Asquiths T-shirts and china mugs, as well as books about bears, greetings cards, and all sorts of small gift items guaranteed to make sure that no one walks away empty-handed.

At the time of writing, there were plans to start stocking bear-making materials, too, including fabrics and stuffing. And it is even possible to buy prints of the paintings hanging in the restaurant. Alternatively, if you would prefer an original portrait of one of your own teddies, the artist happily accepts commissions.

Henley also has a number of antiques shops which can be fertile hunting-grounds for bear lovers, especially those who like to find unusual old accessories for their displays. **Cobwebs** in Bell Street, for instance, often yields something of interest – perhaps even a collectable soft toy or two – while **Rhino Antiques** in Market Place is a similarly good source of bric-à-brac and collectables. **Friday Street Antique Centre** is another place that invites a browse.

Needless to say, a walk round the main shopping streets may also yield some more modern bear-related items, since the town includes a number of gift shops.

If you take time to wander around the town, you will also see some of the three hundred Henley buildings that have been designated as being of either historical or architectural interest. Most are private houses, and therefore not open to the public, but the fifteenth-century timber-framed Chantry house, in St Mary's churchyard, can be viewed by appointment. Nearby are some almshouses, rebuilt in the nineteenth century. There are many interesting eighteenth-century buildings, too – in Bell Street, for instance – while the Kenton Theatre in New Street (opposite Asquiths) is claimed to be one of the oldest in the country.

ADDRESSES

Asquiths, 2 New Street; tel. 0491 571978
Cobwebs, 75 Bell Street; tel. 0491 411486
Friday Street Antique Centre, 4 Friday Street; tel. 0491 574104
Rhino Antiques, 20 Market Place; tel. 0491 411162
Tourist Information Centre, Town Hall, Market Place; tel. 0491 578034

Hertford

The bustling county town of Hertford has a number of interesting old buildings. One of the most splendid is the timber-framed Old Verger's House in St Andrew Street, built in the 1450s. The street contains more timber-framed buildings, as well as Georgian and early Victorian architecture. But bear lovers will probably fail to see any of them as they head purposefully towards **Wigginton's** at Nos 1 and 2.

In fact, there are two Wigginton's shops, on opposite sides of the road. The main building, at No. 2, is full of nostalgic gifts and decorative items, on two floors. Directly opposite, at No. 1, are all sorts of traditional toys, and that includes a good number of teddy bears.

The range is generally identical to that of Wigginton's in Cambridge (page 203), which means that there are plenty of limited editions from companies like Steiff, Hermann, Merrythought and Dean's. They stock the Steiff Classic Bears, too, and also often have some Steiff bears made specially for America.

Canterbury Bears, Big Softies, Bo-Bear Designs and Bedford Bears are some of the other names to be found, along with H. M. Bears, Dormouse Designs and the Muffy Bears from the North American Bear Co.

In addition, artist Pam Howells is making an exclusive Wigginton's Bear, and there could well be more artist bears by the time this book appears.

Of course, there are cuddly bears, too, and popular characters like Winnie-the-Pooh, Rupert and Paddington. So there should be something to appeal to everyone. But don't overlook all the bear-related items among all the gifts, either.

You could find anything from soaps to stationery, pictures to pomanders. There are various ranges of ceramic bears, but there could also be bears beautifully carved from wood, and there are usually a good number of items rarely seen elsewhere.

Then, of course, some of the doll's house furniture in the toy shop may be just right for a bear display. Or what about one of the traditional wooden toys for your bears to play with? Wigginton's is a real treasure trove that keeps you looking again and again.

ADDRESSES

Wigginton's, 1 & 2 St Andrew Street; tel. 0992 551530
Tourist Information Centre, The Castle; tel. 0992 584322

Lamberhurst

A converted oast-house on a working hop farm is the unexpected location for a collection of childhood memories in Kent.

The **Toy & Model Museum** in Lamberhurst is on the A262, just a quarter of a mile off the A21, and some eight miles from Tunbridge Wells. Inside, you'll find a variety of toys, including an extensive OO-gauge model railway, a collection of toy cars, and a model fairground with accurate replicas of fairground rides from the 1920s.

Of particular interest to bear lovers, however, will be the large collection of Rupert memorabilia collected over many years.

Rupert has, of course, a strong Kentish connection, since his creator Mary Tourtel was from Canterbury (page 76) and the Heritage Museum there now has a permanent Rupert exhibition. But the little Lamberhurst museum has a particularly wide range of Rupert merchandising in addition to a collection of the famous annuals.

Easter eggs, money boxes, china, clocks, talcum powder, lamps, rugs, kaleidoscopes, bagatelle games, children's clothing, slippers, children's bicycles, badges, cassettes and videos are just some of the Rupert products that have been produced over the years. They are displayed along with a whole collection of Rupert bears of varying ages, and some Rupert puppets.

There are a few Winnie-the-Pooh and Paddington items on display as well, and a group of teddies is enjoying the inevitable picnic – eating off Rupert china. One or two of these bears are old and worn. But most are far newer, and include a modern Canterbury Bear as well as characters like Sooty, Winnie-the-Pooh and Nookie.

Sometimes, however, there are special exhibits, which may temporarily replace one of the displays. So it is probably safest to telephone first if there is something you particularly wish to see.

A selection of Rupert merchandise is also on sale in the museum shop, and there are generally some teddies on sale from one or two of the craft-type stalls to be found inside the Oast. On my last visit I spotted a few Merrythought limited editions, as well as some cuddly teddies, and a large number of mini-teds from the Far East dressed as everything from sporting bears to artists or pirates.

It is only a small museum, but there is a tearoom serving morning coffee, afternoon teas, snacks and ice-creams, and outside is a picnic area for those who prefer to bring their own food. It is also possible to take a stroll through the woods and around the hop fields, but you may need wellingtons in winter.

ADDRESS

The Toy & Model Museum, Forstal Farm, Goudhurst Road; tel. 0892 890711

Lymington

At first glance, the small Hampshire port of Lymington seems to have virtually nothing of interest to the teddy bear lover.

There is little evidence of anything furry in the High Street shops. The odd cuddly or ceramic teddy can be unearthed in a gift shop, and a haberdashery has a nice variety of ribbon. An **Antique Centre** is also worth a browse. (I found all sorts of interesting props and accessories when I visited, and even one or two relatively recent bears.) But there is really no more than you would find in any other town of similar size.

You'll pass a few more shops as you walk down the cobbled Quay Street to the old town quay, where yachts of all shapes and sizes have their moorings. But Lymington's greatest attraction for bear lovers is not a shop at all. It is a coffee house called the **Bluebird at Lentune**.

It is the name which provides the clue. For if you stop for refreshments, you will find that your every move is being watched by the fastest bear on land or water, Mr Whoppit.

Mr Whoppit was the mascot of Donald Campbell, who repeatedly broke both water- and land-speed records in a succession of *Bluebirds* during the fifties and sixties.

The bear and Campbell first met in 1957, and were soon speeding across Coniston Water together at 239.07 m.p.h. It was Campbell's fourth water-speed record.

For the next ten years they were inseparable. When Campbell set a new record of 248.62 m.p.h. on Coniston Water the following year, Mr Whoppit was there. He was there again in 1959, when they achieved 260.33 m.p.h. When Campbell reached a land speed of 403.1 m.p.h. at Lake Eyre in Australia in 1964, Mr Whoppit reached it as well. And later that same year they were in Australia together for yet another record on water, this time of 276.33 m.p.h.

Even when Campbell lay in a hospital bed after the fastest automobile crash ever, he didn't forget his bear and sent someone back to search for him among the wreckage.

The pair's final journey together was on 4 January 1967, when they returned to Coniston Water for yet another record attempt. All had gone well on the outward run, and a speed of

290 m.p.h. was recorded. Then, on the return, the vessel's nose suddenly rose right out of the water. *Bluebird* somersaulted, and then disappeared.

Campbell himself was never found. But the faithful Mr Whoppit was later discovered floating on the lake and was duly returned to Campbell's widow.

A year later, he went to live with Campbell's daughter Gina, accompanying her on her own record-breaking attempts and helping her set a new women's power-boat record of 122.85 m.p.h. They, too, survived a horrifying accident together (although Mr Whoppit had to be rescued by divers) and in 1990 Mr Whoppit was again there to provide support when Gina achieved a new women's water-speed record of 156.45 m.p.h.

Today, however, he leads a quieter life, keeping an eye on the coffee house's clientele while Gina is busy in the kitchen. A special glass porthole provides him with the perfect vantage point.

Visitors can also take home their own Mr Whoppit – one of the special replicas made by Merrythought as a tribute to the fastest bear on land and water. Replicas of various *Bluebirds* are also on sale, and original *Bluebird* memorabilia can be seen on the coffee house walls.

WendySue '94

ADDRESSES

The Bluebird at Lentune, 4 Quay Street; tel. 0590 672766

Tourist Information Centre, The Car Park, rear of Waitrose, St Thomas Street; tel. 0590 672422 (April–September only. At other times: Southern Tourist Board, 40 Chamberlayne Road, Eastleigh, Hants SO5 5JH; tel. 0703 620006)

Maidstone

As is to be expected from a county town, Maidstone has a large and busy shopping centre, with most of the main High Street shops and the odd larger store catering for everyday needs. Some new arcades also include the kinds of small, specialist business that make for more interesting browsing. It is in one of these newer precincts, the Royal Star Arcade off the High Street, that you will find the town's specialist bear shop, **Especially Bears**.

For more than three years, the shop could be found in the Starnes Court precinct in Union Street. But in September 1993 they took over these more central premises and at the same time set out to expand their range considerably with a constantly changing programme of shop exclusives from names like Bocs Teganau, Susan Jane Knock and Barton Bears.

Their manufactured bears cover a very wide range, from inexpensive (but often unusual) bears made in the Far East to the limited editions from companies like Steiff, Hermann, Merrythought and Dean's. They stock bears in these companies' regular ranges as well, and aim to have a good choice of traditional children's teddies as well as bears for collectors. In addition, they will order any item from these companies' catalogues, should a customer want something that is not in stock.

They are also the sole United Kingdom supplier of a range of Merrythought bears made exclusively for Karin Heller in Germany. A Birthday Bear carries his own accordion. Another wears a dressing-gown, nightcap and slippers, and carries his own candle. A Bee Bear has bees scattered over him. Then there is a whole family of mother, father, child and infant bears, wearing simple bows.

The shop also has its own souvenir teddies, made in the Channel Islands and sporting Especially Bears jumpers. There are character bears like Paddington, Rupert and Winnie-the-Pooh, and popular ranges like Golden Gifts' Tails and Tales.

The range of bear-related items is also exceptionally wide, with a particularly good selection of jewellery and the shop's own T-shirts and sweatshirts. There is a set of four prints of work by local artist Sheila Letchford, and the large range of cards generally includes some published locally as well.

Rubber stamps, tins, boxes, photo frames, stationery, soaps, bookends, bear-sized furniture, giftwrap, a number of books (both story-books and reference books), badges, stitchkits, ceramic and pewter teddies are just a few of the other items generally to be found, making the shop a particularly good source of gifts as well as a variety of bears for both collectors and children.

Another shop of interest to certain bear lovers in Maidstone will be the **Maidstone Book and Print Shop** in Union Street. Their range generally includes a large number of Rupert books, from recent stories costing just a few pounds to old and rare editions at prices running into the hundreds for copies in good condition.

The range is changing constantly, of course, so if you have special wants it is always best to telephone before travelling any distance.

Just a short walk away, at 116 Week Street, is the **Maidstone Antique Centre** which might just yield something of interest for those who collect old props and accessories for their bears.

Maidstone's greatest non-bearish attraction, on the other hand, is the fourteenth-century Archbishop's Palace. Its timbered stable block now houses a museum of carriages – state, official and private horse-drawn vehicles as well as many related exhibits. The collection includes some of the small carriages used by Queen Victoria and her children.

A Heritage Centre tells the history of the Palace, while the original Gatehouse is now home to the Tourist Information Centre. Souvenir Maidstone teddies are among the items on sale there.

In the Palace Gardens is the fourteenth-century parish church of All Saints, one of the largest Perpendicular churches in the country.

From Maidstone there are also river cruises to the nearby Kent Rural Life Museum and the Malta Inn at Allington, between Easter and October.

ADDRESSES

Especially Bears, 29 Royal Star Arcade, High Street; tel. 0622 690939

The Maidstone Book and Print Shop, 38 Union Street; tel. 0622 662878

Tourist Information Centre, The Gatehouse, Old Palace Gardens; tel. 0622 602169/673581

Midhurst

The Sussex market town of Midhurst has a fifteenth-century coaching inn and some lovely half-timbered houses. It is also close to Cowdray Park, famous for its polo. But it is a shop called **Chatterbox** which will be of interest to the bear lover. On sale are babywear, children's wear, toys and gifts, and they aim to have three to four hundred bears in stock, including not only children's teddies but those made primarily for collectors as well.

Among the makes to be found are Steiff (including just a few limited editions), Hermann, Merrythought, Dean's, Nisbet, Big Softies and the North American Bear Co.'s Vanderbear Family. Golden Gifts' Tails and Tales and the equally popular Boyds Collection are there, too, along with some of the character bears from Gabrielle Designs and cuddly teddies from companies like Ty and Russ Berrie.

At the time of writing, only a limited number of artists were represented, although there were bears by Bo-Bear Designs and Bocs Teganau in stock.

Souvenir Midhurst Bears are also on sale, and owner Sue Davies dresses Little Folk bears in a variety of costumes. Some become polo players, of course, while others are fishermen, skiers, cricketers, golfers and French onion sellers.

Clothes are available on their own, again made by Sue, and if anyone has any special requirement, she tries to oblige. In addition, you will find teddy bear greetings cards, some books and various general gift items.

ADDRESSES

Chatterbox, Rumbold's Hill; tel. 0730 812696
Tourist Information Centre, 29A South Street, Chichester; tel.
  0243 775888

Milford-on-Sea

Shopping in the charming Hampshire village of Milford-on-Sea, not far from Lymington (page 109), is a delightfully stress-free experience, with a variety of small shops selling everything from wet fish to gifts, antiques and bric-à-brac. There is a specialist needlecraft shop, too. But of greater interest to the bear lover will be **Milford Models and Hobbies**. You can expect to find around three hundred bears there, of various makes, including Steiff, Merrythought, Dean's, Canterbury, Threadbear and Gund.

They are also a Steiff Club Store, so the range of Steiff bears is particularly good. They take all of that company's limited editions, and they sell Steiff animals, too.

There are many less expensive bears, as well as various bear-related items like postcards, china and jewellery.

As the name suggests, the rest of the shop is given over to all sorts of models and kits, including die-cast, railway items and plastic kits. You can expect to find everything from coach and horses to high-performance cars, and from classic sailing ships to warships. There is even a good number of secondhand and obsolete items.

ADDRESSES

Milford Models and Hobbies, 48 High Street; tel. 0590 642112
Southern Tourist Board, 40 Chamberlayne Road, Eastleigh,
  Hants; tel. 0703 620006

Petersfield

The ancient market town of Petersfield was once a coaching centre on the main road from Portsmouth to London. Now, most through traffic bypasses the town, but the market is still held twice a week (on Wednesdays and Saturdays). The same site, The Square, was being used for the market in the early twelfth century, when Petersfield was founded.

On market days the town really comes to life, but most of its shops and the market stalls are geared to the needs of local residents. So you will find no more small specialist shops than you would in most towns of a similar size. It is the **Bear Museum** which is Petersfield's main attraction for readers of this book.

The Museum is in Dragon Street (the B2070), just a short distance from the station. (Walk down Station Road towards the town centre and turn right along Chapel Street. At the end, turn left and bear left round The Square, continuing on into the High Street. This will bring you on to a main road, Dragon Street. Cross over, then turn right along Dragon Street. The museum will be on your left.)

It is only a small museum, but it was the first of its kind in the country, and has a fascinating collection – even though some of the most interesting and valuable bears disappeared in a burglary after a number of them featured in some books about bears, and also on a series of postcards and notelets.

The museum's owners, Judy and John Sparrow, bought the

117

building in 1979, but it was some time before it began to take its present form. Judy had really wanted to turn it into a dress shop. But the town's main shopping area was just too far away to make that feasible. For a while she concentrated on cats, after finding some splendid ones made of pottery. But that proved to be too limited, so she started selling Carlton Ware, Art Deco and small china items.

Also on display, however, were a number of dolls, which Judy had been collecting since she was sixteen. They had been on display at a tearoom she and John had run, and later in a pub they took over, and gradually Judy had started buying a few to sell, as well as adding to her own collection.

Then, in the early eighties, she bought her first bear. Soon, a couple more had arrived and in no time at all they had started to take over. It is a common occurrence with teddy bears, as many readers of this book will no doubt have discovered.

Soon, Judy and John had started buying bears in earnest, and in 1985 they caused quite a stir when they bought a 1905 Steiff for a then world record price of around £2,000. (A mere five years on, the sale of a bear for £22,000 was hardly noticed.)

They knew by then that they wanted to start a museum and, as it was such a novel idea at that time, they were able to build up a splendid collection for a fraction of the cost that the bears fetch today.

Now, many of the bears are on view to the public. After the burglary, some of the most valuable remaining bears were moved to safety, but those that remain still make up a very interesting collection.

Many are English, but they include a number of unusual examples, like the red and yellow panda produced by Chad Valley, and Merrythought's colourful Twisty Cheeky.

Not all the exhibits are teddy bears. There are some Dancing Dolls and a Donald Duck toy from Dean's, for instance. A whole collection of pandas includes examples by Chiltern, Pedigree and Wendy Boston, while among the polar bears is Dean's version of the mother of the famous Brumas.

Some of the most interesting of the bears are the novelty ones, like the relatively recent Japanese reading and knitting bears. There are musical bears, too, and Chiltern bears on tricycles. A Wendy Boston teddy has an unusual cloth body. There are bears made of sheepskin, too. But others have been chosen simply because they are beautiful old teddies. Some are of unknown make, others are from major companies like Germany's Schuco and Britain's Farnell.

Many of the bears are displayed in cabinets, with information on their origins. But a splendid collection of bear-sized kitchen equipment and other interesting accessories have also been used to create some lively scenes.

There are some fascinating bear-related items, as well, including a beautiful jig-saw and book set and a splendid collection of wooden bears from the Black Forest and Switzerland. Many of these carvings of real bears were not only decorative but also served a useful purpose. The Petersfield collection includes a nutcracker, matchbox and ashtray holder, table brush, bottle stopper, pen holder, blotter, paper-knife, salt cellars and pincushion.

Story-boards tell the story of the first teddy bear, and also show how a bear is made, while more serious collectors will no doubt be attracted by the large display on identification labels and buttons, complete with relevant dates. In complete contrast, the basement is filled with a group of picnicking bears, which include all twelve of the Zodiac Bears made by the House of Nisbet in the 1980s.

Judy Sparrow is also a bear maker, and a few of her own bears are on display in the museum. More are on sale in the museum shop, where there are also a number of Steiff bears, including some limited editions. There are bears by Hermann and Dean's, too, as well as some Merrythoughts, and there are generally some old bears on sale as well.

Bear wear, ceramic teddies and pictures are among the other items which can be bought, as well as various books – including one by Judy herself, featuring many of the museum residents (both past and present). The bears also feature on some stationery items, including postcards, notelets and address books, and you should find a selection of these in the shop as well.

ADDRESSES

The Bear Museum, 38 Dragon Street; tel. 0730 265108
Tourist Information Centre, County Library, 27 The Square; tel. 0730 268829

Port Solent (Portsmouth)

Building started on the new Port Solent marina in 1986. Today, it offers everything the boat owner (or prospective owner) could possibly need – from a deck brush to a wide range of yachts and power boats. Full servicing facilities for the boats are available, while for their occupants there are hot showers and a laundry on hand.

Non-sailors, however, will be more attracted by the six-screen cinema, and by the shops, restaurants and bars of The Boardwalk, where they can enjoy the harbour views and soak up all the atmosphere without even getting their feet wet.

The shops include a number selling clothes of every description, from underwear to oilskins (not to mention wedding dresses and ballgowns). But there is more chance of finding something bearish among the gifts at Fenwicks or the books at Bookends.

Keen needlewomen, on the other hand, will want to check out the wide range of supplies at the needlecraft shop.

Of special interest to all bear lovers is a shop called **Collectif**. They sell a wide range of kits for one-twelfth-scale doll's houses and shops, as well as everything imaginable to go in them. There are collectors dolls, too. But at any one time they also aim to have well over 1,000 bears (despite the teddy's well-known aversion to water).

They are one of the Steiff Club Stores, so naturally stock a good variety of bears from that company, as well as from other manufacturers like Hermann and Merrythought. But there is also a wide range of bears by various British and American artists, many of whom make exclusive editions especially for them.

To date, Bocs Teganau, Bear With Me, Teddystyle, Lillibet, Bearwood Bears, Bo Bears and Barbara-Ann Bears are just some of the British makers who have designed bears specially for them, and new ones are arriving all the time.

Not every bear sold is a so-called collectable, however. There are cuddlies as well, from the likes of the Manhattan Toy Company, Ty and Russ Berrie.

There are also a large number of bear-related items, including stationery, cards and wrapping paper as well as some books and several different makes of ceramic teddies. So there is something to suit most pockets.

Of course, many people travel to Port Solent by sea. But it can be reached just as easily by road. Travelling from the west, leave the M27 motorway at junction 12. Approaching from the east, take the Hilsea exit off the A27. Or, if you are on public transport, there is an hourly bus service from Fratton Bridge, by Portsmouth railway station (telephone 0962 852352 for times).

ADDRESSES

Collectif, The Boardwalk, Port Solent Marina, Portsmouth; tel. 0705 214161

Tourist Information Centre, The Hard, Portsmouth; tel. 0705 826722

Ramsgate

A relatively new arrival on the teddy bear scene, **Bear Thoughts** in Ramsgate opened its doors in October 1993 on the edge of Newington, a small village just outside Ramsgate itself.

Some of the first arrivals were Canterbury Bears, both regular ranges and limited editions, and it is their aim to stock both children's toys and unique, one-off, artist bears, with everything between the two. They plan gradually to expand the number of makes on sale, with both manufactured bears (including limited editions) and artist bears – possibly giving a chance to a number of lesser-known artists as well as some better-known names.

They have various bear-related items, too, including books, plaques, furniture, pictures, tins, musical boxes, ornaments and fridge magnets. They have their own badges, in the shape of a bear's head, featuring a dozen delightful bear-related slogans. And there are honey and beeswax products, including candles and one-ounce (bear-sized!) pots of honey, which are also popular with children.

Rag dolls complement the teddies, and porcelain bisque dolls are hand-made to order.

There is plenty more to see in Ramsgate, too, where you will find everything from a replica of a Viking ship to all the usual attractions of a modern seaside town. The East Kent Maritime Museum is here, and there is a Motor Museum above the Sally Line Harbour. Sally Line ferries depart from Ramsgate, with day trips to France always popular.

At nearby Minster, a museum of agricultural and rural life includes various traditional craft workshops, and the ancient Minster itself can also be visited (although opening times are very limited).

ADDRESSES

Bear Thoughts, 28 Newington Road; tel. 0843 588444
Tourist Information Centre, Argyle Centre, Queen Street, Ramsgate; tel. 0843 591086

Richmond

Although Richmond is just eight miles from Trafalgar Square, and just fifteen minutes by rail from London's Waterloo Station, it has the feel of a bustling country town, with its 2,400-acre park and pleasant river walks. It was Charles I who originally enclosed the park, back in 1637, and descendants of the deer he used to stock it can still be found there today.

Of particular historic interest is the area around Richmond Green, once part of the grounds of Henry VII's Rychemonde Palace. Little of the original Tudor palace remains, but the Gate House can still be seen, along with a row of buildings known as Wardrobe Court. The nearby Georgian houses of Maids of Honour Row were built for the Ladies of the Court of George I.

Near the Green, on King Street, one of Richmond's many gift shops is of special interest to bear lovers. **Quelque Chose** has been steadily increasing its range of bears over the past few years, and now stocks a number of different makes of plush bears as well as an assortment of bear-related items.

Manufacturers whose bears can be found there include Hermann, Merrythought, Dean's, Canterbury, Big Softies, Little Folk, Channel Island Toys and the North American Bear Co., as well as cuddlies from companies like Ty and the Manhattan Toy Company. There are some hand-made collectors bears as well – from makers like Dormouse Designs, Romsey Bears, the Old Fashioned Teddy Bear Co., Jay-Bee, Naomi Laight and Little Treasures. They have Winnie-the-Pooh and the pretty gifts made by Georgia Vienna, and there are also some of their own special limited-edition bears in various sizes.

The range of bear-related items is even wider, with everything from teddy-decorated pine children's furniture to stickers and fridge magnets. You should find any number of household items, like rugs, mirrors, clocks, towels and face cloths, lampshades, waste-paper bins, mugs, coat hooks and towel rails. There are stationery items, including rubber stamps, pens, pencils, greetings cards and giftwrap, and they also sell music boxes, pictures, tins and boxes, book-ends, mobiles, chalk boards, pewter miniatures and teddy bear soaps.

A second shop at Paved Court specializes in dolls, doll's houses and doll's house furniture, but you'll also find a variety of teddy bear miniatures there, both ceramic and pewter.

Any of the other gift shops in the town could have something of interest to the bear lover. There are a number of antique shops and centres, too, but it is a prosperous area, and the range reflects this. Nevertheless, you could still find something interesting to add to a teddy bear display.

ADDRESSES

Quelque Chose, 9 King Street; tel. 081 948 3036 (open
  Monday–Saturday, and Sunday afternoons)
Quelque Chose, 5 Paved Court; tel. 081 948 6636 (closed all
  day Wednesdays and Sundays)
Tourist Information Centre, Old Town Hall, Whittaker Avenue;
  tel. 081 940 9125

Rochester

The City of Rochester-upon-Medway can trace its history
back to the Romans, when it was a fortified river crossing
called Durobrivae, or the Stronghold by the Bridge. Both the
Castle and the Cathedral date from Norman times, but there are
also some fine buildings from the sixteenth, seventeenth and
eighteenth centuries, one of which (the sixteenth-century Eastgate House) is now home to the Charles Dickens Centre.

The great writer spent much of his childhood in the area,
and Rochester turns up frequently in his novels and other
writings. It is 'Our Town' in *Great Expectations*, for instance,
'Cloisterham' in *The Mystery of Edwin Drood*, and a number of the
town's buildings can be identified in other Dickens books.

The town now celebrates its Dickens connections with an
annual Dickens Festival in May or June and with a Dickensian
Christmas in December, both of which are ideal times for a visit.

Rochester's bear shop, too, celebrates the Dickens connec-
tion. They have already commissioned a number of artists to
create special Dickens characters for them. Mary Holden, of Only
Natural, was the first with Mr Pickwick. Then came Fagin by
Shirley Latimer of Crafty Bears and Oliver by Julie and Andrew
Hubbard of Mother Hubbard.

They are just a few of the exclusives that have been made for the shop to date. Some are by such top artists as Naomi Laight, Teddystyle and Bocs Teganau. But the shop also has a reputation for introducing the work of good new artists, long before they become widely known. They were stocking bears by Mother Hubbard, for instance, when few in the teddy bear world had heard of them. And it was at Rochester that I first saw the Kent-made Willow Bears.

In fact, at the time of writing, they had the work of more than thirty different artists in stock, including both top names and relatively new makers – and not just British artists either. America, Belgium, South Africa and Japan were some of the other sources. As a result, the shop can be expected to offer both plenty of variety and some innovative designs.

Not all the bears are artist-made. The **Rochester Teddy Bear Shop** is also a Steiff Club Store, and sells both the limited editions by that company and bears in their regular ranges. They have bears by Hermann, Merrythought, Dean's, Nisbet and Big Softies as well, including many limited editions. There are cuddly Ty bears, the popular Tails and Tales range by Golden Gifts, bears by the North American Bear Co., and popular character bears by Gabrielle Designs.

They try to cater for all pockets. So although even the most discerning collector – at least of modern bears – should find something of interest, there is also plenty on offer for those on a much tighter budget, including many bear-related items.

In fact, the bear shop is actually divided into two halves, with one half selling the bears themselves and the other filled with a wide range of 'bearabilia'. There you will find everything from the popular Colour Box miniatures to stationery and greetings cards. There are book-ends and badges, teddy bear jewellery, books about bears and even knitted teddies, as well as accessories for the bears themselves, including their own passports.

The shop is housed on the first floor of a sixteenth-century building, complete with exposed beams and open fireplaces. In charge is Michelle Chambers. She confesses that her passion is doll's houses. But it is hard to believe that she can devote more energy and enthusiasm to them than she does to her bears.

There is nothing bear lovers like better than to talk about their collections with someone who understands them, and it doesn't take long to discover that Michelle is just such a person. In fact, many of her customers have now become firm friends, and her day is punctuated by the constant brewing of pots of tea – especially welcome when you've a difficult decision to make.

Sometimes she inevitably finds herself tempted, too, and a number of bears have found their way into her own home. But there are even more temptations for her downstairs, where her mother Carol is in charge of a splendid Doll's House Shop. Its wide selection of doll's houses, and all the furniture to go in them, attracts enthusiasts from far and wide – as do the bears upstairs.

Other nearby shops in the High Street also make interesting browsing, for somehow the street has managed to avoid being taken over by the supermarkets and other chain stores which fill most of the country's High Streets. Instead, it is lined with small, mainly independently owned establishments, which maintain all the City's old-world charm.

Included are a number of antique shops, several of which should have an interesting accessory or two for your bears, or even a few actual teddies. There are also no fewer than three bookshops, with **Baggins Book Bazaar** at No. 19 specializing in secondhand books, and always worth a look for books with a teddy bear theme. **Francis Iles' needlecraft shop** at No. 73 may have something of interest for the bear-loving needlewoman, and you could find something bearish in one of the many shops specializing in things for the home.

If you love dolls as well as bears, you may also be interested in the **Dollmakers Workshop** on Northgate, a turning off the High Street itself.

As you walk round, don't forget to take a closer look at some of the interesting old buildings. The Royal Victoria and Bull Hotel on the High Street is, for instance, a 400-year-old coaching inn, mentioned by Dickens in both *Pickwick Papers* and *Great Expectations*. Restoration House is the Satis House of *Great Expectations*. King Charles II lodged there on the eve of his restoration (and also gave the house its name). Now its attractions include Miss Havisham's Room, which has been laid out exactly as Charles Dickens described in his novel.

Many other Rochester buildings appeared in his novels and Rochester is also where you will find Dickens' final home, a Swiss Chalet from Gad's Hill. It now stands in the gardens of the Elizabethan Eastgate House, where you will find the Charles Dickens Centre (largely contained in the 1920s annexe).

Many other buildings are considerably older – like the Norman Castle and Cathedral (both close to the Teddy Bear Shop). Parts of the Roman and medieval walls still remain, too. There are some houses visited by Elizabeth I in 1573, and the Corn Exchange dates from the late seventeenth century. Much of the Guildhall also dates from around that time, and its various collections include dolls and toys.

Chatham and its historic Dockyard are also nearby, and well worth visiting, but opening times vary. Details can be obtained from the local tourist office, or from the Dockyard itself (tel. 0634 812551).

ADDRESSES

Rochester Teddy Bear Shop, 1st Floor, The Dolls House Shop, 68 High Street; tel. 0634 831615

Tourist Information Centre, Eastgate Cottage, High Street; tel. 0634 843666

St Albans

The Romans built their town Verulamium close to the River Ver. One of its citizens, St Alban, became England's first Christian martyr in AD 209, and the Normans built an abbey where he died. Today, the Cathedral and Abbey Church of St Alban still brings numerous visitors into the town, where you will also find the remains of a Roman theatre in which bear baiting was once among the attractions.

Bear lovers will prefer the St Albans of today, where the gift and antique shops make pleasant hunting-grounds.

In fact, you can find both under one roof at 'By George!' – an antique centre and craft arcade in George Street. On one side of the centre, antique dealers offer all sorts of antiques and collectables, and you could discover all sorts of accessories for your bears. On the other side, some forty crafts people offer a wide range of creations. One, **'By George! Bears'**, is a teddy specialist.

Artist Sheila Warren originally called her business Teddy Trivia, and specialized in her own paintings of teddies to suit every occasion. Christian names and letters decorated with teddies proved to be popular christening gifts. But Sheila also painted teddies engaged in various pursuits, from football to scuba diving. Brides and grooms were a perennial favourite, and some challenging commissions included everything from an auctioneer bear to an estate agent.

Sheila's paintings are still on sale at 'By George!'. Among them are a special range of Hobby Bear pictures which include a rugby player, golfer, cricketer, sailor, photographer, juggler, artist and fisherman. But Sheila has also been stocking an ever-increasing number of collectors bears. In addition to those from makers like Steiff, Merrythought, Dean's, Big Softies and Bransgore, there are also artist bears from a number of well-known makers. Bears by Teddystyle, Bocs Teganau, Redditoy and Hardy bears are just a few of those to be found there to date.

There are cuddly teddies, too, and popular ranges like the Boyds Collection, Tails and Tales, and the North American Bear Co.'s Muffy. Teddy bear greetings cards, wrapping paper and some books are also on sale.

'By George!' also has a restaurant, where you can sit and make difficult decisions as to which bear(s) will accompany you home. Or you could head instead for one of the city's beautiful historic inns.

ADDRESSES

'By George! Bears', 'By George!' Craft Centre, 23 George Street; tel. 0707 334782

Tourist Information Centre, Town Hall, Market Place; tel. 0727 864511

Teddington

P art of the Royal Borough of Richmond upon Thames, the small town of Teddington in Middlesex is within easy reach of Hampton Court as well as the eighteenth-century Marble Hill House. So there is every reason to visit the area. But for readers of this book, it is Teddington itself which has the greatest attraction. Among all the gifts at **Pinocchio** in the High Street are a good number of bears.

The shop opened in the late eighties, but it was when the owner's daughter, Sophie Langella, was persuaded to take over as manageress that the bears really came into their own. When she arrived, the only bears on sale were from Steiff. Now the range has widened considerably, with a mix of both manufactured and artist bears, including many limited editions.

They are a Steiff Club Store, and therefore carry quite a range of Steiff bears and animals. Alongside many current limited editions you will generally find a few earlier ones, and if a customer wants any bear that is not in stock, Sophie will do her best to find one.

Other manufacturers represented include Hermann, Merrythought, Dean's, Nisbet, Canterbury, Little Folk, the North American Bear Co. and Gabrielle Designs. But there are also various artist bears, including a number of shop exclusives. The number is increasing all the time, but among the artist bears available to date have been the work of Mother Hubbard, Naomi Laight, Barbara-Ann Bears, Jay-Bee Bears, Norbeary, Oldacre Bears, Bocs Teganau, Shultz Bears and Casbears.

The shop aims to have around two hundred and fifty bears on sale at any one time, and there are also bear-related items like Colour Box miniatures, jewellery, purses, aprons, some clothes for bears, bear-sized deck-chairs and sofas, and a wide range of greetings cards.

Pinocchio prides itself on offering greetings cards for every occasion, and there are naturally many which feature teddies. They have even introduced their own 'Teddart' range, with photographs of bears engaged in a variety of activities, from baking cakes to getting married, or simply feeling poorly. Many of the bears pictured are, or have been, residents in the shop.

There are plans for their own stationery and postcards, too.

Another feature of the shop is the monthly visit by bear doctor Cassie (maker of the Casbears) on the first Saturday of the month. She carries out many of the repairs on the spot, sitting in a corner of the shop in her white coat. But more serious cases are taken away to her 'hospital' and returned the following month.

She sees a wide range of ailments, large and small. Blind, or partially blind bears receive new eyes. Those who have lost their voices (or even those who never had one) are given new growlers and squeakers. Damaged paws are mended, broken joints replaced, new noses sewn, and all the other ills which can befall a bear are tenderly treated. It is a popular service.

It is not all bears at Pinocchio, though. Doll's houses and accessories are also to be found there, as well as dolls (including those by Annette Himstedt), rocking horses, wooden toys, and a wide range of gifts for weddings and other special occasions.

There are several other gift shops and antique shops in the High Street itself while the well-known chains are over the railway bridge, in Broad Street. So it would be quite easy to spend a whole afternoon shopping. Teddington Lock is another popular attraction for visitors.

By car, Teddington can be reached by taking the A316 from Twickenham or by following the signs from Kingston Bridge. Those on public transport can take a mainline train (from Waterloo) or the District Line to Richmond, and then catch the 33 bus to Teddington (alighting at the library for Pinocchio).

ADDRESSES

Pinocchio, 79 High Street; tel. 081 977 8995
Tourist Information Centre, The Atrium, 44 York Street, Twickenham; tel. 081 891 7272

Tunbridge Wells

Tunbridge Wells has seen some changes in recent years, with the opening of the new covered shopping centre at Royal Victoria Place taking custom away from the small shops which once filled the old High Street between the station and the Pantiles.

Several of the small High Street shops – previously good hunting-grounds for things bearish – have now disappeared. On the Pantiles themselves one source of old teddies has closed down. At the time of writing, **Pantiles Collectables** (once the town's main source of modern collectable bears) is up for sale, too, although it has continued to stock a certain number of bears – from Steiff, for instance (including some limited editions), as well as a few Dean's and Canterbury Bears and the budget-priced Tails and Tales. There are also some teddy ornaments and cards.

A shop in the new shopping centre has, on the other hand, been steadily increasing its range of bears. The tiny **Treasure Chest**, situated with lots of other small specialist shops in Ely Court, near the centre's Camden Road entrance, has even become a Steiff Club Store, offering a wide selection of Steiff animals as well as their limited-edition bears.

There are more manufactured bears from Hermann, Merrythought, Dean's, Canterbury Bears and Big Softies, but they have been joined by an ever-growing range of artist bears. These come from all over the country, although Mary Holden's Only Natural bears (made in Tunbridge Wells itself) will no doubt prove popular with visitors. They have a few less expensive cuddlies, too, as well as some Paddingtons and Winnie-the-Poohs.

The shop is also a gift shop, but many of the gifts have some kind of teddy bear connection. There are Colour Box miniatures, Cherished Teddies, and also the exquisitely sculptured Maggy Bears, which are produced in both porcelain and terracotta.

Tins, stickers, doorstops, rubber stamps and greetings cards are just a few of the other bearish items you might find there, in addition to tiny pewter teddy bears and a variety of Pooh merchandise.

A browse round some of the other Ely Court shops might also yield the odd bear-related item. And back in the main shopping centre, it is always worth looking to see what Boots have to offer. This is one of their larger stores, and their gift and household departments often have items of bearish interest – mugs, for instance, and other china.

Lawleys in Monson Road may have some teddy bear china, too, as well as Colour Box miniatures, and there are more Colour Box teddies over the road at **Penny Royal**. Penny Royal has other ceramic miniatures as well, and you should find some teddy bear greetings cards, Winnie-the-Pooh items and even a number of teddies.

There is a larger range of teddies, however, down at **Hooper's**, opposite the station. Their toy department includes both cuddly teddies and Steiff limited editions, and they generally have a few Merrythoughts and Dean's bears – although no limited editions from these companies on my last visit.

Down on the High Street, **Pickwick's** at No. 55 usually has a good selection of bear-related items including ceramic teddies, Pooh merchandise, a large number of greetings cards and cuddly teddies.

Alternatively, if your interest is older props and accessories to add to a teddy bear display, you'll no doubt head for the Pantiles with all the antique shops. The general antique shops on Chapel Place, just before the Pantiles proper, are always worth a look. Or, if books are your special love, you could try **Hall's Antiquarian Bookshop**, also on Chapel Place. They don't often have teddy bear books, but you might just strike it lucky.

It is said that all paths in Tunbridge Wells lead to the Pantiles, and, with or without the bears, it is an area not to be missed on a visit to the town. It takes its name from the small square tiles that paved the walkways during the eighteenth century – bought with £100 donated by Queen Anne (then Princess Anne) after her son, the Duke of Gloucester, had slipped and fallen there. They were replaced in 1793, but some can still be seen at A Day at the Wells and the Museum.

Tunbridge Wells had become a fashionable spa town following the discovery of an iron-rich spring in 1606. The waters can still be taken during the summer months, in front of the nineteenth-century Bath House.

Only a few of the original seventeenth-century columns still remain on the Pantiles, but in the old Corn Exchange A Day at the Wells recreates the town as it was in 1740. (Also in the old Corn Exchange are a number of attractive gift shops to explore.)

The town's other places of interest include a house on Mount Ephraim where William Thackeray once wrote (now a restaurant), and a number of unusual sandstone rock formations – among them the 40-foot High Rocks, a popular training ground for climbers, a mile and a half from the Pantiles.

ADDRESSES

Hooper's, 4 Mount Pleasant; tel. 0892 530222
Pantiles Collectables, 30 The Pantiles; tel. 0892 545440
The Treasure Chest, 1 Ely Court, Royal Victoria Place; tel. 0892 546151
Tourist Information Centre, The Old Fish Market, The Pantiles; tel. 0892 515675

West Horsley

Penny Chalmers is one of those busy people who always seem able to squeeze in something more.

Much of her time is spent running a busy ambulance service, which rescues sick and injured holidaymakers. It's a 24-hour-a-day business, and it has taken Penny herself all over the world. But that doesn't stop her from finding time for other interests. One of them is designing and making her own Little Charmers Bears, which are greatly sought after by collectors.

Some are found in teddy bear shops, and Penny sells her

bears herself at a limited number of fairs. But serious collectors can also visit Penny at home in West Horsley (Surrey) – strictly by appointment – to choose a bear and talk to the artist herself. It is also a splendid opportunity to see the bears in Penny's own collection.

She began making her own bears some years ago now. In those days, though, she used acrylic fur and sold her bears at craft fairs. Then, when the first British Teddy Bear Festival was organized in 1989, she decided to make some bears in mohair to sell there. At the end of the day, hardly a bear was left and since then Penny has found that her bears sell as fast as she can make them.

Even in the early days, when many makers bought their fur by the complete (30-metre) roll and turned out large numbers of bears in the same design, Penny was always trying out something new. Then, as now, she would often make just one or two bears from a particular pattern before moving on to something else.

Often she would be inspired by something she had seen on one of her many trips to America. A qualified nurse herself, she has visited that country numerous times to collect stricken tourists. This has given her many opportunities to investigate new techniques being used by artists there – and also to search out unusual fabrics and trimmings.

She was one of the first British artists to use the clever swivel-tilt head mechanism, for instance – an ingenious device which enables the bear's head to be moved up and down as well as turned around. She was also quick to try out the tiny plastic pellets which many artists now use as stuffing for their bears. Not only do they enable the bears to be posed appealingly, they also give them a pleasing weight, and can help make them delightfully huggable.

Both these innovations came to Britain from America. They inspired British artists to explore other methods of creating bears which could be posed in interesting positions, with some intriguing results.

Penny was also one of the first artists to experiment with fur of very unbear-like colours. Just a few years ago, you could find bears in every shade of beige, brown or gold, with the occasional white or black creation thrown in (although white bears were traditionally poor sellers). But anything else was a real rarity, and stood a good chance of being left on the shelf.

Today, lovers of modern artist bears may buy them in every imaginable shade. There are even whole collections made up entirely of shades of pink or some equally unbearish colour. Mohairs with tips of a contrasting shade have also proved popular, and at fairs you will find everything from bright red bears to designs which use a whole variety of different colours.

Penny has experimented with all sorts of beautiful colours – again often using pieces of fabric discovered on her travels. She also uses more traditional shades, however, perhaps enhancing the bears with unusual ribbons or pretty lace collars or a simple little dress.

Penny really loves her bears, and all that love goes into her designs. She loves to talk about them, too, and to chat with fellow bear lovers. Unfortunately, though, her time is strictly limited, which is why she can only open the bear room to those who are seriously interested in her bears. Otherwise, she would be unable to make even the limited number that she creates today.

If you are interested, however, just give her a ring to make an appointment. Don't turn up on the off chance – she may be off on one of her rescue missions to Australia, South America or the United States. Or she could be driving one of her ambulances across Europe – perhaps on one of her trips to Romania with a vehicle filled with relief supplies. Like so many busy people, Penny still finds time to devote enormous effort to helping others who are less fortunate.

ADDRESS

Penny Chalmers' bears room is in West Horsley, five miles from Guildford (page 97). If you would like to visit, telephone 0483 285134 for an appointment and directions.

Winchester

Winchester's specialist bear shop must be one of the prettiest of them all. Pine shelves are crammed with bears of every shape, colour and size. The relaxed, country feel encourages collectors to linger, safe in the knowledge that no one will object if they take all morning to make a decision.

In fact, there are so many bears to choose from that it is hard to make any decision at all.

Woodruffs' speciality is artist bears. In fact, owner Sandie Whittle was a bear maker herself even before she opened the shop. She had visions of dividing her days between her sewing and the serving of customers. But Woodruffs has proved so successful that her own Worthy Bears have been forced to take a back seat.

Right from the start, however, she has used her inside knowledge to her advantage. Not only can she recognize a good bear when she sees one. She also knows exactly what is involved in the making of a bear and, more important, how long it all takes.

She knew from the outset that the best artists would have long waiting lists for their bears, because there was no way they could ever keep up with the demand. The only solution was to keep planning ahead. If her shop was on enough waiting lists, there would soon come a time when bears started to arrive at suitably frequent intervals, ensuring packed shelves and an ever-changing selection.

It is a policy that has served her well. Many of the bears sell out at an alarming rate, especially with the help of their Woodruffs at Home mail order service for people who cannot get to the shop as often as they would like. But there are invariably new arrivals waiting in the wings to take their place.

The work of well-known makers is complemented by bears from lesser-known artists, which can generally be supplied on shorter notice. Sandie's unfailing eye ensures that collectors will like what they see, even if they don't know the name – yet.

A huge number of artists are represented, with the list expanding and changing all the time, but with British artists very much a speciality. Many create exclusive designs specially for the shop, often in small editions to give collectors the kind of rarity they love. Just about every taste is catered for. Woodruffs keep a watchful eye on current trends, as artists experiment with new techniques and strike out in interesting new directions.

They sell manufactured bears, too, of course. Steiff has a special alcove now that they are a Steiff Club Store, and there are bears from Hermann, Merrythought and Dean's, including each company's limited editions. But soft and cuddly bears by companies like Ty and the Manhattan Toy Company are on sale, too. For although Woodruffs stress that they are a teddy shop, not a toy shop, they understand that bear lovers may have widely differing tastes.

A great deal of attention is paid to the display of the bears. They like to have bears engaged in various activities, to bring them to life. They generally try to have some old bears on sale alongside all the new although, like many other shops, they find them increasingly hard to find – at least at reasonable prices.

There are also plenty of bear-related items, among them a wide range of teddy ornaments, some jewellery, books, greetings cards and other stationery. A range of bear wear is made specially for them, too (waistcoats are especially popular). So bear lovers will find no shortage of choice.

As Sandie also loves nothing better than to talk about bears with fellow lovers, a visit to the shop is an outing in itself, whether you're buying or not.

Of course, Winchester itself has a good deal to offer non-bear lovers, too, so it is a good destination for a full day out.

Its Cathedral, for instance, is more than nine hundred years old, although it has been much altered since its earliest days. Its nave is one of the longest in Europe. It is where both Henry IV and Mary Tudor were married, and Jane Austen is buried there, as are the Anglo-Saxon Kings of England.

Winchester was also at the heart of Alfred the Great's Kingdom of Wessex. The Round Table in the medieval Great Hall is, however, a thirteenth-century construction. The Great Hall itself was built in the twelfth century by Henry III, during an almost complete rebuilding of Winchester Castle.

The City also boasts a number of interesting museums, among them the City Museum which includes reconstructions of some old shop interiors. The Winchester City Mill is another popular tourist attraction, close to City Bridge.

Nearby, also in Bridge Street, is a little shop called **Collector's Corner**, which stocks a few teddy bears from leading manufacturers as well as some doll's house miniatures.

There are plenty of other shops to browse around, with a number of gift shops selling soft and huggable teddies. The **Toy**

Cupboard in St Georges Street also has some of Merrythought's children's teddies among their soft toys.

It is worth exploring some of the back streets as well as the main thoroughfares, and if you are a collector of teddy bear books, the antiquarian bookshops could be worth investigating.

ADDRESSES

Collector's Corner, 23 Bridge Street; tel. 0962 849933
Woodruffs, One Kings Head Yard, St Thomas Street; tel. 0962 877738
Tourist Information Centre, The Guildhall, The Broadway; tel. 0962 840500

Windsor

Windsor now has a long tradition of being a good town for bear lovers. When Joan Bland opened her little **Asquiths** teddy bear shop in George V Place it was something totally new. Ten years on, there are three Asquiths shops, and dozens of other teddy bear specialists can now be found all over the country.

It all started when Joan's aunt, who had been a GI bride, came over for a visit from America. She wanted to take a teddy bear back with her, as a present for a grandchild, but searched in vain for the kind of teddy she remembered from her own childhood.

It reminded Joan of her own childhood teddy, and of how sad she was when her mother threw it away. She realized that there must be countless other people with similar memories, and a similar affection for bears but, like her aunt, unable to buy them. The idea of a specialist teddy bear shop began to form in her mind.

At the time, Joan was a partner in a small design and promotion company called Asquiths Designs. While looking for an office for the company, she came across one with a little shop attached to it and knew immediately that it would be just right for bears. Within two hours she had started proceedings to buy it. Ten years on, it is still there, stuffed full of bears and bearish items.

In the early days, the collectable bears came from major German companies like Steiff and Hermann. English manufacturers were not yet making many bears for the collectors market, and bear makers hand-crafting bears in their own homes were very few and far between.

Some bears came to the shop from those early British 'bear artists', however – although that term had not yet been coined to describe them. But others were designed by Joan herself, with outworkers employed to make them up for her. The range grew rapidly as more and more fabrics became available and provided inspiration for new designs.

Gradually, word of the shop began to spread, and collectors began to travel from far and wide to visit it. Four years later, a much bigger shop was opened just a few minutes' walk away, over the river in Eton (page 94). The extra space means that the Eton shop now offers an even greater choice for collectors. But many also seek out the original little Windsor Asquiths, which remains crammed with bears for collectors as well as less expensive teddies and a number of exclusive bearish gifts. The latter include special magnets, like a guardsman teddy, and there are mugs, T-shirts, gift bags and postcards.

There are Colour Box miniatures, too, and Colour Box have also made a special miniature of Archie, one of the many exclusive Asquiths bears. The miniature is only available from the Asquiths shops.

Such gift items are invariably popular with passing tourists, who flock to Windsor Castle – one of the most popular destinations for visitors to Britain. Those teddy lovers with an interest in dolls and doll's houses will want to visit the Castle, too, to see Queen Mary's Doll's House, with its exquisite furniture and luxurious decorations.

There are many full-size buildings of historical interest elsewhere in the town. Sir Christopher Wren completed work on the Guildhall, for instance, while Nell Gwynn is said to have lived in Church Street.

Of more recent date is Windsor and Eton Central Station, still in use as a railway station but now also the home of various crafts stalls. It is a good place to look for some unusual bearish creations, like the wide variety of dressed bears by **Collectable Crafts** discovered on my last visit. The bears themselves are inexpensive imports, but they are then dressed by Collectable Crafts' Sheila Norman, who can be seen machining away throughout the day. Clown bears are apparently very popular, but the range also includes beefeater, guardsman, flower lady, city businessman, policeman and policewoman, bride and groom, chimney sweep, fishmonger, nurse, artist, surfer, tennis bear, footballer, snooker bear and hiker.

There are some more new bears, including Canterbury Bears and Dormouse Designs, at **Old Boys Toys** in River Street, which also sells numerous die-cast toys.

Windsor naturally boasts many general gift shops, too. I found a particularly wide range of bear-related gifts at **Raffles** in Thames Street – among them some souvenir teds wearing Windsor jumpers in various colours. **Talents of Windsor**, on the other hand, offers 'Fine Art and Craft' from Britain and Europe, including the delightful Maggy Bears. These exquisite, finely detailed little sculptures in terracotta or porcelain show teddies engaged in all sorts of activities. The superb craftsmanship means that they are highly collectable.

143

So, with the larger Eton Asquiths also just a stone's throw away, it is little wonder that Windsor is such a popular haunt for anyone with a love of bears.

ADDRESSES

Asquiths, 10 George V Place, Thames Avenue; tel. 0753 854954

Collectable Crafts, Windsor & Eton Central Station, Thames Street; tel. 081 658 4862

Old Boys Toys, River Street; tel. 0753 842003

Raffles of Windsor, Curfew Yard, Thames Street; tel. 0753 831320

Talents of Windsor, 12 Church Street; tel. 0753 831459

Tourist Information Centre, Central Station, Thames Street; tel. 0753 852010

Witney

One of the best known of all British teddy bear shops is **'Teddy Bears' of Witney**, in Oxfordshire. It was one of the very first teddy bear specialists, and carries a huge range of bears for sale. Some very interesting residents are on permanent display, too, so it is little wonder that many collectors name it as their favourite shop.

Ian Pout and his wife Jane started selling antiques in Witney in the mid-seventies. In the early eighties, they started to introduce some teddy bears, and within a few years the bears had become their speciality. These days, they are particularly well known for their huge range of *modern* bears, although they aim to have a good selection of older teddies on offer at any time as well.

They are one of the few shops to produce regular catalogues, and a look back over the last few years provides a graphic example of the way in which the teddy bear world (and collectors' tastes) have changed.

Just a few years ago, all the modern bears illustrated in the catalogue were from manufacturers like Steiff, Hermann, Merrythought and Canterbury Bears, with limited editions few and far between and most of the bears intended to appeal to children as much as to collectors.

By 1989/90, however, they had noted 'a surge in demand for the best quality limited-edition bears' and correctly predicted that this trend would continue. Limited editions from Steiff, Hermann and Nisbet were listed, as well as a large number of other manufactured bears. But the catalogue also contained a further hint of things to come. Tucked in among all the manufactured teddies was a single hand-crafted bear, made in Yorkshire. A supplementary catalogue included another, this time handmade in Wimbledon.

It was in 1991, however, that the so-called 'artist-made' bears really came into their own. The manufactured bears were still there, including many limited editions. But so, too, was the work of several top artists – not just from Britain but from America as well. Today, many specialist shops also have artist bears from a number of different countries, including America. But when Ian Pout first started bringing them to Witney, they were very much a rarity in this country.

In addition, the 1991 catalogue advertised a large number of bears made exclusively for the shop. Now this is a major trend, but again the Witney shop was one of the pioneers.

Each year since then has seen a bigger and better catalogue – so beautiful that they have become keenly sought collectors' items in their own right. Each has offered a still wider range of bears, with the 1993–4 edition listing nearly two hundred different designs in all, with nearly seventy of them exclusive to the shop. And that represents just a fraction of the range available to personal visitors.

All the popular manufacturers are represented, of course, with a good number of limited editions as well as the companies' regular ranges. But the shop also sells many manufactured bears which are available nowhere else. They have had exclusive editions made for them by Steiff, Hermann, Merrythought, Dean's, Big Softies and Clemens.

In addition, they have bears carrying the revered Schuco and Bing names. Older bears from both these German companies are today eagerly sought by collectors. Now new bears are being produced from the original patterns, and the Witney shop lost no time in obtaining some of them.

Collectors of artist bears will also find themselves spoilt for choice, with huge numbers of bears from all over Britain and America, as well as from any other country where good-quality bears are made. Australia, Canada, the Netherlands and Ireland are just a few of the sources to date.

There are dressed bears and bare bears, bears in a huge variety of fabrics and colours, tiny bears, giant bears and everything in between. Some have splendid costumes, beautifully worked down to the last minute detail. Others wear a simple ribbon, or even nothing at all, relying simply on an irresistible face to capture the heartstrings of some collector.

Although the shop carries a huge variety of highly collectable bears, there are plenty of less expensive offerings, too – often just that bit different from bears commonly found elsewhere. So it is a rare bear lover indeed who walks away empty-handed.

There are some bear-related items on sale as well, and again you will find some unique offerings. The range of greetings cards is particularly wide, and the postcards include some that are exclusive to the shop. There are also pictures, books, stationery, ceramic miniatures, mugs and jewellery, so all in all it is the kind of shop where you keep going back for one more look, and find something new every single time.

Lovers of old bears are not forgotten either, with a constantly changing selection on sale, along with some interesting bear-related items.

Many more are on permanent display, and include a number who have become major celebrities over the years.

Possibly the best known of all is the bright red Alfonzo, bought at a Christie's auction in 1989. The price of £12,100 was a world record for a teddy bear at the time, a reflection not only of the little bear's rarity but also of his fascinating history.

The button in his ear proved that he was a German Steiff bear, but it emerged that Steiff had no records of ever having produced a range of these bears. The only explanation they could offer was that he was made specially for Harrods in London, who often asked for toys to be made to order for their special customers.

In this case, the customer was the Russian Grand Duke George Mikhailovich, who bought the bear as a present for his four-year-old daughter Xenia in 1908.

The bear's early years were spent mainly in the family's house in the Crimea, almost next door to the Tsar's own villa. But from time to time he would travel north to Petersburg to visit the Princess's grandfather, a son of Tsar Nicholas I.

The bear accompanied Princess Xenia everywhere, and he was with her when she and her mother travelled to Buckingham Palace in 1914 to holiday with King George V and Queen Mary.

They were there when war broke out and prevented them from returning home. They stayed with Queen Alexandra at Marlborough House for a while, before taking a house in London's Chester Square.

They were still in London when the Princess's beloved father was shot at the Peter and Paul Fortress in 1919. The bear was to be a much-treasured reminder of him and would stay with Xenia until her death in 1965.

By then, the Princess was living in America. She had married the heir to a tin fortune, and Alfonzo lived with her on Long Island for more than forty years. After her death, he moved first to Connecticut and then to Vermont, where he was looked after by the Princess's daughter Nancy until his journey to the Christie's auction in 1989.

Now he is on permanent display at the Witney shop, who also commissioned his original makers, Steiff, to make 5,000 replicas of the bear exclusively for them (complete with his distinctive clothes – little trousers with braces, topped by a Cossack-style tunic). At the time of writing, however, stocks were very low, and most will have been sold by the time this book appears.

Many felt that it was one of the finest replicas ever to have been made by Steiff. Even the Princess's own daughter was shocked by the likeness. The only difference she noted was the bear's nose, as the original had been half kissed away.

A miniature sculpture of Alfonzo by Colour Box sold out even more quickly than the Steiff replica. But a second Colour Box miniature of the bear is now being produced.

Another very special Steiff bear on display in the shop was bought at London auction house Phillips. Called Othello, he is a rare black bear, made in 1912.

Steiff records revealed that he was part of a whole consignment of black bears sent to Britain that year. There were five sizes in all, with some bears being made in a short mohair and some in mohair with a longer pile. Only 494 were made in the longer pile. The 19-inch Othello was one of them.

Six months earlier, another of these bears had fetched a staggering £24,200 at auction. Although the condition of this second bear was less pristine, bidding was again fierce, and Ian was forced to part with £8,800 in order to add him to his collection.

The following year, Steiff produced a full-size replica of the bear. Like the original, it was made specially for the British market, but this time in a limited edition of 3,000. In 1992, a 16-inch version was introduced in a worldwide edition of 7,000.

The resident collection at 'Teddy Bears' of Witney includes many other interesting bears. A beautiful off-white mohair Steiff bear, for instance, is believed to be one of the first created specially for the British market. Another Steiff, apricot coloured and in splendid condition, dates right back to about 1905. A bear king skittle was created even before the first teddy bear, in the 1890s, while a special shop display item is much more recent, dating from the 1950s.

There are many more interesting and appealing British bears, too. Barnaby is a lovely 1930s Merrythought – reproduced in a limited edition of 600 specially for the shop. Replicas of a splendid 1930s Dean's bear called Bertie have also been created by his original makers, while Yorkshire's Big Softies were commissioned to produce faithful copies of another 1930s bear in the collection. All these replicas have been exclusive to the Witney shop.

Also on display is a distinctive 15-inch Merrythought bear created to commemorate the Queen's Coronation in 1953. His head and arms are red, his body white and his legs blue. Forty years on, Merrythought produced a special boxed edition of the bear, limited to 5,000 worldwide.

A much older English bear is the 1915 Master Teddy, made by the Buckinghamshire-based Chiltern Toy Works. He has distinctive googly eyes, and is still dressed in his pink checked shirt and blue felt trousers, with the original cardboard tag still attached.

Another splendid bear still carrying his original card label is a Bellhop Bear (or *Messenger-Bär*) from the German company Schuco. These distinctive bears in their red felt jackets and hats and black trousers were first made in 1921, and are now much sought after by collectors. Unlike most seen today, however, this particular example also still has his little leather bag across his shoulder. By moving the bear's tail, his head can be made to nod both up and down and from side to side. This so-called Yes/No mechanism was patented by Schuco in 1921.

A beautiful early American bear dates from around 1906/7 and was made by the Ideal Novelty and Toy Company just a few years after its founder, Morris Michtom, and his wife Rose made their very first toy bears. They had been inspired by a cartoon in the *Washington Post* in which President Theodore Roosevelt, a keen hunter, was shown refusing to shoot a tethered bear. It was this incident which led to the teddy bear being given its name.

Bears by England's J. K. Farnell and Chad Valley are also on show – the latter including a number of early bears carrying a variety of different buttons. There are novelty items, too, like a teddy bear muff from around 1905–1910, along with a photo of it being worn by its original owner. A box of teddy bear soap is of a similar age, but the early battery-operated bears from Japan are of much later vintage.

With so much to see, it is not surprising that many collectors find themselves spending more time in this shop than in any other they visit. Even those unable to buy are able to enjoy seeing all the bears, which are invariably beautifully displayed to show them to their best advantage.

The shop itself is two hundred years old, one of the many attractive old buildings in this pretty market town. Witney is, of course, best known for its blanket industry, which dates back to at least the seventeenth century. These days, however, its wide range of shops bring visitors from a wide area into the town.

Many are attracted by the large number of antiques shops, several of which will make interesting browsing for those who like to incorporate old 'props' and accessories into displays of their bears. Any gift shop could also contain something of bearish interest, so it is a town where many hours can be spent in leisurely browsing.

Witney is just twelve miles to the west of Oxford, with buses from Oxford running every fifteen minutes (service 100). Alight at the Methodist Church for the teddy bear shop.

ADDRESSES

'Teddy Bears' of Witney, 99 High Street; tel. 0993 702616
Tourist Information Centre, Town Hall, Market Square; tel. 0993 775802

SOUTH-WEST and WALES

Bath

Most towns attracting large numbers of visitors have their share of attractions for bear lovers, and Bath is no exception. Not only do the bears appeal to passing tourists in such towns; serious collectors will often travel considerable distances to see them, knowing that they can combine a bear hunt with an interesting day out for the whole family. In Bath, however, although there are a number of shops selling collectable bears, the majority are not teddy bear specialists.

The **China Doll** in Walcot Street, for instance, sells mainly dolls and doll's houses, as the name suggests. But, as manageress Caroline Nevill is a real arctophile, they also have a number of bears.

Among them are some by leading German manufacturers Steiff and Hermann, including the collectable limited editions. But there are hand-crafted artist bears, too, of which a number are usually exclusive to the shop. In addition, alongside all the doll's house miniatures, there are often some unusual miniature bears to be found.

The shop's parent company is **Tridias**, whose shop in Bennett Street has been selling toys for nearly thirty years. They include a large number of teddy bears, both collectable ones and cuddly soft toys.

Again, they stock a range of Steiffs, including the limited editions. Also on the shelves are bears by other manufacturers, like Merrythought, Dean's, Hermann, Canterbury, Nisbet and Gund. But when I last visited, the range of artist bears was fairly limited.

Another toy shop, Eric Snook's **The Golden Cat** in Abbeygate Street (by Marks & Spencer) also has a good number of manufactured collectables – by Steiff and Merrythought, for instance – as well as lots of cuddly toys.

A place of rather different bearish interest in Bath is the **Paddington and Friends** shop in Abbey Street. It is not all bears. Other children's favourites are there, too, like Noddy, Thomas the Tank Engine, Babar and Beatrix Potter's popular characters. But there is an especially large number of Paddingtons.

The range of Paddington items on offer is changing all the time, but you'll generally find both Paddington and his Aunt Lucy in various sizes, as well as a wide range of other Paddington merchandise.

The special miniature suit-case is often popular with collectors, and I discovered duvet cover and pillowcase sets, babies' bibs, T-shirts for all ages, embroidery kits, photograph albums, a large number of stationery items, children's aprons and tote bags, rattles, toothbrushes, postcards, games, jigsaw puzzles and even a set of five wooden Paddingtons that nest inside each other like Russian dolls.

Needless to say, there are also a large number of Paddington books.

The shop also stocks Rupert and Winnie-the-Pooh items, but Pooh lovers will find many others at the **Disney Store** in Union Street. In addition to the cuddly toys, I discovered slippers, mugs and other gifts there, as well as videos of Winnie-the-Pooh cartoons.

Bath also has a branch of the **English Teddy Bear Company**, in Abbey Church Yard, right opposite the Pump Room. All their bears are made specially for the company, some from mohair and others from acrylic fabrics. There are both jointed and unjointed bears, while some are dressed and some not.

Other items on sale include teddy bear clothes and special English Teddy Bear Company mugs, jams and biscuits.

Naturally, there are also bears in some of the many other gift shops in Bath. Mementos, next to the Pump Room, has some dressed in special Bath sweaters or Roman Baths T-shirts, and there are more souvenir teddies in the gift shops actually inside the Roman Baths complex. They include inexpensive little bears wearing Roman Baths medallions.

The Roman Baths are just one of the many attractions that bring vast numbers of visitors to Bath every year. Splendid Georgian crescents and terraces include the magnificent sweep of thirty houses which make up the renowned Royal Crescent. Then there is the Abbey, famous for its fan vaulting, which dates from the sixteenth and nineteenth centuries. It is also claimed that the only British church with more monuments than this one is Westminster Abbey in London.

Bath is a perfect city for leisurely strolls, exploring all the small streets and interesting shops with just about every kind of speciality.

In Bartlett Street, towards the north of the city, there are two antiques markets, directly opposite each other. Both the **Great Western Antiques Market** and the **Bartlett Street Antiques Centre** contain a wide variety of stalls, and either could yield an interesting old bear if your timing is right.

The weekly **Bath Antiques Market** at nearby Guinea Lane and **Paragon Antiques Market** on the adjacent Paragon could be worth a visit early on Wednesday morning, too.

Bears themselves, however, may prefer a morning coffee with crumpets and honey in the elegant Pump Room, where suitably gentle music is provided by the Pump Room Trio. Or the unique Sally Lunn bun can be taken drenched in honey at the oldest house in Bath, where Sally Lunn herself began baking her famous buns back in the 1680s.

All in all, Bath can provide a splendid day out, or weekend break, for any bear lover. You may not find that special bear, but you can have a wonderful time looking for him.

ADDRESSES

The China Doll, 31 Walcot Street; tel. 0225 465849

Bartlett Street Antiques Centre, 5/10 Bartlett Street; tel. 0225 466689

English Teddy Bear Company, 8 Abbey Church Yard; tel. 0225 338655

The Golden Cat (Eric Snook's), 2 Abbeygate Street; tel. 0225 463739

Great Western Antiques Market, Bartlett Street; tel. 0225 310388

Paddington & Friends, 1 Abbey Street; tel. 0225 463598

Tridias, 6 Bennett Street; tel. 0225 314730

Tourist Information Centre, The Colonnades, 11–13 Bath Street; tel. 0225 462831

Bideford

For bear lovers, Bideford's main interest is not its busy, narrow streets, the boats which take visitors to tiny Lundy island, or the sixteenth-century bridge across the Torridge, with twenty-four different arches. It is a cottage some miles away where artist Trudy Friend has set up her **Smithy Art Studio**.

Trudy, a qualified art teacher, and her husband Michael have turned their North Devon home into a comfortable guest house for up to six visitors, who can combine their stay with expert tuition in drawing or painting. And one of Trudy's specialities is teddy bears.

Trudy welcomes both beginners and more experienced artists and uses a questionnaire to devise a course specially tailored to their interests and capabilities. She believes that anyone can learn to draw an acceptable picture – they just have to learn to look at things in the right way.

Not everyone decides to paint bears, of course. The surrounding countryside offers plenty of interesting landscapes and seascapes. Some guests choose to paint buildings, and animal lovers will find pigs, Shetland ponies, a horse and a goat among the occupiers of the cottage's ten acres. Plants and still life are two other favourites.

There is a choice of medium, too. Oils, water-colours, pastels, acrylics, ink, pencil, charcoal – even appliqué. Materials not available from the studio itself can usually be found in nearby Bideford if guests do not already have their own.

Two hours of concentrated tuition are provided each morning for a very reasonable sum, and an extra hour is available in the afternoon for those who want it. At other times, Trudy is generally on hand to sort out any problems, and guests can make use of the studio whenever they wish. At the end of their stay, they receive a list of helpful tips, and there is also the possibility of postal tuition for those who wish to take their study further.

Many teddy lovers bring one of their own favourite bears to paint, but some borrow one of Trudy's, or even buy one of the locally made bears that are usually on sale in the studio.

Some even bring a bear and don't paint it at all, leaving it for Trudy to paint while they disappear each day to explore the surrounding area. But many combine mornings of drawing or painting with afternoons enjoying the local attractions, of which there are many.

It is only a short drive to picturesque Clovelly, for instance. This unique village's only transport is donkeys and sledges, and its steep cobbled street descends some four hundred feet in under half a mile. Bears are not in great supply there, but the new Visitor Centre does offer inexpensive souvenir teddies wearing a special Clovelly sash.

The Gnome Reserve at West Putford, near Bradworthy, is another popular attraction, with its collection of over 1,000 gnomes and pixies (open March to October). Lovers of Tarka the Otter, on the other hand, head for the Tarka Trail, which starts not far away, in Barnstaple.

Dartington Crystal is made in Great Torrington. The fascinating Quince Honey Farm (page 170) in South Molton is easily accessible, and it is even possible to make excursions into Cornwall – to Tintagel (page 176), for instance.

The nearest town is a few miles away, however, so those without cars are more restricted – although arrangements can be made for transport to places of local interest. Transport from Barnstaple station can also be organized for guests arriving by train and, once at the cottage, some people will find that there is no reason to set foot outside at all.

Accommodation can be either bed and breakfast, half board (dinners are excellent), or even full board if required. There are TVs and tea-making facilities in the rooms, and the studio even offers a selection of suitable take-home gifts, including bears and some of Trudy's own work. (Animals and teddies are her specialities.)

Some of her drawings are being made into greetings cards, and these are also on sale.

ADDRESSES

The Smithy Art Studio, Stowford Moor Cottage, Collingsdown Cross, Buckland Brewer; tel. 0409 261325

Tourist Information Centre, The Quay, Kingsley Road, Bideford; tel. 0237 477676

Budleigh Salterton

Until the outbreak of the Napoleonic Wars, it was fashionable for the wealthy to spend their winters abroad. In the early nineteenth century, however, they were forced to seek alternatives closer to home, and Budleigh Salterton on the East Devon coast was one place which found favour, with its dramatic red cliffs and sheltered pebbled beach.

Victorian novelist Anthony Trollope was one of many famous visitors, and Sir John Millais used the sea wall as the setting for his painting of *The Boyhood of Raleigh*.

Today, the town is still popular with tourists seeking peace and tranquillity. They divide their time between the beach and a street of small, privately owned shops – among them **Budleigh Bears**.

Owner Barbara Madell has been collecting bears for quite a few years, after falling in love with a small old teddy at an antique fair. As her collection of both old and new bears began to grow, she began to dream about a shop of her own, and late in 1992, the dream became a reality.

The small shop is just right for teddies, which include the work of several local artists as well as some from further afield. Mother Hubbard, Redditoy, Hardy Bears, Bear With Me, Bridon Bears and Childhood Treasures are just a few of the makers whose bears have been sold so far.

There are also manufactured bears by British companies like Merrythought, Dean's, Nisbet and Big Softies, as well as Germany's Hermann and the American company Gund.

Those who prefer cuddly teddies will find some here, too, as well as various bear-related items. Designer bear wear is particularly popular.

For those who are already loaded down with Devon cream, honey, fudge and other goodies (or for those unable to get to the shop) Barbara will also post most of her bears anywhere in the United Kingdom.

If you are in Devon, however, Budleigh Salterton is a pretty place to visit. In fact, its numerous hanging baskets full of flowers have previously won for the town the Britain in Bloom competition.

There are several other shops which may provide something of bearish interest, too. Maybe the antique shop will yield a lucky find, and china shops are always worth a look, while stationers **Lesley's**, in the High Street (a continuation of Fore Street), has a number of bears. Among them are bears by Steiff (including some limited editions), Nisbet, Little Folk and Golden Gifts, and they have bears in special Budleigh Salterton jumpers, which make popular souvenirs. Books, stationery, Colour Box miniatures and other teddy bear gifts are also on sale there, as well as various teddy greetings cards.

ADDRESSES

Budleigh Bears, 28 Fore Street; tel. 0395 443641
Lesley's, 49 High Street; tel. 0395 443954
Tourist Information Centre, Fore Street; tel. 0395 445275

Hay-on-Wye

This quiet Marches town, on the Breconshire side of the river Wye, is now world famous for its secondhand books. It boasts more than twenty major bookshops, all of them independently owned, so if you love books this is the place to browse away a day.

The local Tourist Information Bureau can supply a complete list of all the shops, some of which carry a general range while others are more specialist. The larger ones are open 364 days a year, so if you are in the area on a Sunday it is still worth a visit.

It is said that you will find a million volumes in the town, so there should be something for the teddy bear lover among them. You may have to search hard, but book lovers will surely not mind that.

Of more direct interest for bear lovers, and also open every day of the year except Christmas Day, is **Mr Puzzle's Jigsaw World and Teddy Bear Wonderland**. They always have over a thousand bears in stock, with prices ranging from about £1 to £1,750. But the majority are under about £30, and they generally offer a wide selection of bears costing less than £10.

For collectors there are bears from companies like Steiff, Hermann, Merrythought and Nisbet, including various limited editions. Other manufacturers represented include Little Folk and Golden Bear, while there are also plenty of character bears like Paddington and Rupert.

There are also cuddlies galore, of every shape and size. But there are some artist bears as well. At the time of writing, they included the work of Bocs Teganau, the Old Fashioned Teddy Bear Company, Worthy Bears, Carolan and Haydn Bears.

Guarding them all are a number of six-foot Merrythought bears – dressed as policeman, guardsman, beefeater, highlander, hobo, Sherlock Holmes and Chelsea Pensioner – and the bears on sale can include everything from cyclists and pilots to chefs, golfers and cricketers.

There are plenty of bear-related items, too, among them cards, giftwrap, badges, brooches, mobiles, wall hangings, clothes and puppets. But not everything in the shop is related to bears. As its name makes clear, its other speciality is jigsaw puzzles, and there are even more of those than there are of the bears.

They aim to have over 2,500 different ones in stock, with anything from four to 8,000 pieces in each. So they cover every range of difficulty, from those which anyone could complete in just a minute to the puzzle claimed to be the World's Most Difficult.

There is more to see in the town, too. The most interesting historical building is its Norman castle, originally built around 1200. Since then, however, it has suffered repeatedly at the hands of both the Welsh and the English between the thirteenth and fifteenth centuries. In 1971, it was acquired by a bookseller, but six years later it was severely damaged by fire for the second time this century. Now it is occasionally open to the public.

Many of the town's old buildings have had their timber and plaster hidden by rendering. But bear lovers will be pleased to note that the Bear in Bear Street has been restored, exposing its original frontage, which dates from the sixteenth or seventeenth century.

ADDRESSES

Mr Puzzle's Jigsaw World & Teddy Bear Wonderland, Y Gelli Chambers, 10 Broad Street; tel. 0497 821440
Tourist Information Bureau, Oxford Road; tel. 0497 820144

Honiton

The market town of Honiton in East Devon is best known for its lace. The Allhallows Museum contains a fine collection, and there are lace-making demonstrations there during the summer months. In the High Street there is also a special lace shop, but bear lovers will probably be more interested in the various antique shops.

Honiton Antique Toys, for instance, has a number of older teddies as well as dolls and a host of other toys, including tin toys and various games. Being old bears, the range can never be predicted. But on my last visit I saw a number of interesting English bears, so it is worth seeking them out.

Occasionally, bears can be found in other antique shops in the town, and they are also good hunting-grounds for the kinds of props and accessories that are just right for teddy bear displays. It is a place for quiet browsing where you might just find something really special.

ADDRESSES

Honiton Antique Toys, 38 High Street; tel. 0404 41194/42831
Tourist Information Centre, Dowell Street East Car Park; tel.
  0404 43716

Launceston

Collectable teddy bears are rather few and far between in Cornwall, but some have found their way to the old market town of Launceston, once the Cornish capital. Today the town is dominated by the Norman Castle, built in 1066 and offering splendid views of Dartmoor and the Cornish countryside.

A quilting exhibition has become an annual event, with many of the quilting supplies coming from **Windmill Patchworks**. It is there that you will also find quite a few bears.

They have Steiffs (including some limited editions), Dean's and Merrythought, as well as the Boyds Collection and Golden Gifts' Tails and Tales. Character bears like Winnie-the-Pooh, Rupert and Paddington are on sale too, along with cuddly teddies from companies like Ty and some locally made bears.

In addition, they stock various teddy-related items, including mugs, jewellery, ornaments, boxes and pictures.

The shop sells everything from Indian print clothes to Caithness glass, jewellery, music boxes, wooden toys and much more. But teddies feature throughout. They can also be found in the café, which offers coffees, lunches, Cornish cream teas and home-made cakes. On warm days many people make use of the secluded tea garden.

ADDRESSES

Windmill Patchworks & Café, 23 Westgate Street; tel. 0566 775076

Tourist Information Centre, Market House Arcade, Market Street; tel. 0566 772321

Llantrisant

Shops selling teddy bears for collectors seem to be rather thin on the ground in Wales. But Llantrisant in Mid Glamorgan, home of the Royal Mint, has **Traditional Toys**, a shop whose stock generally includes more than three hundred bears. Among them are various bears for collectors.

There are bears from a number of major manufacturers – Steiff (including some limited editions), Merrythought, Hermann and Dean's. Big Softies and Bedford Bears are there, too, as well as cuddlies from Ty and bears from the Boyds Collection. Small selections of bears by other manufacturers can usually be found as well.

At the time of writing, the range of artist bears is fairly limited. Their main line is Sue Schoen's Bocs Teganau – hardly surprising with Sue herself living just four miles away. But they obtain bears by other artists as and when they can.

There are some bear-related items, too, like book-ends, doorstops, ceramic teddies, water-colours, prints and greetings cards. But some of the non-bearish items on sale may also be of interest to those who like to set up interesting displays. The shop sells reproduction Victorian and Georgian rocking horses, for instance, as well as children's desks and chairs, and a variety of wooden toys (trains, whips, tops and so on).

Those who love dolls or doll's houses as well as teddies will find these on sale too, in addition to one-twelfth-scale doll's house miniatures.

Llantrisant also boasts some other craft-type shops, and a craft and design centre, so you could find something bearish in one of those as well.

The town is one of the oldest in South Wales, and there are

a 900-year-old castle and church for those with an interest in historic buildings.

Traditional Toys, 6 Bull Ring; tel. 0443 222693/229015
Tourist Information: Pontypridd Historical and Cultural Centre, Bridge Street, Pontypridd; tel. 0443 402077

Plymouth

During the Second World War, Plymouth lost over 20,000 of its buildings, including over forty churches. So it is hardly surprising to find that the busy town centre has relatively little of historic interest. Perhaps more surprising is the lack of interesting bears in the extensive, and largely pedestrianized, main shopping centre.

It is, however, just a short walk to the historic Barbican, with its maze of streets lined by small specialist shops, some of them housed in listed buildings.

The building at 54 Southside Street was built at the end of the eighteenth century. A family called Millman bought it at auction in 1864, and for many decades it was a jeweller's and pawnbroker's. Now it is the home of **Dolls and Miniatures** which, in addition to doll's houses, doll's house miniatures, and dolls large and small also stocks a good number of teddy bears.

Steiff and Merrythought are two of the makes stocked. Bears by Hermann, Dean's and a number of other makers are also available, and there are naturally a good number of tiny teddies – the furry variety, as well as ceramic and pewter ornaments.

The Barbican is full of other small shops selling everything from locally made fudge and other goodies to gifts from all over the world. It is always worth looking for an exclusive teddy among the hand-made jewellery and pottery, but a visit to the **Antique and Bric-à-Brac Market** in Southside Street could be even more rewarding. The chances of finding an appealing old bear may be small, but it is the kind of general market where you could find some unusual bear-sized accessories to add extra interest to a bear display. A bear collection can really be brought to life by carefully chosen 'props', which can often be picked up for just a few pounds – or, at a car boot sale, even just a few pence.

Parade Antiques, on the Parade, is another potential hunting ground. On my last visit I also saw some lovely old bears there but, as is so often the case these days, they were from the owner's own collection and not for sale. They had been put out on display to encourage anyone with a bear to *sell* to bring it along for him to see – and possibly add to his collection.

The Barbican also has a number of other attractions, like the distillery producing two million bottles of Plymouth Dry Gin each year, and a similar quantity of vodka. The Mayflower Steps are where the Pilgrim Fathers gathered before their voyage to the New World in 1620, and some of the pilgrims stayed in nearby Island House.

Many of the old warehouses surrounding the busy Sutton Harbour have now been turned into homes and restaurants. But the Victorian fish market on the quay is still very much in business, with its scents adding extra atmosphere to the whole area.

Sir Francis Drake himself once lived near Sutton Harbour, and a pleasant waterside walk will soon bring you to the famous Hoe.

Dolls & Miniatures, 54 Southside Street, The Barbican; tel. 0752
663676

Barbican Pannier Market, Southside Street; tel. 0752 221256

Parade Antiques, 17 The Parade; tel. 0752 250019

Tourist Information Centre, Civic Centre, Royal Parade; tel.
0752 264849

Sidmouth

On Christmas Eve, 1819, the Duke and Duchess of Kent
arrived in Sidmouth, East Devon, together with their new
daughter, the Princess Victoria. Within weeks, the Duke had
succumbed to pneumonia after being caught in a sudden snow-
storm. But by focusing attention on the town, he had assured its
future as a fashionable resort.

Many of the houses built by visiting gentry have now been
converted into hotels, but the air of quiet elegance persists. You
won't find loud amusement arcades in Sidmouth, or even many
buckets and spades. It is a place for quiet strolls along the
promenade, beside a sea that can be more red than blue, thanks
to the red sandstone cliffs surrounding the bay.

Equally relaxing is a browse round the many small shops
which make up the pretty town centre. Like most resorts,
Sidmouth has its fair share of gift shops, but there is none of the
brashness found in most tourist attractions. There are also two
shops of interest to bear lovers.

Puddleducks, in Old Fore Street, specializes in wooden toys,
but a few shelves are given over to collectable bears. They will
usually include a number by manufacturers like Steiff, Hermann
and Dean's, perhaps with a few limited editions. And there are

also some hand-made artist bears, often including a few by local artists.

In fact, the shop's owner Tereza Jarvis has started making bears herself, and generally has a few of her own creations on sale as well. They can be personalized, too, to make special wedding, christening or anniversary presents.

A number of other bear-related items are also usually on sale – teddy mobiles, perhaps, and clocks or book-ends. Wicker prams, chairs and settees are similarly popular with teddy collectors, and many cannot resist the wooden toys themselves. The chunky trains, cars and pull-along toys go beautifully with traditional teddies.

Tereza has also opened a doll's house shop above Suzanne, the florist in the Market Place. The miniatures include various teddies – in pewter and porcelain, for instance.

In addition, on my last visit, the florist itself had some attractive stone bears. For bear lovers they would make an ideal alternative to garden gnomes, although I gather many people cannot bring themselves to leave the bears out in the cold!

Field's department store is in Market Place, too, and boasts a Vintage Toy and Train Museum on its first floor. As with so many toy museums, however, bears are conspicuous by their absence. There are plenty of cars by Corgi, Matchbox and Dinky Toys, as well as clockwork vehicles, trains, Meccano construction sets, jigsaw puzzles and lead soldiers – but no bears.

Better for bear lovers is **Reflections** in the High Street. The shop sells a variety of gifts and die-cast models and its range of bears is limited. But they usually have some by Merrythought, Little Folk, Big Softies, Nisbet and Ty, among others.

Of course, Sidmouth's many other gift shops also often have cuddly teddies and teddy gift items on display. So although the town may not be a suitable hunting-ground for the really serious collector, the bear-loving visitor should feel very much at home.

Collectors of artist bears, on the other hand, will feel even more at home a few miles away at **Higher Knapp Farm**, just outside Sidbury. The farm offers bed and breakfast accommodation and, as it is also the home of bear artist Lynda Graves, it is an ideal choice for any collectors visiting the area.

Lynda has a collection of her own, dominated by Rory. A seven-foot grizzly bear made by the French company Aux Nations, he used to live at the Cotswold Teddy Bear Museum's shop in Broadway. Now he presides over a gathering of bears old and new, which includes an interesting selection of bears by Lynda's fellow artists from both Britain and America.

Lynda is only too happy to show them to any of her guests who are interested.

When she is not cooking mammoth breakfasts for her overnight guests, she can usually be found in her workroom, busily stitching away at her latest creation. She began making bears a number of years ago now, when she needed work that could be combined with looking after her youngest child. It wasn't long before collectors began to appreciate the appeal of her designs and the standard of craftsmanship, so now she is kept busy working anything up to eighteen hours a day to try to satisfy the demand.

Several local shops stock her bears – although they tend to disappear as soon as they arrive. But Lynda is also happy for collectors to visit her at home and make their choice from any bears available – provided that they ring first to make an appointment.

As Lynda loves to talk bears while she works, it is an excellent opportunity for anyone with a genuine interest in bear making to see just how it is done.

Bear making is made up of many stages – the cutting out; machining of the body, limbs and head; inserting the eyes; jointing; stuffing; embroidering the nose and so on. It is painstaking work, and only one or two bears will be made in a day. If clothes are made, too, completion will take even longer.

Lynda often buys rather than makes the clothes she uses to dress her bears, however, and is always on the look-out for interesting accessories for them. So she spends many a Sunday morning exploring the local car boot sales. She knows every one of them, as well as all the good local shops, and is only too pleased to point her guests in the right direction.

In fact, the farm is within easy reach of Budleigh Salterton (page 158), Taunton (page 174) and Honiton (page 162) as well as Sidmouth, so it is in an excellent situation for anyone whose ideal holiday combines beautiful countryside with a major bear hunt.

Lynda also runs the local South West Bear Group, who meet once a month, to talk about their latest finds or newest creations.

ADDRESSES

Lynda Graves, Higher Knapp Farm, Sidbury; tel. 0395 597720
Puddleducks, Old Fore Street; tel. 0395 515999
Reflections, 113 High Street; tel. 0395 516001
Tourist Information Centre, Ham Lane; tel. 0395 516441

South Molton

It is not just teddy bears that have a well-established love of honey. Wild bears are known to have a fondness for it, too. But how many bear lovers know anything about the way in which honey is made?

The **Quince Honey Farm** in North Devon (just north of South Molton) explains it all with a mixture of fascinating displays and informative videos.

There is film of the bees at work. The extracting of the honey is shown, and the bottling process. The relevant equipment is also on view, and at certain times it can also be seen in action. However, as the annual crop (from 1,500 hives) can be bottled in just fifteen days, the video is an essential substitute for much of the year.

Other exhibits include protective clothing and samples of beeswax products, and there is an interesting video showing the making of both dipped and moulded beeswax candles. Most intriguing of all, however, are the hives themselves.

Some open up to show the activities of the bees, with magnifying glasses strategically placed to give an extra close-up view. Other displays show the kinds of habitat chosen by wild bees, like a typical roof space, a hollow log, and even a pillar box. All are kept behind glass, enabling the bees to be watched at unusually close quarters, yet still in absolute safety.

A well-stocked gift shop sells the farm's own honey in a variety of different containers – some of them bear-shaped. There is honeycomb, too, and honey fudge, as well as beeswax candles, beeswax polish, soap and creams. There are empty honey pots, too, and a host of souvenirs, including badges, pencils, mugs and thimbles. Aprons, oven gloves, peg bags, tea cosies and other household items have been produced in a special Quince Honey Bee design. But for those with a more serious interest in the bees themselves, there are also a number of informative books.

In the market town of South Molton itself, the interesting buildings include a fifteenth-century church and eighteenth-century town hall. Markets are still held every Thursday, and on summer Saturdays, and there are various antique shops to browse around.

ADDRESSES

Quince Honey Farm, North Road; tel. 0769 572401
Tourist Information Centre, 1 East Street; tel. 0769 574122
 (summer only)

Tourist Information Centre, North Devon Library, Tuly Street, Barnstaple; tel. 0271 388583 (all year)

Swanage

Most people visit the Dorset town of Swanage for its traditional seaside attractions and the lovely countryside of the surrounding 'Isle of Purbeck'. Designated an area of outstanding natural beauty, its coastline offers some spectacular views, making the area a perennial favourite with walkers.

The atmosphere in the town itself is relaxed, too, with an interesting aspect to its architectural heritage. In the nineteenth century, when much rebuilding was taking place in London, several interesting structures were salvaged and brought to Swanage, earning it the title 'Little London by the Sea'. A particularly fine example is the façade of the Town Hall, once the façade of London's Mercer Hall. Its designer was a pupil of Sir Christopher Wren.

Bear lovers, however, will find themselves heading for nearby Institute Road, at the eastern end of the High Street and to the south of Shore Road. For in the Swanage Leather and Knitwear Shop, just fifty yards from the beach, they will find a **Teddies Corner** crammed with bears.

The shop's owner Jennifer Bulbeck has only a small area in which to squeeze her bears. But she has managed to fit in everything from a fairly comprehensive range of inexpensive gift bears (costing from about £1 upwards) to some Steiff limited editions.

Among the other manufactured bears are the German Hermann and Grisly and England's Merrythought, Dean's and Little Folk. They stock the Boyds Collection, too. But Jennifer also tries to obtain a good number of artist bears, patiently adding her name to waiting lists if necessary in order to get what she wants.

As a result, the range is quite wide, with both well-known names and the less familiar. Among those who have supplied bears to date are Appletree Bears, Barbara-Ann Bears, Bear With Me, Bo-Bear Designs, Bolly Dolls and Bruin Bears, Fluff and Stuff, Imagine, Mister Bear, Redditoy, Romsey Bears and Teddystyle. They have had some American bears, too. But the range of artist bears is changing constantly, and the numbers and makes will vary. With popular artists invariably snowed under with requests for their work, shops often find themselves faced with a long wait for new arrivals.

Teddies Corner also has a variety of bear-related items, including ceramic teddies, as well as magnets, thimbles, greetings cards and postcards.

Places of interest within easy reach of the town include the famous Corfe Castle (five miles away) and the beautiful Blue Pool (eight miles). Or you can watch wooden toys and animals being made from storm-felled trees at Purbeck Farm Crafts at Knitson Farm (Corfe Castle). You may find one that is just the thing to include in a display of bears.

ADDRESSES

Teddies Corner, 11 Institute Road; tel. 0929 422264

Tourist Information Centre, The White House, Shore Road; tel. 0929 422885

Taunton

The county town of Somerset does have some interesting old buildings, among them the gabled and timbered Tudor House, the eighteenth-century Market House and the fourteenth-century Castle Bow, once an entrance to Taunton Castle. But many visitors are attracted not by its history but by its comprehensive shopping centre.

Bear lovers will head straight for the **Honey Pot**, situated right at the top end of the High Street. Owner Judith Stacey is determined to offer collectors something just a bit different. So within just a month of the shop's opening, her selection included artist bears from America, Canada, Germany, France, Ireland and Britain, not to mention some Almost South Pole Bears which had travelled all the way from New Zealand.

They were soon followed by bears from Australia and Holland, and as new artists emerge in an ever greater number of countries, Judith is constantly on the look-out for interesting examples of their craft. A real enthusiast herself, she has a keen eye for a good bear.

She also sells bears by many British artists, of course – including some by fellow members of the local South West Bear Group. The thriving club is run by local artists Deborah Canham and Lynda Graves (see Sidmouth, page

167), and holds monthly meetings at which members can discuss their latest purchases or creations, and generally 'talk bears' to their hearts' content. At least two members have been sufficiently inspired to start shops of their own. Judith is one of them.

She also sells some unusual bear-related items, again carefully chosen to offer something out of the ordinary. In fact, even the less expensive cuddly teddies on sale tend to be just that little bit different from those seen everywhere else.

Another Taunton shop also offers some collectable bears. **Minor Detail** in Riverside Place, a small pedestrian precinct off St James Street, is primarily a children's clothing shop. But one corner is devoted to bears. A number of collector bears, by German manufacturers Steiff and Hermann and by Britain's Merrythought and Dean's, are stocked as well as some cuddly toys, and there are a few artist bears as well. So it is worth a visit if you are in the town.

Of course, in such a large shopping centre, there are also a number of shops selling cuddly toys and bear-related gifts, but on Mondays there is an extra attraction. The **Taunton Antiques Market** in Silver Street is said to be the West Country's largest one-day antique market, with some hundred and thirty dealers offering a wide range of antiques and collectables. This may include an interesting bear or two, although as old bears become ever more hard to find, the chances of this will decrease.

The stalls also offer a wide range of other items, from furniture to jewellery. So this is just the right kind of place to rummage around for the interesting 'props' and accessories which can really bring a teddy bear collection to life.

You could find some old doll's clothes or children's clothes, or a pretty antique lace collar, or maybe a simple necklace that is just right for a bear. Wooden boxes, old china and worn toys are just a few of the other things to look out for. It is a wonderful market to browse around. Even if you cannot find anything you wish to buy, you should find plenty of inspiration.

ADDRESSES

The Honey Pot, 32 High Street; tel. 0823 352205
Minor Detail, 11 Riverside Place; tel. 0823 254484
Tourist Information Centre, The Library, Corporation Street;
  tel. 0823 274785

Tintagel

Cornwall seems to favour pixies rather than teddies and is therefore one of the less fertile hunting-grounds for the serious collector. The **Teddies Kitchen** in Tintagel did sell collectable bears. But new owners took over in 1993, and decided not to stock them. Nevertheless, they say they will be continuing the teddy theme in their restaurant, where framed teddy bear postcards and advertisements adorn the walls, and a teddy gift shop will continue to sell less expensive cuddly teddies and some other bear-related items.

So this is surely the place to go for your Cornish cream tea, after working up an appetite on the steep climb to and from Tintagel Castle – said to have been the birthplace of King Arthur in 452.

Teddies Kitchen also serves cooked breakfasts, lunches, snacks and evening meals. But if it is a traditional Cornish pasty you are after, the Pengenna Hotel and Tea Garden is a good place to try one. If your timing is right, you can watch the pasties being made, and marvel at the volume of filling crammed into them, before sampling the results in the restaurant or out on the lawn.

Like most popular tourist resorts, Tintagel is filled with many other eating-places as well as countless gift shops. Some of the shops do have bears and bear-related gifts, but again the teddies tend to be more cuddly than collectable, and many of the gifts are of the kind found in shops all over the country.

The **Pendragon Gallery**, for instance, has a special Pooh's Corner, selling a variety of Pooh merchandise, including the soft toys.

On the other hand, a shop selling mainly older and second-hand items might just yield a small accessory for one of your bears. (There were lots of new bear-sized Cornish scrumpy jars on my last visit.)

The Tintagel Toy Museum proved disappointing for a teddy lover, being filled largely with cars by Corgi, Dinky Toys, Matchbox, Tri-ang and others. There were a few dolls, too, but when I visited, teddy bears were nowhere to be seen.

There are other non-bearish attractions. The historic Castle offers splendid views of the Atlantic. King Arthur's Great Halls are constructed from more than fifty different types of Cornish stone, and there is a fourteenth-century manor house that became a Victorian Post Office.

You will also find plenty of Cornish pixies. But bears have yet to mount a counter-attack. There is, however, lots of Cornish honey to take home for them, including a delicious blend of honey with clotted cream.

ADDRESSES

Teddies Kitchen, Fore Street; tel. 0840 770761

Tourist Information Centre, The Clease, Camelford; tel. 0840 212954 (summer only)

Tourist Information Centre, The Crescent Car Park, Bude; tel. 0288 354240 (all year)

Totnes

South Devon's Totnes is a perfect place for browsing. The old streets are crammed with interesting buildings and small shops, many of which sell hand-crafted goods.

Of greatest interest to bear lovers is, of course, **The Bear Shop**, centrally situated in the part of the High Street known as The Narrows. Once the town's West Gate could be found there. Now it is full of little shops and eating-places.

The Bear Shop is crammed with bears of various makes, including the Steiff limited editions. The most popular ones sell out as soon as they reach the shelves. Bears by Hermann, Merry-thought and Dean's are some of the other manufactured bears they sell, and they try to stock bears by a variety of different artists as well. Some of the artists are widely known, others may be relatively new local artists whose work is only available in the South-west and is therefore ideal for those seeking a souvenir of a visit to the area. (And, of course, some of these unknown artists can go on very quickly to become major names in the teddy bear world.)

Owners Lin Morgan and James Sturges try to give the shop a specific theme, and the window displays always arouse a good deal of interest among passing shoppers. During Wimbledon fortnight you could find quite a few of the bears dressed for tennis, for instance. At other times they might adopt a nautical look. The shop actually stocks a range of exclusive sweaters, with different designs for different occasions. Specially personalized ones can also be ordered at just a small extra charge.

The sweaters have been so successful that the shop now also has a range of other bear-sized clothes.

They offer a teddy portrait service as well, for those who fancy owning a painting of their favourite bear(s).

They also try to have a few old bears on sale, or you could

just be lucky enough to find one at **Past & Present** – an antique shop just up the road at number 94. The shop is owned by Lin's partner James, but Lin confesses that many of the bears that come into the shop simply go straight home with them. She does, however, find many good props for her bear displays in the antique shop, so if you like to make interesting displays with your bears, it is a good place to look for accessories.

The town is full of other shops selling gifts or hand-crafted items, books or antiques, many of which may have something of interest to bear lovers. Many are in the steep main street (Fore Street/High Street) and in the new undercover shopping area on The Plains, and it is easy to lose a whole day exploring them and some of the adjacent streets.

But there are many beautiful old buildings to see, too. In the main shopping street are merchants' houses from the sixteenth and early seventeenth centuries, as well as the red sandstone of St Mary's Church and the famous arch of the East Gate. Nearby is the ancient Guildhall, built on the site of a Norman Priory, and the Norman Castle offers fine views over the town and towards Dartmoor.

The various museums include a well-known collection of vintage cars at the Totnes Motor Museum, and the town also offers boat trips on the River Dart. A steam railway runs along the Dart Valley from Buckfastleigh, stopping at Littlehempston station. (A footbridge from there to the Totnes side of the river is now planned.)

So all in all, Totnes is a place which should have something to please everyone.

ADDRESSES

The Bear Shop, 75 High Street, The Narrows; tel. 0803 866868
Past & Present, 94 High Street; tel. 0803 866086
Tourist Information Centre, The Plains; tel. 0803 863168

Wimborne Minster

People travel from a wide area to shop in this small Dorset market town. In addition, its famous twin-towered Minster, dating back a thousand years, attracts large numbers of tourists. Many of them find their way to Janet and John Hopkins' traditional toy shop, known as **Serendipity Toys**.

Indeed, now that they are a Steiff Club Store they have found that their members come from all over the country, popping in to see them each year when they return to the town on holiday.

Their range of Steiff bears naturally includes various limited editions – and you should find some from previous years as well as the current range. They stock many of the other Steiff animals as well, while there are more bears from Gund and Dean's.

Another attraction for bear lovers is the lovely teddy bear cards painted by local artist Christine Groves. In fact, she often borrows Steiff bears from the shop to act as her models.

Serendipity also sells a wide range of other toys. So if any of your bears like to play, you might find something here to put on display with them.

ADDRESSES

Serendipity Toys, 5 Crown Court, The Square; tel. 0202 841693
Tourist Information Centre, 29 High Street; tel. 0202 886116

Yeovil

Yeovil is a modern town whose main attraction is its shops, which attract visitors from a wide area. One shop in Middle Street specializes in sewing-machines and haberdashery. But part of it, known as Teddy's Corner, has been given over to teddy bears and the owners have managed to cram an extraordinarily good selection into the limited space available.

They aim to have over three hundred different bears in stock at any one time, and that doesn't include the soft toys that are available for the non-collector. In order to offer as wide a choice as possible, they will only display one example of any design. As a result, their selection is every bit as good as many a shop selling nothing but bears.

They stock limited editions by all the major manufacturers like Steiff, Hermann, Merrythought and Dean's. But there are also bears by some thirty different British artists, including both well-established names and up-and-coming makers. Mother Hubbard, Bear With Me, Malvern Bears, Barton Bears, Redditoy and Bearwood Bears are just some of those whose creations have been stocked to date.

Owners Fran and John Farquharson always try to include some fairly local makers among their artists, so these make ideal souvenirs. But they also sell traditional teddies wearing Yeovil Bear jumpers.

Naturally, as a shop which specializes in sewing, they also have some teddy bear kits for those who want to have a go at making a bear themselves.

For those making a day trip, other nearby attractions include the Fleet Air Museum at Yeovilton, six miles from Yeovil itself. More than fifty historic aircraft are to be found among the exhibits, which cover every aspect of the aviation history of the Royal Navy.

ADDRESSES

Teddy's Corner, J. J. & F. Farquharson, Middle Street; tel. 0935 75803

Tourist Information Centre, Petter's House, Petter's Way; tel. 0935 71279

CENTRAL
AND EAST

Abbey Dore

When Charis Ward arrived at **Abbey Dore** (near Hereford) along with fifteen horses, five dogs and a number of cows, she certainly had no thoughts of opening her overgrown garden to the public. That came about almost by accident some years later, by which time long hours had been spent taming the wilderness. Today a constant stream of visitors makes its way there during the opening season. Many are garden lovers. But some are not interested in gardens at all. For them, the attraction is an old cowshed, for it is there that Charis Ward's elder daughter, Sarah Sage, has created her **Bears' Loft**.

At first sight it appears that the bears in the loft are on permanent display. Some are busily engaged in washing, ironing, sewing and similar homely pursuits, with the help of a splendid collection of old furniture, kitchen equipment, games and other props. More bears are occupied by seasonal activities, from making crackers and decorating the tree at Christmas to fashioning flower hats in the summer or collecting autumn conkers. It is almost like a 'living' museum.

But look closer and you will find that every bear on display has a price tag. For this is not really a museum at all, but a highly original shop.

Although most of the props are part of a permanent collection, and therefore not for sale, the bears themselves can be purchased, and they should include something to appeal to every kind of collector.

In all, there are about forty different makes to choose from, with both manufactured bears and the work of a variety of British artists. There are bears by Steiff, Merrythought and Dean's, for instance, including many limited editions. Germany's Clemens bears are also to be found, as well as Britain's Canterbury and Little Folk. The latter are particularly active in the displays, thanks to their willingness to adopt very human-like poses.

Sometimes, bears of a single make will be gathered together to create a special display. When I visited, it was Merrythought's turn, with a large number cosily gathered round a kitchen table. Here, the bears often get together to discuss things of current interest in the bear world (like the plight of the real bears). But one small group was also busy sewing a dress, while another large bear was busy typing.

The boxed limited editions, however, cannot be used in such a way, and are simply housed on shelves along with some of the artist bears. There is a good selection to choose from. Of course, the actual bears will change frequently, as artists are constantly introducing new designs, usually in very small editions. But some of the names to be found there so far have been Little Charmers, Atlantic Bears, Mister Bear, Naomi Laight, Bocs Teganau, the Old Fashioned Teddy Bear Co., Imagine, Bedford, Bearwood and Willow Bears.

Then, of course, there are plenty of cuddly bears – many of them downstairs in the old cowshed. Perfectly at home among all the old mangles, irons, butter churns and a host of other kitchen, garden and dairy implements are bears by companies like Russ Berrie and Golden Bear, and others wearing special Bears Loft jumpers.

Numerous bear-related items are on display, too. Colour Box

miniatures and other teddy bear ornaments, tins, mugs, some pictures, stationery and so on are all for sale.

There are more bears in a conventional gift shop, along with a whole range of more general gift items, many of them with a flower or garden theme.

The artist bears on sale there generally include some lovely shop exclusives, and you may find the work of a few artists not represented in the loft itself. When I visited, there were exclusives from Bocs Teganau and Lynda Graves, for instance, and I spotted both Barton Bears and Mary Holden's Only Natural.

I also discovered more Colour Box miniatures there, as well as greetings cards, stationery, Paddington Bears and other Paddington merchandise, a good selection of Old Bear products, more cuddly bears (by Ty, for instance), inexpensive little dressed bears from Holland, and a good deal more. With the shop in two sections, one of which is on two floors, there is plenty of space, and a good deal of choice.

One interesting bear is a permanent resident, however, by the name of Alistair Marmaduke Way. A cuddly teddy, made in the Far East, he could easily be overlooked, as he is tucked away behind a counter. But if you are visiting, do ask Sarah about him. For this bear had an extremely interesting life before coming to stay at Abbey Dore Court, and it is all recorded in a splendid album that he carries with him.

It tells how he travelled down to the Falklands and to Russia, flew with the Red Arrows and on a Chinook helicopter. He took part in a road race round the Isle of Wight and in a fly-past to commemorate the Battle of Britain. He was at a motor-racing grand prix in Australia, and even found himself on an aircraft of the Queen's Flight with the Princess Royal.

He had his own NATO travel order. Certificates confirm that he completed a Flight Attendant's Course, a Dental Assistant's Course and a Parachute Course, among others, and there is a delightful passing out letter from his commanding officer.

All in all, he is a splendid example of how a very ordinary bear can be made extremely interesting. He also features on one of three exclusive postcards, and there are special Alistair badges, with the proceeds given to charity.

Over in the Stables, a restaurant offers a variety of home-made food, including light lunches and cream teas. The cooking is done by Sarah herself, before the gardens open, and you'll find both hot and cold dishes (many of them vegetarian), with a selection of salads – not to mention a wonderful choice of home-baked cakes. Ploughman's lunches are also popular, with local Abergavenny cheeses.

Various edibles can be purchased here to take home, as can still more bear-related items, as well as other gifts with a garden theme.

Elsewhere, a small nursery has a variety of plants for sale, with clematis, shrubs and herbaceous perennials among the specialities. There is a range of pots, too, and a splendid selection of bearish garden ornaments, some clearly copied from beautiful old bears.

The garden itself will be of interest both to connoisseurs and to those who simply love gardens. Even if gardens are, for you, simply somewhere to sit when the sun shines, you'll love it here. It is a haven of tranquillity, with the only sounds the rushing of the River Dore and the mooing of the nearby herd of Jersey cows. Those interested in plants, however, will find many unusual shrubs and perennials to be admired, as well as the euphorbia collection of the National Council for the Conservation of Plants and Gardens.

It is a place where people often go to spend just an hour and end up staying all day, enjoying the garden, eating in the restaurant and, of course, falling in love with all the bears in a very different kind of shop.

Unfortunately, buses are few and far between, so you will need to be quite dedicated to reach the gardens by public transport. But by car, they are just two miles west of the A465, halfway between Hereford and Abergavenny.

The gardens' summer opening is from the third Saturday in March to the third Sunday in October, from 11.00 a.m. to 6.00 p.m. (closed on Wednesdays). But bear lovers will find even more attractions on the last Sunday in July, which has become an annual Teddy Bear Sunday. On that day, various extra stalls are set up, selling even more bears and bear-related items. There are competitions for visiting bears, and (weather permitting) they can go parachuting or ballooning. Each year, about five hundred bear lovers (and many of their bears) attend the event, which each year raises a substantial sum for the chosen charities.

Outside the main season, the shop and Bears' Loft are also open in the weeks before Christmas, from early November to Christmas Eve, with visitors welcomed by a hot drink and mince pies. Then, from Boxing Day to the New Year, the gardens are opened to the public, too, with all visitors being welcomed by warming mulled wine or punch.

Anyone in the area in January or February is also invited to telephone if they want to see the Bears' Loft – but during those months it is open strictly by appointment only.

If you can drag yourself away from Abbey Dore, there is lovely countryside to explore, and much to see in nearby Hereford, with its eleventh-century cathedral and various museums (one devoted to cider-making). The market town of Abergavenny, on the other hand, has the ruins of an eleventh-century castle, and the compact town centre contains many craft and antique shops. There is also a **Museum of Childhood and Home** with about thirty bears, most of them dating from the fifties or before, with both Steiffs and early English bears among them. Antiques and crafts are also on sale here. The antiques section generally includes some early teddies, while newer, generally locally made, bears can be found in the crafts section.

ADDRESSES

Abbey Dore Court Garden; tel. 0981 240419/240279

Museum of Childhood and Home, Market Street, Abergavenny; tel. 0873 850063

Tourist Information Centre, Town Hall Annexe, St Owens Street, Hereford; tel. 0432 268430

Tourist Information Centre, Swan Meadow, 2 Monmouth Road, Abergavenny; tel. 0873 857588

Birmingham

Like any big town, Birmingham has a number of shops where bears can be found. But the specialist will head straight for **Teddies of Birmingham** in Temple Street.

The shop has had quite a chequered history, with several changes of address over the past three years or so. Their active Teddy Bear Club has ensured that collectors always knew where to find them, however, and they intend to put down strong roots at this nicely central location, just a short walk from New Street station.

You should find bears by most of the leading manufacturers there, including the Steiff limited editions (if they haven't already been sold), Hermann, Merrythought, Dean's and so on. But they also have ranges aimed at those who prefer a cuddlier teddy, like the ever-popular Ty and Manhattan Toy Company bears. There are generally some Paddington Bears in stock as well.

There are artist bears, too, and this is something they are working to expand, paying special attention to local artists. In this way, they can offer something a bit different for collectors, which is why they are planning to increase their range of shop exclusives as well.

They also generally have a few older bears on sale, although these often disappear as soon as they arrive.

You should find plenty of teddy-related items, too. The range changes all the time, but they usually have ceramic and pewter miniatures, Winnie-the-Pooh merchandise, a large number of greetings cards and a selection of bear-making kits.

An extra dimension is added by the area set aside for collectors to enjoy a quiet coffee while making a difficult decision, or simply to sit and chat with other collectors. It is an ideal place for meetings (of their club members, for instance), and they plan to exploit this to the full.

Of course, Birmingham has much more to offer the visitor. It is England's second city and, in addition to all its shops, there are museums and galleries and historic buildings – including two cathedrals. But if you are a chocolate lover, no visit to Birmingham would be complete without a trip to **Cadbury World** in nearby Bournville. It is easily accessible by road, rail and even canal, but it is always advisable to book your tour in advance, especially at the busiest times like weekends and school holidays.

They reckon that most people spend an average of around two hours on their visit. But dedicated chocaholics can easily spend a good deal longer seeing all that there is to see – including teddies.

You can smell the chocolate long before you enter the factory itself, but you are soon handed a bar to satisfy any cravings, and there will be plenty more before your tour is complete.

The exhibition begins with a look at the cocoa tree and the history of chocolate, and there is a chance to taste the cold, spicy chocolate drink loved by the Aztecs. (Bear lovers will no doubt notice that it contains honey as well as cocoa and assorted other ingredients like vanilla and chilli). You can learn about the discovery of chocolate by the Europeans, and how it finally arrived in England at the time of Cromwell. And you can see one of the famous chocolate houses frequented by chocolate lovers like Samuel Pepys.

Of course, there is plenty of Cadbury history, too, from tea dealer John Cadbury who also sold chocolate in his Birmingham shop, to the building of the factory and its associated village in Bournville, and the creation of the first Dairy Milk bars nearly ninety years ago.

The process of making chocolate, from cocoa beans to finished product, is described, and then it is time to move on to the factory part of the tour, with another chocolate bar for sustenance.

Sadly, for reasons of hygiene, it is not possible to see the chocolate actually being made and put into the moulds. But there is a video to fill the gap, and then a chance to see the packaging plant at work. Best of all, however, is the Demonstration Area, where chocolates are made by hand, with the minimum of mechanical help.

There, you can see various centres being produced and dipped in chocolate, and there is a chance to taste some of the results. You can also see moulded chocolate novelties being made, and it is these that will no doubt attract the attention of any bear lovers. For they include chocolate teddy bears, which are also on sale in the Cadbury World shop.

Before you reach it, however, there is still more to see, not to mention the gift of another chocolate bar.

Examples of early packaging, catalogues and promotional gifts are on display. There's a chance to see how a number of favourite bars are made. Another film gives an insight into the making of one of the famous television commercials. Advertisements from four different decades can be viewed, and there are even some made for various overseas markets, like the Middle or Far East.

Finally, you reach the Cadbury World shop, where those moulded chocolate teddies are not the only items of interest to bear lovers. I found no fewer than six different kinds of souvenir teddy, not to mention the teddy puppets. None were what would normally be called 'collectables', but neither were the prices collectors' prices.

Needless to say, there is also a huge range of Cadbury chocolates and biscuits, including hand-made chocolates exclusive to Cadbury World. A variety of small gift items is on sale, some of which could be used in a teddy bear display. And for those who still haven't had enough chocolate, a restaurant offers not only meals and snacks but a large number of chocolatey desserts, all made in their own kitchen.

A nearby building houses the Cadbury Collection, with its displays of Cadbury memorabilia. A Factory Trail gives visitors an impression of the sheer scale of the complex, and of course it is possible to see the garden village of Bournville itself. A successful experiment in town planning, it provided accommodation for both factory employees and others, and is still thriving today.

ADDRESSES

Cadbury World, Linden Road, Bournville; tel. 021 433 4334; reservations 021 459 9116

Teddies of Birmingham, 43 Temple Street; tel. 021 643 2820

Birmingham Convention & Visitor Bureau, 2 City Arcade; tel. 021 643 2514

Broadway

I have to confess that the Cotswold village of Broadway is one of my personal favourites. The village is concentrated around a single busy street, but virtually all the buildings are of beautiful Cotswold stone. Many now house gift and antique shops, much frequented by the visitors who flock to the area, especially during the summer months. But one has become something of a

Mecca for teddy bear lovers, for it is the home of a truly superb museum.

The **Cotswold Teddy Bear Museum** was the brainchild of Wendy and Colin Lewis, who moved to the area from the Wirral a number of years ago. Wendy had been collecting bears for some time and, like many collectors, found that they were taking over every bit of her home. Each time a new bear was brought home, the others had to be crammed even more tightly together to make room.

Eventually, she and her husband Colin began to think about the possibility of a museum. Many other collectors have done the same, but the difference in the Lewises' case was that they made it all come true.

Wendy had also started buying bears to sell, and was building up a successful business, working from her home in the Wirral. She sold many bears at antique and teddy bear fairs, but it was only natural that eventually she would start thinking in terms of opening her own shop. When she and Colin started looking for suitable premises, however, they also had the museum very much in mind.

The building they chose is situated in Broadway's main street, with two bow windows making it one of the prettiest shops anywhere. Soon, shelves were filled with a wide range of bears for sale, and work had begun on converting a back room into the long-planned museum.

They had for some time been acquiring bears specifically for a museum, gathering together interesting examples from leading makers and also seeking out bears with interesting histories. Colin became a familiar face at fairs, always one step ahead of the crowd. Before most people had had time to get their bearings, Colin had completed his circuit of the stands and was already on his way back to his car, carrying all his spoils. Many a collector's heart would sink when they saw him. If Colin was there, they knew that many of the best bears would already be gone.

Now, however, all collectors can benefit from his zeal. There may be far fewer interesting old bears on sale these days, but in the Broadway museum large numbers can still be admired, if not bought.

Wendy and Colin, however, decided that running the museum was not what they wanted to do, and in the summer of 1993 it came under new ownership. It is now in the hands of Monica and Des Carpenter, who are continuing to add to the collection whenever the opportunity arises.

Some of the bears in Wendy Lewis's private collection naturally went with her when the museum was sold, but it is believed that there are still some eight hundred in residence. There are also other animals and many dolls, not to mention all sorts of interesting old toys and accessories, making up a total of something like 1,700 exhibits in all.

It is a delightfully cluttered museum, with some of the bears displayed in bear-sized room settings and others packed on to shelves. Best of all, however, is the fact that a very large number of the bears have labels giving details of their makes and approximate dates. Those with no interest in such matters can simply enjoy the bears. But those seek-

ing to identify bears of their own, or simply to learn as much as possible about the bears made by the various companies, will welcome all the information that is given.

A very large number of companies is represented. Many of the main manufacturers have a whole section devoted specially to them, with more of their bears scattered around the other displays.

A group of old Steiff bears, for instance, includes one of their so-called centre-seam bears, dating from 1906. These bears were actually the result of the company's efforts to obtain more bears from a given piece of mohair. Six complete heads could normally be fitted across the width of the mohair. But a seventh could be added if the bear was given an additional seam down the centre of his head. As there were thus far fewer of these 'centre-seam' bears than of those with no such seam, they are now much sought by collectors.

Another old Steiff in the group was made in 1904 and was actually the mascot of Gainsborough Rugby Club. He still wears his original rugby kit.

Others date from the 1920s, the 1940s and the 1950s, and there are also some old Steiff animals here. But elsewhere in the museum you will find a whole collection of open-mouthed Steiff 'Zotty' Bears, dating from the 1950s, and a Noah's Ark scene created with miniature Steiff animals made between the late 1920s and the 1960s.

There are more Steiff bears in the so-called 'Pride of Place' display, which includes a number of residents with interesting stories to tell. One white Steiff made in 1910 was owned by a German Jewish family and escaped to England with them in 1939. Later, he travelled widely with his owner, who worked as a freelance foreign correspondent all over the world. More recently, he could be seen in the television series *Trainer*.

Another 1910 Steiff belonged to a former servant of the German emperor William II, while an even earlier one was found under the floorboards of a camp for German prisoners of war when it was dismantled in 1949.

A complete case is given over to Steiffs of far more recent vintage. A large number of the limited-edition collectors' bears produced since the early eighties can be seen here. Among them are some produced exclusively for the British, American or German markets, as well as some created for individual shops, including London's Harrods (see page 31) and 'Teddy Bears' of Witney (page 144).

There are many other German bears in the museum – from leading companies like Bing, Schuco and Hermann. But there is also a particularly good collection of British bears by a host of different makers.

Today, it is the bears once made by the London-based J. K. Farnell which often fetch the highest prices, and there are a large number of these to be found here. One case contains a whole collection. Many date from the 1930s and 1950s, but one is from the 1920s and clearly shows the influence of Steiff bears on some of the early creations by this British company. Also here are a musical bear from the 1930s and a 1950s teddy nightdress case, as well as various other Farnell animals.

Many more Farnell bears are included in other displays around the museum. One is an early, and very rare, pin-jointed bear. It is claimed that another was once owned by A. A. Milne, writer of *Winnie-the-Pooh*.

Merrythought, based in Ironbridge (page 213), is also well represented, with a whole hospital scene created entirely from Merrythought bears, old and new. Many date from the 1930s, and include a rare example made from brown alpaca as well as one of the distinctive 'Dutch Teddies', with wide Dutch-style trousers made of corduroy. There are some 1930s pandas, too, and a whole variety of the popular 'Cheeky' Bears with their wide grins and bells in their ears. Among them is a special Bedtime Cheeky, dressed in pyjamas and bright red dressing-gown and produced exclusively for the museum shop. He was a copy of a bear which was originally made by Merrythought in the 1970s.

A few other modern limited editions will also be found here, as well as a Merrythought version of Yogi Bear, made in the 1960s. Elsewhere, a whole case is crammed with Merrythought animals and cartoon characters, including Donald Duck, Thumper the rabbit from *Bambi*, and Lady from *Lady and the Tramp*.

A large number of Chad Valley bears, made in Wellington (page 259), are also to be found, with many included in a Li'Bear'y setting. Among them are beautiful bears from the late 1920s and the 1930s, as well as some fully jointed Sooty Bears made in the 1950s. Chad Valley made Sooty glove puppets for many years, but they also produced some complete Sooty Bears, like those here – one of which was made specially for a London department store.

Other Chad Valley bears include a 1950s nightdress case and a polar bear cub produced to mark the birth of the famous Brumas. There is also a large 1953 Coronation Bear, with some parts made in red fur, some in white and some in blue, while a bear from the 1930s is in an unusual yellow colour.

Elsewhere, a whole case is given over to a large Chad Valley version of Snow White and the Seven Dwarfs, while another contains a rare complete set of Goldilocks and the Three Bears, dating from the 1930s.

One display case contains a large number of bears made by Dean's between 1920 and 1960. They include one of the distinctive, and highly collectable, bears inspired by the real animals at London Zoo. Designed by Sylvia Wilgoss, who joined the company in 1952 and became their chief designer four years later, they were either sitting, standing upright, or on all fours, and there were both black bears and polar bears. It is one of the latter, first made in 1955, which can be found at Broadway.

Also on display are a number of other toys made by Dean's, among them a pair of dancing dolls and some gollies.

There are a good number of Chiltern bears in the museum as well. A number are 1930s Hugmee Bears – now extremely popular with collectors. But earlier and later bears will be found, too, including an unusual 1930s skater and a roly-poly bear of similar age, along with many made in the 1950s.

Various other British makes are also on view – Peacock, for instance, and Wendy Boston. In addition, a number of exhibits carry the Pedigree name. Some were made in England, others after their soft toy production moved to Belfast.

There are bears from the Republic of Ireland, too, but also on display are bears from all over the world.

The French contingent includes one made by the well-known Martin company, and a group of 1930s bears still carrying their original price tags. A Dutch bear is made from typical cotton plush fabric. There are bears from Poland, Israel, China and Japan, and a number of bears come from the new owners' homeland of Australia. They include creations by Joy Toys, Berlex and Verna.

Several American makers are represented. In addition to traditional bears by such well-known companies as Ideal and Knickerbocker, there is also an early novelty bear, whose eyes light up electrically.

Other novelties, from various countries, include musical bears and a number of mechanical bears – drummers, a violin player, a knitter and a drinking bear, for instance. There are pandas by Dean's, Chiltern, Merrythought, Wendy Boston, Pedigree and others. (Look out for the one with red pads!) And there is a stunning collection of blue bears, again from many different companies. As I said at the beginning of this book, such a collection in an unbear-like colour really stands out amongst all the usual browns and beiges. This display illustrates that perfectly.

Another case is devoted entirely to a single bear, who goes by the name of Lieutenant Peter Paul Rubens. Made in 1908, he now has a whole trunk of belongings, including several sets of clothes and a couple of toys. He also brought with him his own pipe and tobacco pouch, a glass tankard, a chair, a suitcase and some photographs. One shows him as a very young bear, along with his original owner. Another, taken in 1916, shows him wearing the same military uniform as he is wearing in the museum.

Modern bears have not been overlooked, with one case containing examples of more recent manufactured bears by companies like Canterbury, Dean's, Hermann, Little Folk, Merrythought, Nisbet and Steiff. Another contains bears by a large number of British artists. Barbara-Ann Bears, Barton Bears, Brian Beacock, Bearwood Bears, Bocs Teganau, Charnwood Bears, Dormouse Designs, Jo Greeno, Maddie Janes, Susan J. Knock, Naomi Laight, Little Charmers, Malvern Bears, Anita Oliver, Pamela Ann Designs and Sirius Designer Bears are just some of the names to be seen there.

Elsewhere, a number of modern character bears, including Pudsey, Sooty and Super Ted, are on display.

A fascinating collection of old bearabilia includes bears of wood, metal and china, along with other bear-related items. But the museum is not all bears, in spite of its name. There are also a good many dolls of various ages, makes and countries of origin. A large number of other toys either have their own displays or are used as accessories for some of the bears.

So there is a good deal to see, and it is well worth allowing time for a really thorough look. Who knows? You may even find a bear remembered from your own childhood, or one that you have been trying to identify.

In addition to the museum, there is a shop selling a whole range of bears and some bear-related items. At the time of writing, the new owners had only been in residence for a few months, and will no doubt introduce certain changes as they begin to settle in. But they plan to continue stocking bears by all the major manufacturers as well as a good selection of British artist bears.

You should therefore find bears by Steiff, Hermann, Merrythought and Dean's, including plenty of limited editions. But the Steiff limited editions tend to sell out quite quickly, as this is a well-known shop which attracts a large number of serious collectors as well as many casual visitors.

They have the Steiff Classic Bears as well, but there are also less expensive ranges like Golden Gifts' Tails and Tales and the cuddly Ty bears. Special souvenir bears, made in the Channel Islands, are on sale too, wearing jumpers of various colours carrying the name of the museum.

The range of artist bears to be found changes constantly. They sell quickly in a shop which is so frequented by collectors, and those available will depend very much on which artists have fulfilled an order just prior to your visit. Some bears come from far afield, like the Devon-based Bear With Me, the Welsh Bocs Teganau, Dorset's Hardy Bears, and Mother Hubbard from Sussex. Others are more local, like Ledbury's Malvern Bears, Redditoy from Redditch, and Leamington Spa's Teddy Boys 'n' Girls, which have proved especially popular.

A number of editions are exclusive to the shop, and an inexpensive museum bear is made specially for them by Mme ZuZu.

Visitors carry the bears off to all corners of the world, as the Cotswolds are a 'must' for anyone touring Britain.

With so many tourists browsing round the shop, especially during the summer months, there should always be a good selection of pocket-money items on sale, too. I found plenty of inexpensive teddies, as well as stickers, brooches, pencils and so on, and also some special Cotswold Bear Museum rulers and pens. There was also a good number of Colour Box miniatures and tiny pewter teddies to choose from, not to mention a large number of greetings cards and various teddy bear postcards (some of the latter exclusive to the museum).

When it first opened, the shop was well known for its large selection of splendid older bears, too – many of them found by Colin during his forays to find bears for the museum. These days, interesting older bears are becoming ever more difficult to find. But Monica and Des aim to keep as many in stock as possible. The number will, however, depend very much on their future availability.

Some of the other shops in Broadway may have the occasional bear-related gift, or even a few teddies, although I saw no other collectables on my last visit. You may, however, find some accessories for your bears. And even if you don't, it is a lovely village to browse around. Most of the shops are spread out for some distance along the main High Street, but don't miss those in the new Cotswold Court, reached through an archway near the village green. It includes a number of small specialist shops, including one whose window is filled with sweet jars containing all sorts of childhood favourites.

There are plenty of charming tea shops and restaurants in the village, if you need time to sit and ponder a purchase. Or you can simply saunter along admiring all the lovely stone buildings which help give the area its unique character.

ADDRESSES

Cotswold Teddy Bear Museum, 76 High Street; tel. 0386 858323

Tourist Information Centre, Cotswold Court, The Green; tel. 0386 852937

Cambridge

A vast number of visitors flock to Cambridge each year, quite apart from the hordes of students who swell the population during term time. But although it is no longer the sleepy market town of old, it has firmly refused to go the way of so many other tourist resorts, with every other shop displaying take-home gifts for the tourist. The souvenir shops are there all right, and many of them have something of interest for those who love bears. But it would be easy to spend a whole day enjoying the city's attractions and still miss seeing most of its bears – unless you know where to look.

The specialist **Bears & Things**, for instance, is in the modern Grafton Centre, a short walk from the main city centre shopping area, close to the Newmarket Road (the A1303). Pedestrians will find that it is clearly signposted from the bus station (and there is a regular bus link between the rail and bus stations).

The shop attracts both tourists and collectors, so owner Lin Reid tries to ensure that she has something to suit every pocket. There are highly collectable bears from companies like Steiff, including some limited editions. But

201

there are also some inexpensive souvenir bears, made in the Far East and sporting a Bears & Things sash.

Bears by Hermann, Dean's and Merrythought are also sold, including the limited editions. There are some by Little Folk, too, as well as cuddlies by Ty and the popular Tails and Tales by Golden Gifts. Paddington is especially popular with visitors from America and Canada, and Winnie-the-Pooh and his friends are perennial favourites.

There are some artist bears, too, with those by Bearaphernalia's Sarah Cox generally in great demand. Not only is Sarah a local resident, she can also be found stitching away in the shop on certain days of the week.

One of her creations is an alpaca bear called Eden, made specially for Bears & Things. But she also does a number of dressed bears, with the graduates naturally proving particularly popular. She happily accepts commissions, too, if someone has another outfit in mind.

There are usually bears from several other artists as well, including the odd shop exclusive.

Another unique aspect of the shop is related to owner Lin's love of music from Peru. Anyone who has read the Paddington stories will know that this famous bear originally hailed from Peru. So there is some Peruvian jewellery on sale, as well as a number of intriguing musical instruments from that country – all displayed, of course, along with their Paddington Bears.

Lin also has a keen interest in antiques, and there are generally a few old soft toys on sale, although you are more likely to find animals like dogs and lions than you are to find a teddy bear. Bears do appear from time to time, but are rarely allowed to settle in before heading for new homes.

Old children's china decorated with teddy bears is another of Lin's special interests and, although it is not at all easy to track it down these days, she tries to keep a number of pieces on the shelves.

She also has her own collection of juvenilia, and sometimes brings pieces like prams or books or china into the shop to liven up the window display. These are not for sale, but may give you ideas that you can adapt to your own teddy bear collection.

More modern bear-related items are on sale, however. These generally include various ceramic miniatures – including tiny pocket-money pieces – as well as a good range of Winnie-the-Pooh merchandise, some teddy bear brooches, greetings cards, postcards and so on.

The shop is busiest during the summer and in the weeks before Christmas, so that is likely to be when you will find the greatest variety of bears on offer. But they try to ensure that they have something for everyone throughout the year, and especially that there is something to suit every pocket.

Cambridge also has a branch of the **English Teddy Bear Company**, on King's Parade, where they sell their own range of English-made teddies and various other items featuring teddy bears. Most of these are produced specially for the company.

The bears themselves are both jointed and unjointed, with some made of mohair and others of synthetic plushes. Some are dressed, while others remain 'in the fur'. There are also English Teddy Bear Company mugs, badges, tea towels, biscuits and preserves, as well as T-shirts which include some special Cambridge designs. One features a cycling bear, for instance (since cycling is such a popular form of transport for the students), while another is on a punt.

Punting on the River Cam is, of course, a much-loved Cambridge pastime. These flat-bottomed boats can be hired by visitors – complete with chauffeur in the summer. One place where punts can be hired is beside Magdalene Bridge, just a stone's throw from another easily overlooked source of bears.

Wigginton's, on Quayside, is a huge gift shop, packed with decorative objects of all kinds, beautifully displayed on Victorian-style pine furniture (which can also be bought). One of their specialities is traditional toys – and that, of course, includes teddy bears.

In fact, the collectable bears have their own special shop within a shop, and most of the leading manufacturers are well represented. The range of Steiff bears includes both limited editions and the very collectable Classics range, and they often have some of the bears made specially for the American market as well.

The Hermann bears also include a good number of limited editions, and there are more from English companies like Merry-thought and Dean's.

Other English bears include those by Canterbury, Big Softies, Bedford and Bo-Bear Designs, as well as H.M. Bears and Dormouse Designs. The North American Bear Co.'s Muffy is there, too, and manager Jane Holt is expecting a gradual increase in the number of artist bears stocked by the shop, as these become more and more sought after by collectors.

Pam Howells, for instance, of Pamela Ann Designs (see Crowland, page 210) is making an exclusive Wigginton's Bear, with an Edwardian-style lace collar in keeping with the nostalgic feel of the shop itself.

Although all these collectables are to be found in the special teddy bear section, there are even more bears among the vast array of other gifts crammed into the delightful shop. There are plenty of cuddlies, for instance, while character bears like Winnie-the-Pooh, Paddington and Rupert are well represented – not just by the bears themselves but by all sorts of related merchandise, including tins, stationery and an ever-changing selection of other items.

There is a special Wigginton's souvenir bear as well, made in the Channel Islands and wearing a special Wigginton's Cam-bridge Bear jumper.

More soft bears are dotted around the shop, with new ones appearing all the time, so it is impossible to give a comprehensive list. There are ceramic bears, too, and bears made of wood. But careful exploration will reveal a huge variety of other 'bearabilia', with the range changing on just about every visit.

Among the items I found were pictures, money boxes, bookends, a wide variety of stationery, soaps, perpetual calendars, chalk boards, pomanders, teddy bear story-books and greetings cards. Some ranges are widely available, while other pieces are more exclusive, guaranteeing that most browsers will find something to appeal.

They also sell doll's house furniture, including some larger scale pieces that could be just right for bears. Traditional wooden games and toys also often look good as part of a teddy bear display, and you'll find a colourful selection of those here. Or perhaps a pretty lacy cushion will provide just the effect you want. Again, you will find plenty of choice.

Of course, there are other gift shops in Cambridge with something of bearish interest. You will also find some bears in **Robert Sayle**, a John Lewis store in St Andrew's Street. They have both cuddly children's bears and some of the mohair Merrythought bears specially made for John Lewis, while their gift department includes some of the Merrythought limited editions.

Most visitors, however, will also want to spare some time to explore the city's many other attractions. The oldest college dates back to the thirteenth century, so visitors will find a splendid range of architectural styles within the town. Many college courtyards can be viewed at certain times, and the Gothic King's College Chapel is one of many that are open to the public. One of the best views of the chapel is from the grass of The Backs, which run alongside the river and which are a popular picnic spot in summer.

The city's academic history has given rise to many excellent museums, including those of zoology, geology, archaeology and anthropology. Then there is the world-famous Fitzwilliam Museum, whose treasures include antiquities from Egypt, Greece and Rome as well as a huge collection of English pottery and porcelain.

A Folk Museum looks back at local life in the more recent past, while the famous Round Church dates back to the twelfth century, and is one of only four round churches in England.

ADDRESSES

Bears & Things, 67 Eden Hall, Grafton Centre; tel. 0223 323657
The English Teddy Bear Company, King's Parade; tel. 0223 300908
Robert Sayle, St Andrew's Street; tel. 0223 61292
Wigginton's, 3 Quayside; tel. 0223 302165
Tourist Information Centre, Wheeler Street; tel. 0223 322640

Colchester

B ritain's oldest recorded town, Colchester was made the capital of Britain by the Roman Emperor Claudius, and its huge Norman castle was actually built on the site of a Roman temple.

The temple had been destroyed by Queen Boudicca, who sacked the city and killed its inhabitants in AD 60. Today the Castle Museum contains one of England's best collections of Roman treasures.

The town contains many other relics of its colourful past. Some buildings still bear the scars of Civil War bullets. Timbered medieval houses in the Dutch Quarter are where Protestant refugees from the Low Countries settled in the sixteenth century. The ruins of the Norman St Botolph's Priory can still be seen.

It is shops, however, which attract many visitors to Colchester. New shopping areas are combined with medieval lanes and alleyways to provide a splendid mix of major stores and small independent shops. It is the kind of town you can visit with a long and diverse list of hard-to-find items, and go home with every single one.

Even bear lovers have not been forgotten. For on Sir Isaac's Walk, right in the heart of the town centre, they will find Colchester's **Bear Shop**. Part of the town's original Roman wall lies beneath the old building, and it is reputed to have its very own ghost. But there are no reports of it venturing into the shop, where everything is much more modern, including the bears.

Margaret Chapman has looked after the shop since it opened in 1990 and was soon welcoming collectors from all over Essex, as well as from London and even further afield. In little more than a year, the shop's success encouraged owner Robert Stone to open a second in Norwich (page 228), and the two now carry broadly similar ranges, with just a few local variations.

The Colchester shop, for instance, has more bears by local artist Susan Jane Knock, who lives in nearby Witham. It also has a particularly good range of bears by Naomi Laight and Mister Bear, both of whom are Essex-based. Visitors to the town are always especially pleased to find bears with a local connection, and the Colchester shop is lucky in that it has some particularly good names to choose from.

Like the Norwich shop it has a good range of artist bears from further afield, too – although generally not from outside Britain, in order to keep prices more within reasonable limits. Bocs Teganau, Bo-Bear Designs, Imagine, Jay-Bee, Pamela Ann Designs, Just Bears and Bear Bits are just some of the names they have stocked so far.

They also have Bear Shop exclusives from artists like Teddystyle and Crafty Bears, and also unique, one-off bears whenever the opportunity arises.

The ideas come from both Margaret and owner Robert, and the two different viewpoints help to give a nicely balanced selection. In addition, if customers start asking for bears from a particular artist, Margaret and Robert will always make an effort to obtain some to satisfy the demand.

They visit as many fairs as they can, so that they can see the bears 'in the fur', rather than relying on catalogues. So although the range is constantly changing and expanding, the quality remains high.

In fact, some collectors will visit the shop twice a week, just to see what is new, and it is not at all unusual for someone to spend a couple of hours deciding which one to take home.

Luckily, there are bears to suit every pocket, ranging in price from just a few pounds to several hundred.

Most of the major manufacturers are represented. There are limited-edition Steiffs, as well as bears from their regular and Classic ranges. You should find Hermann bears, too, while the English makes include Merrythought and Dean's. The Bear Shop stocks limited editions by all the companies, but they also have some of the bears made with children rather than collectors in mind. In fact, their children's range even includes a special shop exclusive made by Merrythought in a rich-looking mohair, in three sizes.

In addition, you should find Paddington Bears, and Winnie-the-Pooh and his friends, as well as a good number of cuddly teddies, like those by the Manhattan Toy Company. They also sell Golden Gifts' popular Tails and Tales bears.

There is also a selection of bear-related items, which is changing all the time but will generally include some ceramic and pewter teddies, teddy bear brooches, stationery and greetings cards.

Local craftspeople have not been forgotten either. A range of painted celebration spoons has teddies incorporated into the designs, for instance. The spoons carry a personalized message, depending on the occasion, and the design can be adapted to suit both the event and the recipient. A sports lover could receive a spoon showing a bear playing their favourite game, while a ballet lover may prefer a bear in a tutu. This adaptability makes the spoons popular gifts.

Also locally made are some unusual wall plaques which feature real fabric teddies in the design.

The combination of numerous quality bears for collectors and a large number of teddies for children has proved very successful. It is a particularly busy shop, that people return to again and again.

Of course, other shops in the town may also yield certain bear-related items, but there are other places to see during a visit, too. The Hollytrees Museum includes Victorian doll's houses and other toys; railways buffs, on the other hand, will head for the East Anglian Railway Museum at Chappel & Wakes Colne station.

The East Anglian countryside immortalized by John Constable is also just to the north of the town, including the village of Dedham and the famous Flatford Mill.

ADDRESSES

The Bear Shop, 3 Sir Isaac's Walk; tel. 0206 577345
Tourist Information Centre, 1 Queen Street; tel. 0206 712920

Crowland

The little Lincolnshire town of Crowland, or Croyland, may not seem the most obvious place to find something of unusual interest for the teddy bear lover. Its main claim to fame is its Abbey.

Nearby, however, is a variety of shops, and it is one of these, **Pamela Ann Designs**, which is of special interest to bear lovers. For 'Pamela' is bear maker Pam Howells.

On sale in the shop (open Mondays, Wednesdays, Fridays and Saturdays, and at other times by appointment) are some of Pam's latest creations, as well as various gift items. But Pam also uses the building as her workroom. So this is one of the few places where you can actually see a bear maker at work, surrounded by piles of mohair and other fabrics in a great variety of colours and pile lengths (not to mention all the other tools of the bear maker's trade).

Pam is no newcomer to the bear-making business. She has been creating bears all her working life. In fact, her very first teddy was made when she was just eight or nine years old and confined to bed with rheumatic fever. She fashioned his joints from paper-clips.

She went to art school when she was fifteen, but two years later took a job as assistant to the chief designer at the Chiltern factory in Pontypool. Within eight months the chief designer had left and Pam took over her job.

Over the next ten years, she produced hundreds of new designs for the factory, although not all of them went into production, and they included other animals as well as the teddy bears. Dogs, cats and rabbits were the main lines, but there were numerous different versions of each.

The company had its origins in the late nineteenth century

when Josef Eisenmann set up his export agency Eisenmann & Co. in Germany. Their main export was toys. In 1913, however, Eisenmann set up a toy factory of his own in Chesham, Buckinghamshire, producing first dolls and later teddy bears and other toys. When Josef died six years later, the business was inherited by his son-in-law Leon Rees.

A year later, Leon went into partnership with a friend who worked for the well-known soft toy company J. K. Farnell. The new company, H. G. Stone & Company, soon established a reputation for itself as a maker of quality soft toys, including teddy bears. They opened a second factory in Tottenham, London, in 1921 and introduced the trade name Chiltern in 1923. The distinctive Chiltern Hugmee Bears first appeared that same year, and today are much loved by collectors.

After the Second World War, a magnificent new factory was opened in Wales, and it was here that Pam Howells began her career as a toy designer.

By the time she left, ten years later, the company had been taken over twice – the second time by another firm well known for its teddy bears, Chad Valley.

Pam and her husband moved to Peterborough, and for a while Pam did some freelance designing. But it is now twenty years since she set up on her own, and began to rent her little workshop in Crowland. In those days, it was toys rather than collectables which filled her days, and she still designs and makes a wide range of appealing animal toys as well as the ever-growing number of teddy bears for collectors.

She continues to design toys and kits for manufacturers, too. Yet despite such a busy schedule, she always finds time to chat to collectors, either in her shop or at the many teddy bear fairs she attends. (She can usually be seen busily stitching away even there.)

She has an amazing memory for all the bears she designed during her Chiltern years, and for many of the other Chiltern bears created long before her own time at the factory. She also has a unique perspective on the teddy bear world, having experienced it from the side of both the manufacturer and the teddy bear 'artist'.

It is just a short walk from Pam's shop to the Abbey. Its history dates back to the eighth century, when King Ethelbald set about building the first Croyland Abbey in memory of St Guthlac, the founder of a religious community in the area (then known as Crulande). A century and a half later the wooden structure was burned to the ground by the Vikings. Another fire, in 1091, destroyed a second abbey, and the building of its replacement was also hampered by a fire (1143), not to mention the earthquake twenty-five years earlier. Later, Cromwell's cannon would cause considerable destruction again.

The town's other landmark is its triangular Trinity Bridge, built in the fourteenth century at the meeting point of two streams. The water now runs through underground pipes, leaving the bridge in splendid isolation in the middle of the town.

ADDRESSES

Pamela Ann Designs, 12 West Street; tel. 0778 344152
Tourist Information Centre, Ayscoughfee Hall, Churchgate, Spalding; tel. 0775 725468

Ironbridge

A book published in 1912 refers to Ironbridge as 'an uninteresting and somewhat squalid town'. Today, visitors flock there from all over the world, to enjoy both the splendour of the Gorge itself and the rich history of an area that was at the very heart of the Industrial Revolution. The region has also became famous for its soft toys, and at one time it was believed to produce greater quantities than any other area in the world.

The Gorge itself is part of an area rich in such minerals as coal, iron ore and limestone, and its iron works were responsible for a whole string of innovations. Among them was the construction of the world's first cast-iron bridge, opened on New Year's Day 1781. It is still there to be admired today.

Also still to be seen are cottages built by craftsmen attracted to the area in the seventeenth and eighteenth centuries. There are terraces built by the Coalbrookdale Company to house their workers, like Carpenters Row built in 1783. And there are also grander homes, owned by the ironmasters.

With so many of the old buildings still remaining, Ironbridge affords a rare insight into the way life was lived in the town's heyday, an insight that is being strengthened by the work of the **Ironbridge Gorge Museum Trust**.

The Trust is also responsible for a number of museums and other places of interest in and around the town. Some, like the

Museum of Iron and the Coalport China Works Museum, tell the story of some of the products for which the area is famous, while Blists Hill Open Air Museum is a complete reconstruction of a turn-of-the-century town in which various craftsmen demonstrate their skills.

For teddy bear lovers, however, the most interesting part of the Trust's work will be their **teddy bear shop and museum** next to the **Merrythought** factory, just a few minutes' walk from the Iron Bridge itself.

On display are some of the teddy bears and other toys made by Merrythought since it was founded more than sixty years ago. Today, early examples of the company's teddy bears are highly prized by collectors, and each year Merrythought also produces a whole range of new bears specially designed with collectors in mind. Most of these are made in strictly limited editions.

The company, registered on 10 September 1930, was the brainchild of W. G. Holmes (grandfather of the current Managing Director) and his partner G. H. Laxton, who founded a Yorkshire spinning mill in 1919. It produced mohair yarn from imported mohair.

One of their major customers was the Huddersfield-based Dyson Hall & Co. Ltd. But during the twenties, Dyson Hall found a steady decrease in the demand for their mohair cloth. Eventually, they were taken over by Holmes and Laxton, who decided that, by opening a toy factory, they would provide themselves with a regular outlet for their fabric. The new company was called Merrythought Ltd.

Its first two directors were H. C. Janisch, formerly head of sales at the West London toy company J. K. Farnell, and C. J. Rendle, who had been in charge of toy production at the renowned Chad Valley Company in Wellington (page 262), not far from Ironbridge. So there was plenty of experience on which to draw, especially as Rendle brought with him a number of fellow Chad Valley employees. One of them was Florence Atwood, a deaf mute who would design most of the toys made by the company up to 1949.

The new company rapidly acquired a reputation for producing top quality toys and within months it moved from its original temporary accommodation to larger premises by the River Severn. It is still there, although the factory has seen further expansion over the years.

The past sixty years have, on the other hand, seen relatively few changes in the ways in which the bears are made. In the early days, the only machines were sewing machines and a machine to cut the felt pads. Today, most of the cutting and stuffing is carried out with mechanical help. But the basic bear-making process has remained very much the same.

To date, few collectors have been able to see this for themselves. With so much of the work being carried out by hand, the presence of onlookers inevitably causes quite a disruption, and tours have therefore been discouraged. But at the time of writing, Merrythought are considering the possibility of introducing a limited number of factory tours during the summer months. These would, of course, need to be booked in advance.

As the factory makes only limited use of outworkers, such a tour is unusually interesting. Typically, the first stage after cutting out is all the machine sewing. The body pieces (generally four) are joined together, as are the pieces that make up the head. The ears are pieced together, the arm and leg seams stitched, and the foot and paw pads are attached after the sewing of the distinctive Merrythought label to one of the feet.

Safety eyes are inserted next, with a little mechanical help to fix them firmly in place. Then the body, head and limbs are all turned the right way out.

The head, legs and arms are machine-stuffed at this stage,

before the jointing begins. This fascinating process, known as 'fitting up', fixes the head and limbs to the body, but still allows them to be rotated.

After stuffing of the body, again by machine, the bear moves on to the finisher, who attaches the ears, hand-sews the back seam on the body, stitches the claws and, most important, adds the nose and mouth which give the bear its character.

Finally the bear is brushed, both by hand and with a mechanical device, and the fur around the nose and eyes is carefully trimmed. A ribbon is tied round its neck, a paper 'swing ticket' attached to the bear's tummy or ear using a staple gun, and the bear is then packed in a polythene bag or a special box ready for dispatch.

Of course, not every bear is made in exactly the same way. Merrythought has produced numerous different designs of bear over the years. Some are jointed, some not. Some dressed, some not. Some have fur heads and paws but bodies of cotton or felt or another smooth fabric.

Particularly popular with collectors are the lovely mohair Magnet Bears, with their gentle faces and distinctive stitching on their paws. Early ones not only bore a Merrythought label on a foot but a pewter button in their ear or on the back, just below the shoulder.

In those days, of course, these bears were bought mainly for children, not as collectables, but there was also some adult interest in teddy bears and other soft toys. Toy dogs, for instance, were carried as fashion accessories – they were much less trouble than the real thing. Later, teddy bears, too, were adopted as a fashion accessory, and companies like Merrythought produced them in all the latest fashion colours. Presumably, though, these bears were simply thrown away when the fashions changed, and not kept in attics like so many treasured childhood toys. Very few of them are seen today, which of course makes them highly collectable.

Some bears were also turned into novelty items, like muffs

and slippers, and Merrythought was particularly well known for its nightdress cases. In fact, the company still makes some today.

In the postwar years, Merrythought also produced a large number of character toys, and several examples of these are on display in the adjacent shop run by the Ironbridge Gorge Museum Trust. There is Walt Disney's Yogi Bear, for instance, a Sooty muff (produced for a while in the early sixties), the dog Bonzo, and a Winnie-the-Pooh puppet and nightdress case. There is also a rare Albert Bear, who is featured in a delightful series of books by Alison Jezard.

Merrythought was also one of the first companies to produce toy pandas – even before the arrival of a baby panda at London Zoo in 1938 led to a massive demand for the animals in every shape and form. A panda toy and a panda nightdress case are both on display in the Ironbridge shop.

One of the most distinctive of all the Merrythought toys, however, is the grinning Cheeky bear, which first appeared in the design trial books in 1955, and went on sale in 1957. Several versions of this lovable bear can also be seen here, as well as his ancestor, Punkinhead, who was made for a Canadian department store for a number of years.

The shop sells bears in the current Merrythought range (and will order any which are not actually in stock). They have some teddy bear books, and a number of teddy bear gifts and pocket money items, too. And there are usually one or two special souvenirs featuring Merrythought bears, like mugs, postcards and badges.

There are other gift shops in the town, which may also have some bear-related items on offer. But collectors will be drawn instantly to the **Ironbridge Toy Museum**. The museum shop sells a wide range of toys, but as the bears have threatened to take over, they were given their own Bears on The Square Shop next door.

They have some bears made exclusively for them by Merrythought, like the cuddly Bernie (named after one of the Museum's owners), and an Indecisive Bernie, with a special neck mechanism that enables him to nod his head up and down as well as turning it from side to side. There is a sweet Baby Bernie, too, and Bernie's girlfriend Jenny.

They stock the German Steiffs and Hermanns as well, including the limited editions and some of the Steiff animals. But they also have an ever-changing selection of artist bears in a wide range of sizes, colours and styles. They especially like to have bears that no other shop has, which makes them of extra interest to collectors. Work by many top artists can generally be found there, and they also try to encourage newer names – the big stars of the future.

In addition, there are Paddington Bears and a good number of cuddly soft toys, as well as inexpensive souvenir bears wearing special Ironbridge Bear jumpers. Plenty of small items for children are also on sale.

The Museum itself is a sheer delight, too, with a splendid selection of childhood memories which is increasing and improving all the time. You will see everything from cars, trains, boats and planes of various makes to a fascinating range of kitchen and household toys not to mention the games, toy theatres, space toys, soldiers and farm animals, and a collection of Pelham puppets.

Among the dolls are a large number by England's Peggy Nisbet, and there is also a rapidly growing collection of teddy bears and other soft toys.

There were once no fewer than three major manufacturers of soft toys in this part of Shropshire – Merrythought in Ironbridge, and both Chad Valley and Norah Wellings in Wellington (page 262). In recognition of this, the Museum is developing a very special collection of toys created by these companies.

Chad Valley's huge output included toys of virtually every description, among them large numbers of teddy bears and other soft toys, including dolls. For some years, Norah Wellings designed toys for them, but in 1926, she left to form her own company. She is best known for her distinctive cloth dolls, but there were also a few teddy bears and teddy bear nightdress cases, which are much sought by collectors.

The Museum collection includes many unusual examples from these three local factories, as well as various bears and bear-related items from further afield. Unlike many such museums, they have decided to concentrate on toys from Britain – a fitting choice for a museum in an area with such a rich toy-making tradition.

ADDRESSES

Merrythought Ltd; tel. 0952 433116
Ironbridge Gorge Museum Teddy Bear Shop; tel. 0952 433029
Ironbridge Toy Museum, The Square; tel. 0952 433926
Tourist Information Centre, The Wharfage; tel. 0952 432166

Lichfield

The **Bear With Us** shop in Lichfield, Staffordshire, is one of those delightful teddy bear shops where collectors know they are welcome to pop in just for a chat. Owner Gloria Walsh loves to talk about her bears. The only problem is that the shop is crammed with so many appealing faces that bear lovers find it impossible to leave empty-handed.

Gloria works hard to provide her customers with something different. She specializes in hand-made artist bears, and is always trying to find good new artists, before everyone else discovers them. Many of these go on to become leading names in the teddy bear world.

Of course, Bear With Us stocks bears by well-known artists, too, and Gloria is constantly commissioning artists to make a range of bears exclusively for the shop. She also tracks down artists in other countries and, because she likes to see as many of the bears as possible before buying them, she has even visited America to seek out good but lesser-known bears from there as well.

British artist Pam Howells (see Crowland, page 210) was also commissioned to make a special 'house' bear, who was actually conceived even before the shop was opened. Writer and lexicographer Dr Samuel Johnson was born in the town and, passing his birthplace one day, Gloria and her former partner Gaynor Fryer began to wonder what kind of bear would have been found in its attic, if bears had been around in the eighteenth century.

They decided he would be grey and distinguished because, according to Johnson himself, the verb 'to bear' means 'to carry with distinction'. So of course the Johnson Bear would have to carry himself with distinction as well.

The image is heightened by a pair of bear-sized spectacles. Word has it, however, that they are also used to help him decipher the tiny type on the miniature newspaper under his arm. It is a much-reduced copy of the very first *Lichfield Mercury*, dated 7 July 1815 (there's a notice of the Abdication of Bonaparte on its back page). The paper is still being published today and apparently actually sponsored the creation of these miniatures.

Each anniversary of the shop sees the creation of other 'house' bears with a Lichfield connection. Erasmus, for instance, was named after Charles Darwin's grandfather Erasmus Darwin, who had a medical practice in Lichfield. Dame Oliver's namesake was a schoolmistress in the town.

The shop stocks modern manufactured bears as well, like Steiffs (including limited editions), Dean's and a good number of Merrythoughts. Merrythought were even commissioned to make a hundred replicas of two delightful old Chad Valley bears, exclusively for sale here.

There are a good number of bear-related items, too, including ornaments, pictures, jewellery, pewter items, embroidery kits, books, greetings cards and plenty of small pocket-money purchases for children. So it is very difficult to walk out with nothing at all.

Visitors to the town will also find that there is quite a bit more to see, like the Cathedral with its three spires and the Samuel Johnson Birthplace Museum. Lichfield House, on Bore Street, is a beautiful Tudor building from 1510 (now a café and shop), and its neighbours include a Georgian townhouse (now home of the Tourist Information Centre) and the Victorian Guildhall.

There are picturesque timber-framed buildings in Quonians Lane and The Close, among others, and Bear With Us itself is four hundred years old. Apparently, bear baiting once took place outside.

There are several antique shops in the town, too. Try **Cordelia and Perdy's Antique Junk Shop** on Tamworth Street. When I was last there, the bears on display turned out not to be for sale, but it is just the place for a good rummage for interesting accessories for your bears.

ADDRESSES

Bear With Us, 7 Greenhill; tel. 0543 250410
Tourist Information Centre, Donegal House, Bore Street; tel.
  0543 252109

Lincoln

With its ancient castle, splendid cathedral and other historic buildings, Lincoln attracts a large number of visitors each year. Among them are many who love bears and head straight for **No. 9 Gifts and Games**, situated right on Steep Hill.

Now, however, the shop is up for sale, and no one can tell when it will finally change hands and whether the new owners will want to keep it as a bear shop. So if you are planning a special visit, it would be best to telephone first to see whether the shop is still there.

As long as it is, you can expect to find some two to three hundred bears on sale at any time (many more before Christmas). They include bears from makers like Steiff (including their limited editions), Merrythought, Canterbury Bears, Dean's, Nisbet, Bedford Bears, H.M. Bears and the Old Fashioned Teddy Bear Company. There are Big Softies, too, including a special Lincoln Bear, carrying the city's coat of arms and available only through the shop.

You should find some American artist bears as well (by Everyday Heroes, Jeannie Major and Tender Treasures), and Britain's Little Treasures are also usually in good supply.

There are bear-related items, too, including miniatures, fridge magnets, postcards and greetings cards, as well as some exclusive items, like the shop's own special coasters.

As the name suggests, however, it is not all bears. They also sell many games, like chess, backgammon, mah-jong, dominoes, Chinese checkers and playing cards.

Luckily, the shop is right at the bottom of Steep Hill which certainly lives up to its name, with a one-in-four gradient. (It looks, and feels, even worse!) However, if you make the effort to climb up to the cathedral, you will find not only spectacular architecture but also some more exclusive bears. In the **Cathedral Shop** are chorister and choir master bears, made specially for the cathedral by H.M. Bears.

On the way up to the cathedral, you will pass the famous twelfth-century Jew's House, and many other interesting old buildings, while the city's other attractions include the National Cycle Museum and the Museum of Lincolnshire Life.

ADDRESSES

No. 9 Gifts and Games, 9 Steep Hill; tel. 0522 510524
Tourist Information Centre, 9 Castle Hill; tel. 0522 529828

Loughborough

It only takes a handful of customers to fill Loughborough's **House of Bruin**, but it is a place that collectors travel considerable distances to visit. One of its attractions is its wide range of bears, of course. But the enthusiasm of owners Sue and Frank Webster helps to make the shop extra special. It is the kind of place where collectors drop in just for a chat, without feeling any pressure to make a purchase, although many find all the temptations simply too hard to resist.

It comes as some surprise to learn that it was neither Sue nor Frank who started it all, but Sue's brother-in-law, Ned. Sue's sister Irene, Ned's wife, was a doll collector, and Ned finally got fed up with simply following her around all the toy and antique fairs she attended. He decided to start collecting bears, which were often to be found at the same events.

Sue and Frank were themselves buying and selling general antiques at the time, and started looking out for bears for Ned. Then they found that they were getting hooked too. It was Irene and Sue who opened the House of Bruin, in 1989.

Sadly, Ned has since died and Irene later remarried and moved away. But Sue continued on her own, with help from husband Frank and also from Irene's equally enthusiastic daughter.

An important feature of the shop since its earliest days has been the repair service it offers for owners of old and injured bears. Frank started undertaking some repairs when he and Sue were dealing in general antiques. Sometimes they would come across a teddy in such a sorry state that they knew no one would want him. Frank would set to work on some careful restoration before the bear could be sold.

These days, however, it is Sue, not Frank, who does most of this work, especially since Frank began creating his own Charnwood Bears.

He used to work as a textile engineer, rushing home to make bears in the evenings after an already long day. It meant that he could only manage to produce them in very small numbers, and they were sold only through the House of Bruin, but word soon spread among collectors that here was an artist to watch. Eventually he took the plunge, and started making his bears full time.

There are still only a handful of men working as bear artists in Britain (in America, the number is far greater), but bear collecting isn't solely the preserve of women, as many people believe. There are many male collectors amongst the House of Bruin's regular clientele. In fact, Frank has found that they tend to be even more enthusiastic, although some have difficulty admitting their hobby. Perhaps Frank's own enthusiastic presence helps.

The shop specializes in British artist bears, with as many designs exclusive to them as possible. Work by many of the British bear world's top names fills the shelves, and collectors are encouraged to pick the bears up for a cuddle. Nothing has a fixed place. Sue and Frank believe that homeliness is more important than perfect order.

There are bears by major manufacturers, too. Steiff, Hermann, Merrythought, Dean's and Nisbet bears are generally to be found, including each year's limited editions.

Other shelves hold a good number of bear-related items, ranging from ornaments to tins to greetings cards.

Above all, however, Sue and Frank pride themselves on offering a friendly and personal service. They love the bears themselves (they have a large collection of their own) and the shop is treated more as an extension of their home than as a place of business. They believe that bears don't need to be sold, they sell themselves, and any bear lover who has fallen for a pleading face will surely agree with them.

Loughborough's other places of interest include its bell foundry. The Bell Foundry Museum can be visited on many days, and a carillon of nearly fifty locally made bells has been incorporated into a First World War memorial. The steam railway is another popular attraction, and the Donington Collection, with its vintage vehicles and classic racing cars, is just a few miles away.

ADDRESSES

The House of Bruin, 4 Ashby Square; tel. 0509 210488
Tourist Information Centre, Wards End; tel. 0509 230131

Ludlow

Ludlow in Shropshire has been called one of the most beautiful towns in Britain. Its medieval street pattern has survived almost unchanged, and the town contains close to five hundred listed buildings from a variety of periods. Dominating them all are a castle built by the Normans in the late eleventh century, and one of the largest parish churches in the country, dating from the fifteenth century.

As always in a town which attracts many visitors, you will find a good number of gift and craft shops, but a shop of special interest to bear lovers started life as a ladies' boutique. Now bars are trying hard to take over.

You should find about a hundred of them in the **Little Paws** section of Martyn's Boutique, in the High Street. Among the makes to be found there are Dean's, Merrythought, Steiff (although at the time of writing no limited editions), Romsey Bears and cuddly teddies from Ty. But they are constantly increasing their range of artist bears. Among those stocked to date have been Bocs Teganau, Heritage, Hartrick, Mother Hubbard, My Old Teddy and Wimblebury Bears. Some have been shop exclusives.

They also have bear-related items, including painted sweatshirts, jewellery, prints, china, stationery and greetings cards.

ADDRESSES

Little Paws at Martyn's Boutique, 10b High Street; tel. 0584 875286

Tourist Information Centre, Castle Street; tel. 0584 875053

Malvern

These days the most popular activity amongst visitors to this Worcestershire town is probably walking. The surrounding hills and countryside offer some stunning views, and the Malvern Hills actually became the first preservation area in Britain.

In Victorian times, however, it was the springs which flowed from those hills that provided the greatest attraction. The town became a fashionable watering place, and those days have left their legacy in the buildings and layout of the present town.

The town is often used as a base for visiting the Cotswolds and Stratford-upon-Avon (see Broadway, page 191, Stow-on-the-Wold, page 241, Stratford-upon-Avon, page 243, Witney, page 144, etc.), where bear lovers will find plenty of interest. But they will also not want to miss **Treasures of Childhood Past** in Malvern itself. This small shop sells a whole variety of old and antique childhood items, including antique dolls, doll's houses, doll's house miniatures, toy theatres and paper dolls.

They also aim to have thirty-five to forty-five old bears in stock at any one time. Often there are more. Naturally the range of makes changes constantly, but could include Steiff, Schuco, Bing, Merrythought, Chad Valley, Farnell, Pedigree, Ideal and others that are equally collectable. There will also be some of unknown make, for a charming face has just as much appeal for many collectors as a prestigious label.

The shop also sells various teddy-related items, and often has old teddy photos and old china decorated with teddy bears. You may find bear-sized hats and other accessories, too. So if you love old things, this is a place you will enjoy visiting.

The town also has one of the most splendid parish churches in the country. And of course you can taste the famous Malvern Water, now bottled by Schweppes at Colwall.

Sir Edward Elgar was born at nearby Broadheath, where his birthplace has been turned into a museum. Visitors can also follow a special Elgar Route, which traces places that were of significance in the composer's life.

ADDRESSES

Treasures of Childhood Past, 43 Wyche Road; tel. 0684 560010
Tourist Information Centre, Grange Road; tel. 0684 892289

Norwich

N orwich has been a major market town for centuries, with the market held on the same site for more than nine hundred years. Then, from the seventeenth century onwards, small speciality shops also started to spring up – drapers, ironmongers, booksellers and many others. At that time, Norwich was Britain's second city, and over the next two hundred years, as Britain developed into what became known as a 'nation of shopkeepers', more and more retailers set up businesses in the town.

That legacy remains today. In addition to all the well-known High Street chains, you'll find a warren of small pedestrianized lanes and alleyways housing all sorts of specialist shops.

One of the best known is Coleman's Mustard Shop and Museum in Bridewell Alley, set up more than twenty years ago to promote one of the city's oldest industries. Nearby, Hovells have been selling baskets for well over a hundred years, continuing a family tradition that dates back a good deal further.

It is Elm Hill, not far from the site of the earlier Saxon market, which beckons bear lovers. Not only is the cobbled street one of the prettiest in the city, with many buildings dating from

the sixteenth and seventeenth centuries, but one of those buildings also houses the extremely busy **Bear Shop**.

Owner Robert Stone hated sitting in an office all day, and
longed to find a viable alternative. But even when he opened his
first Bear Shop in Colchester (page 206), he employed someone
else to run it for him and continued with his daily trudge to the
office. The shop's huge success encouraged him to think of opening
a second one, however, and when he did, it gave him the perfect
excuse to give up his job at last and run the new business himself.
Now, Monday mornings are greeted with a huge smile, and there
are many more smiles from the constant stream of customers.

The shop attracts collectors from all over Norfolk and from
far beyond as well, and it does not take long to figure out why. It
may not be large, but it is absolutely packed with bears to suit
nearly every taste and pocket. Add to that the warmest and
friendliest of welcomes, and you have an irresistible combination.

In stock are bears by many of the major manufacturers,
including the Steiff limited editions as well as their regular and
Classic ranges. There are Hermann bears from Germany, too
(again including limited editions), while Britain's Merrythought
and Dean's are also well represented. They have a good many
collector bears from these companies. But they also have some of
their bears for children, to satisfy the demand for good-quality
traditional bears made in Britain. They have even had a special
range of Merrythought bears made specially for them, in a lovely
rich-looking mohair, and in three sizes. Although they are
suitable for children, they will have just as much appeal for many
older bear lovers.

There are plenty of soft and cuddly bears as well, generally
made in the Far East and covering a wide range of prices (from a
few pounds upwards). The ever-popular Paddington and Winnie-
the-Pooh are there, too. But one of the great attractions for
collectors will be the splendid range of bears from numerous
British artists.

Many of the top names are there. I counted well over twenty on my last visit. But you will also find some good new artists represented, as well as a number of local makers whose bears are often exclusive to the shop. These are especially popular with visitors, who are often looking for something with a local connection.

From slightly further afield, the Essex-based Naomi Laight and Mister Bear have been two long-time favourites. But other bears come from all over the country, with the work of Bocs Teganau, Mother Hubbard, Hartrick Bear Company, Bo Bears, Bear Bits, H.M. Bears, Imagine, Jay-Bee Bears and Susan Jane Knock among the bears on sale to date. But the number is increasing all the time, as any good new artist that Robert sees will instantly be asked if they can make something for him.

He has, however, opted to concentrate on British rather than American bears, to keep the prices within more reasonable limits.

The artist bears also invariably include a number of shop exclusives. Janet Clark of Teddystyle and Shirley Latimer of Crafty Bears are just two of the artists who have designed bears specially for the Bear Shop. In addition to the special limited editions, they have also had many totally unique, one-off bears, from a number of different makers.

There is a good deal of originality among the bear-related items on sale as well. Local artist Rita Evans will paint your bear in oils, pastels or watercolours, for instance, and there are some of her inexpensive small pastels of bears on sale in the shop.

Some unusual wall plaques, on the other hand, feature genuine fabric teddy bears, while hand-painted celebration spoons can be specially created to suit the occasion or the recipient. In addition to a personalized message, they can feature bears engaged in all sorts of activities, like sports or ballet or deep in a book, to suit the interests of the person concerned.

The shop generally has a good selection of Oscar and Bertie

merchandise, too, since the artist concerned (and the bears) live in Norfolk.

Then there are ceramic and pewter miniatures, and on my last visit I also found a whole variety of different brooches, as well as bookmarks, pens, hand-painted tiles and teapot stands, stationery, greetings cards, wrapping paper and a good deal more.

There are more bear-related items, including Winnie-the-Pooh ranges and a selection of greetings cards, at the **Elm Hill Craft Shop** at number 12. They have a few traditional bears, as well – I spotted a Canterbury, a Bedford Bear and several Steiffs (especially miniatures) on my last visit .

The antique shops are worth exploring too – not so much for bears or even bear-related items as for the odd prop or accessory. **Elizabeth Lake**, at number 32a, has some lovely antique lace and period clothes, for instance, as well as all sorts of 'Victoriana and Bygones'. Over the road in Wrights Court, **Philip Milne's** Antique Shop (next to the taxidermist) may also yield something to include in a display.

If you like browsing round antique shops and centres, you'll find several more as you walk around the town. Some of the specialist gift and craft shops could also yield something for the bear lover, and the huge range of new toys at **Langleys** in the Royal Arcade naturally includes some bears.

There are a few older bears on permanent view in the Toy Room of the Strangers' Hall Museum, but most of them date from the fifties and sixties, and they are not the museum's main attraction. Dolls are present in larger numbers, dating from the early nineteenth century onwards, and there is also a wide range of other toys and games. Again, many date from the fifties and sixties, and will be instantly remembered by those who played with them then.

Early this century, this medieval merchant's house became

one of the first folk museums in Britain. In addition to the Toy Room, it now includes a whole range of period rooms. Some have furniture from the seventeenth century, and there are a Georgian dining-room, a Regency music room, and Victorian parlour and nursery.

Another old merchant house is now occupied by the Bridewell Museum, which includes some fascinating looks at the working life of the city.

A Norman castle, Norman cathedral, and more than thirty medieval churches are among the city's many other places of interest, although very few of the latter are actually used for church services today.

ADDRESSES

The Bear Shop, 18 Elm Hill; tel. 0603 766866
Tourist Information Centre, The Guildhall, Gaol Hill; tel. 0603 666071

Nottingham

Nottingham's large shopping centre attracts shoppers from a wide area. Most of the usual High Street stores are there. In addition, department store **Jessop & Son** is one of the John Lewis Partnership, so their toy department should include some of the bears made for the company by Merrythought. Their gift department, on the other hand, should have some limited editions from Merrythought and Dean's, as well as perhaps one or two from Steiff.

However, Nottingham bear lovers often head for **A Bear's Life**, situated about a mile and a half from the city centre, on the main A52 Derby Road (near the Queen's Medical Centre).

There they sell bears of various makes, including Steiff, Merrythought, Hermann, Dean's, Canterbury and Bo-Bear Designs. They have a particularly good range of Steiffs, with animals as well as bears, including some of the life-size studio range.

Bo Bears are also making a number of limited editions exclusively for the shop – including a bear called Warwick, after the bear and ragged staff in the coat of arms of Warwickshire County Council.

You will also find bear-related items like cards, jumpers and a range of leatherware, and they have some teddy bear mugs, which are again exclusive to them.

Everything is displayed on pine furniture, and the shop's bow window helps to add to its atmosphere.

You may also want to include Nottingham Castle on your itinerary. If you do, look out for the old Nottinghamshire stoneware in the ceramics collection. You will see that some of the jugs are in the form of brown bears.

For those who love lace, on the other hand, another port of call will be the Lace Hall, which tells the story of lace making in Nottingham over some two hundred years. A quite different story is covered by the Tales of Robin Hood – fittingly situated in Maid Marian Way.

ADDRESSES

A Bear's Life, 361–363 Derby Road; tel. 0602 423366
Jessop & Son, Victoria Centre; tel. 0602 418282
Tourist Information Centre, 1–4 Smithy Row; tel. 0602 470661

Nuneaton

Situated to the north of Coventry, Nuneaton was the birthplace of Mary Ann Evans, who wrote under the name George Eliot. Today, it is a busy market town, and bear lovers will be pleased to note that its shops include one of particular interest to them.

Called **Teddies & Treasures**, it usually has around 250 new bears in stock, and at the time of writing you could find around 50 old ones there as well.

They have bears from various manufacturers, among them Steiff, Hermann, Merrythought, Dean's and Big Softies, including limited editions from each of these companies. There are cuddly bears from companies like Ty and Russ Berrie, and also popular characters like Paddington and Rupert.

In addition, they stock bears by various artists, including some made specially for them. Teddy bear cards are on sale, too.

ADDRESSES

Teddies & Treasures, Co-op Arcade, Abbey Street; tel. 0203 353409

Tourist Information Centre, Nuneaton Library, Church Street; tel. 0203 384027

Rickinghall

The Suffolk village of Rickinghall, hidden away between the ancient Suffolk town of Bury St Edmunds and the busy Norfolk market town of Diss, is an unexpected source of bears for collectors. But **Breklaw Crafts** aims to have between fifty and sixty in stock at any time.

Owner Barbara Walker prefers to stock artist bears rather than the products of major manufacturers. So the range generally includes the work of makers like Bocs Teganau and Bearwood Bears, as well as some Canterbury Bears and Big Softies. Bransgore, the Old Fashioned Teddy Bear Co., Jay-Bee and H.M. Bears are among the other names found there so far, and there are also the Breklaw Bears made by Barbara herself.

Some books and cards are also on sale.

ADDRESSES

Breklaw Crafts, The Corner Shop; tel. 0379 898330
Tourist Information Centre, Meres Mouth, Mere Street, Diss;
  0379 650523

Shrewsbury

Ann Richards is well known to teddy collectors – even to many who have never visited her Shrewsbury shop. She just bubbles over with infectious enthusiasm, and anyone who has met her at a teddy bear fair knows just how much she loves her furry charges.

That love of bears is very evident in her Shrewsbury shop, **Peggotty**, situated in the Victorian Arcade alongside a variety of other interesting small businesses. Peggotty is really quite tiny. In fact, it is more window than anything else. But it is crammed with a splendid selection of beautiful bears, and collectors are actively encouraged to hug and cuddle any that catch their eye.

There are bears from all the major manufacturers. Steiff limited editions usually disappear as soon as they arrive, but that still leaves plenty of other Steiff collectables, like their popular Classics.

There are Hermanns and Merrythoughts, too, including limited editions, as well as bears by Dean's, Big Softies and other companies. But Ann is well aware of current trends, and has been turning her attention more and more to the individually made artist bears. She tirelessly scours the country looking for new designs, and visits as many fairs as she can to seek out the best of the new artists and to gather as many bears as she can from the better-known names who can never supply enough to keep up with the demands of collectors.

Many artists make exclusive editions and even one-off bears specially for the shop. They sell so fast that the range changes constantly, but some of those whose work has been on sale to date are Little Charmers, Mister Bear, Crafty Bears, Bear Bits, Blossom Bears, Mother Hubbard, Naomi Laight and Bocs Teganau.

Peggotty also has a few bear-related items like cards and teddy bear jewellery, but the bears themselves have taken over most of the available space. There are, however, some less expensive cuddlies as well as all the splendid collectables.

It is a shop that would be worth a visit wherever it was situated. But an extra bonus is that Shrewsbury is such a lovely town. Almost totally surrounded by the River Severn, it was a settlement at least as far back as the year 901, and by the time of the Norman Conquest there were already 252 houses. It grew to become a major trading centre for Welsh wool and cloth.

Today, one legacy of its long history is an abundance of interesting and picturesque old buildings, like the half-timbered Tudor buildings scattered about the town, the stone-built Market Hall, which dates from 1596, and various fine churches – not to mention the intriguingly named Bear Steps.

Shrewsbury is also a major shopping centre. There are

modern, covered shopping precincts, like the Pride Hill Centre. But there are also many narrow streets and passages, to make browsing a real joy. Small, specialist shops abound (like those in the Victorian Arcade), and some of these may offer the odd bearish item. But outside Peggotty, I found few actual bears on my last visit, apart from some soft toys at **J. C. Pickering's** toy shop on Mardol, not far from Peggotty itself.

The town also boasts a number of antique centres, however. Those in Frankwell and Princess Street are probably the most likely prospects for bear lovers. As usual, bears themselves may not be too plentiful, but bear-related items and interesting accessories are distinct possibilities.

ADDRESSES

Peggotty, 23 Victorian Arcade, Mardol; tel. 0743 246230
J. C. Pickering, 26 Mardol; tel. 0743 362730
Tourist Information Centre, The Music Hall, The Square; tel. 0743 350761

Stamford

In 1967, Lincolnshire's Stamford was the first town in Britain to be declared a Conservation Area. Neither the Industrial Revolution nor the out-with-the-old-and-in-with-the-new mentality of the twentieth century was permitted to wreak havoc on the stone-built town. Its streets remain filled with beautiful medieval and Georgian buildings, among them a twelfth-century priory, five medieval churches and a hospital which dates back to the fifteenth century.

No fewer than six hundred buildings of architectural or

historical interest are crammed into an area measuring just 1,000 m by 400 m. Together they make up around half of all the listed buildings in the county.

It is a busy little town which nevertheless maintains a delightfully relaxed atmosphere, with plenty of coffee-houses and tearooms encouraging you to linger awhile. You can even enjoy homemade food in the company of Paddington and some of his bear friends at **Paddingtons** in Ironmonger Street.

Then there is a whole **Room for Bears** at Perfect Presents in St Mary's Street.

Pat Garner and her husband John opened the original Perfect Presents in Stamford's Red Lion Street in 1989. Gradually, however, bears started trying to take over, and at the end of 1992 they moved them all to a new home, where they could have a whole upstairs room to themselves.

They stock bears by most of the major manufacturers. The Steiffs include some of their Classic bears as well as a few limited editions. There are limited editions from Merrythought and Hermann, too. But you will also find the popular Tails and Tales by Golden Gifts, as well as cuddly teddies from the Manhattan Toy Company, Ty and Gund. In addition, there are souvenir Stamford Teddies, made in the Channel Islands, and inexpensive bears from China in special Room for Bears jumpers.

Paddington is well represented, and usually available in a variety of sizes, while you will generally find Pooh and his friends there as well.

These days, however, Pat finds she is fighting a constant battle to keep up with the huge demand for artist bears. She aims to have a large number in stock at any time, but bears by some of the most popular makers disappear as soon as they come in. Nevertheless, you should find the work of a large number of different artists, even if in some cases it is just a single bear.

Among the names found there to date have been Bocs Teganau, Mother Hubbard, Little Treasures, Willow Bears, Only

Natural, Dormouse Designs, H.M., Romsey and Bo Bears. In addition, the range generally includes work from a number of miniaturists.

They try to have a number of older bears on sale, too, mainly of English manufacture.

Alongside all the bears, Perfect Presents stocks a wide variety of general gifts, and many of these again have a bearish theme. Some can be found in the Room for Bears, but there are more among all the other gifts which fill the rest of the shop's two floors.

The range is changing constantly, but on my last visit the list included a large number of different ceramic teddies, as well as bottle stoppers, letter openers, coat hooks, music boxes, mugs, and even teddies made from recycled paper. There were all sorts of items featuring Winnie-the-Pooh and his friends, among them money boxes, book-ends, picture frames and clocks. Pooh featured on some of the stationery, too, and the many greetings cards included some unusual 3-D creations by a local artist.

John Garner himself also creates unique 3-D cards using tiny resin teddy bears. The cards can be tailor-made for just about any occasion, and even personalized with the recipient's name if required. As they are totally hand made, no two will ever be exactly the same.

You could also find the odd teddy or teddy-related item at other shops in the town, a number of which sell various gifts.

The children's shop **Jeunesse** at 14 St Mary's Street has some cuddly bears, for instance, and I also found a few attractive bearish gifts there. Some of their children's fashions might prove to be just right for a bear as well, and they stock some lovely traditional wooden toys which can look just right in a teddy display.

There are various antique and craft shops to explore, too. For example, the Stamford Antique Centre in the Exchange Hall in Broad Street brings together around forty different dealers selling everything from large items of furniture to small collectables. I found a few old toys there on my last visit, as well as all sorts of small items that could be used to enhance a display of bears.

Broad Street was once a market area and many of its limestone buildings date from the eighteenth century. But it is here that you will also find the late fifteenth-century Browne's hospital, one of Stamford's many interesting buildings. These medieval almshouses were built by a rich wool merchant for ten poor men and two women, but were partly rebuilt and enlarged in the nineteenth century. Today there are six double and five single rooms, as well as a hobbies room.

You will find some fine Georgian buildings in Barn Hill and All Saints' Place, and it is here that you will also find the Stamford Museum, telling the history of the town and of Britain's oldest provincial weekly newspaper, the *Stamford Mercury*, founded in 1712.

Another exhibit is a life-size model of the 53-stone Daniel Lambert, who died in 1809 and is buried in Stamford. The model wears clothes actually worn by Lambert himself. They so impressed America's 'General Tom Thumb', who visited the town thirty-three years after Lambert's death, that he left a suit of his own tiny clothes to be displayed alongside them. They, too, are now worn by a life-size model.

A Victorian brewery has been converted into another museum, which includes a licensed refreshment room. But when it comes to refreshments, few places could beat the ivy-clad courtyard of the George Hotel.

At least three kings have stayed at this sixteenth-century coaching inn (among them Charles I and William III). It stands on the site of the House of the Holy Sepulchre, where the Knights of Saint John of Jerusalem were entertained. Black-robed Crusaders once walked in its gardens. Today, its famous gallows sign still welcomes the honest traveller, and offers a warning to highwaymen.

ADDRESSES

Room for Bears, Perfect Presents, 9a St Mary's Street; tel. 0780
480528
Paddingtons, 12 Ironmonger Street; tel. 0780 51110
Tourist Information Centre, Stamford Arts Centre, 27 St Mary's
Street; tel. 0780 55611

Stow-on-the-Wold

The old market town of Stow-on-the-Wold is the highest in the Cotswolds. Once it was famous for its sheep fairs. Now, it is high-class antique shops which help to attract visitors.

Most will hold few attractions for those wanting inexpensive bits and pieces to add interest to a bear display. But there is still plenty to appeal to bear lovers of all kinds.

Lovers of oldies will head for **Park House Antiques** in Park Street, a general antique shop which invariably has a good number of bears as well. Many bears from the shop and from the owners' own collection have featured on greetings cards and postcards published by Perspectives Photographics. The keen-eyed may still be able to spot some of the props used to bring the bears to life.

The cards are on sale in the shop, as are all sorts of interesting old collectables, some of which are bear-related. They also have a large selection of dolls and doll's clothes, and it is just the kind of place to look for things like beautiful old prams and cots which make such a good basis for a display.

A very different shop, but of equal interest for the bear lover, is the specialist **Bears on the Wold** in the Talbot Court precinct in Sheep Street. They, too, often have some old bears in stock, but they also sell a wide range of more modern collectables.

241

Some are by manufacturers like Steiff, Hermann, Merrythought, Dean's and Canterbury, and include many limited editions. But there are also bears by a wide range of artists, with new designs arriving all the time.

Teddystyle, Bocs Teganau, Apple of My Eye, Naomi Laight and various American artists are among those whose bears have been sold to date.

Others are beautifully made by Jane Galbraith, daughter of the shop's owner, Eileen Evers. They tend to sell out as fast as she can make them, however. For many collectors, being able to buy a bear from the artist herself is a very welcome bonus, and Jane can be found in the shop most mornings.

Another speciality of the shop is some attractive cottage-style painted furniture, like bear-sized chairs and benches and pretty shelves which set off a group of bears to perfection. Eileen also keeps an eye open for other suitable display aids, like prams and sledges, which are similarly popular with her customers.

There are some inexpensive cuddly bears, too, and Golden Gifts' Tails and Tales, as well as some bear-related items like postcards, brooches, magnets, ceramic miniatures and Winnie-the-Pooh items for those with less money to spend.

Stow also has its share of gift shops, and is a relaxing place for an afternoon of strolling and browsing, since nothing is too far from its central market square. A large part of the town has been designated a conservation area, and there are many buildings of historical interest, mostly built of the mellow Cotswold limestone for which the area is so famous. Narrow alleyways off the square were once used not only as short cuts but also on sheep fair days, when the sheep were driven through them to make counting easier.

ADDRESSES

Bears on the Wold, 11 Talbot Court, Sheep Street; tel. 0451
870133
Park House Antiques, Park Street; tel. 0451 830159
Visitor Information Centre, Hollis House, The Square; tel. 0451
831082

Stratford-upon-Avon

Stratford is one of those places that seems to have everything – numerous buildings of great historical interest, a beautiful river, fine theatres, good restaurants. It also has more bears in more places than possibly any other town in Britain. In fact, it was only on my fifth visit that I even found time to look round any of the Shakespeare properties. There were simply too many bears to distract me.

First stop for most bear lovers will, of course, be the **Teddy Bear Museum**, opened by Gyles Brandreth and his wife Michèle on 4 July 1988. They chose American Independence Day because it was an American President, Theodore Roosevelt, who gave his name to the teddy bear.

It is only a small museum, housed in one of Stratford's many beautiful old buildings (it was a farmhouse in Elizabethan times). But its various displays convey a good deal of teddy bear history (although experienced collectors will already be familiar with much of the information).

The 'Teddy Roosevelt Hallway', for instance, contains a large copy of the newspaper cartoon which played such an important part in the birth of the teddy bear. Published in *The Washington Post*, its inspiration was a bear hunt undertaken by

President Roosevelt while in Mississippi to settle a border dispute in 1902.

The hunting expedition had not been a success. At the end of the day, the President had not shot a single bear. Anxious not to disappoint him, his hosts eventually managed to capture one and tethered it to a tree, so that the President could be sure of a trophy to take back with him. Roosevelt, however, refused to be so unsportsmanlike, and the moment was soon immortalized by cartoonist Clifford Berryman.

His drawing, captioned 'Drawing the line in Mississippi', caught the attention of New York shopkeeper, Morris Michtom. His wife Rose made some toy bear cubs to be sold in his shop, and legend has it that Michtom asked the President for permission to call the toys 'Teddy's Bear'.

Although no evidence of this request exists, there seems to be little doubt that it was indeed this incident which gave the teddy bear its name.

Michtom, incidentally, had so much success with his toys that he went on to found the Ideal Novelty and Toy Company, which was to become one of America's biggest toy manufacturers. In 1968, it became the Ideal Toy Corporation.

In addition to the cartoon, the museum's homage to the President includes a photograph of Roosevelt himself, and there is also an impressive carved hall stand featuring real bears as opposed to teddies. Smaller versions of these carved wooden bears come in all sorts of guises and sizes, like inkwells or ashtrays or all sorts of other useful items, and are very popular with collectors.

Most of the museum is, however, devoted to teddy bears rather than bears in the wild, and the exhibits come from more than twenty different countries. Many have been collected by Gyles and Michèle during their own travels. But others have been added since the museum opened, so the displays are evolving all the time.

Among the new additions, for instance, is a bear by artist Naomi Laight. He was intended as one of the prizes in a draw held at the British Teddy Bear Festival in August 1990, but is still waiting for the holder of the winning ticket to come and claim him.

Then there is the French teddy bear given by the people of France to Britain on the eve of Bastille Day 1989, the 200th anniversary of the French Revolution. The French Ambassador, who made the presentation, said that it was offered as a symbol of Franco-British friendship.

Bob and Sabine de Beer, on the other hand, were a gift from Dutch department store the Bijenkorf, whose lovable Bob actually sparked off Holland's whole teddy bear fever.

Then there is Steiff's William Shakesbear, one of 2,000 of these bears made exclusively for the Museum. Marmaduke, on the other hand, is the Museum's logo, turned into a real teddy bear by Britain's Big Softies. Both are on sale in the Museum shop.

Many of the museum's residents are older, however. The Bedroom, for instance, is filled with representatives from the first six decades of this century. Some of the bears are German, like the huge Steiff which sits on the bed. Others are made by well-known British companies like Chad Valley or Chiltern, while some are inevitably of unknown origin. They sit playing card games or looking at old photographs, or simply enjoying each other's company in a friendly room setting rather than a sterile display case.

The Music Room holds bears of more recent vintage, with some from manufacturers and others from various artists. They include the work of those who were making bears long before the term 'bear artist' was first heard in this country.

They are quite a cosmopolitan group, too, with bears from Australia, Japan, Zambia, North America and Holland, as well as one of the sheepskin creations by Swedish maker Anna Rooth, who now lives in England.

One of the Irish Theme bears made by Cork's Joan Hanna (of Craft-T Bears) has also been included, with clothes typical of those worn in her area at the turn of the century. He carries a miniature turf creel of a kind still in use today. This more modern creation gives some indication of how much the work of British bear artists has progressed in just the few years since the museum opened.

More relatively modern bears (both manufactured and early artist bears) are taking part in a Teddy Bears' Picnic elsewhere in the Museum. But both the Library and the so-called Hall of Fame are filled with further teddy bear history.

The Library, for instance, includes a tribute to actor and arctophile Peter Bull, whose books and appearances on radio and television did so much to publicize the wonderful world of the teddy bear. Many of today's keenest collectors cite Peter Bull's books as a major factor in the development of their hobby.

The museum's exhibits include a copy of the first of these, *Bear With Me*, as well as the later *Teddy Bear Book*, published in a signed and numbered, boxed limited edition by British bear manufacturer the House of Nisbet. There are also three versions of the Nisbet Bully Bear, named after Peter, and some of the delightful little Bully Bear books which he wrote about the antics of this bear.

Needless to say, there are also some other very collectable teddy bear books in the library, among them John Betjeman's *Archie and the Strict Baptists*. In addition, there are a number of bears loaned or donated by various celebrities.

The bejewelled teddy of romantic novelist Barbara Cartland is there, for instance, and bears belonging to Richard Baker, Richard Briers, Liza Goddard, Bonnie Langford and Derek Nimmo are among others who have been enjoying long stays at the Museum. Neil Kinnock's Islwyn visited for a while, too, but his place has now been taken by a modern bear in a Labour

T-shirt. Lady Thatcher's bear Humphrey, on the other hand, is represented by a photograph, taken outside No. 10 when it was the house he called home.

Other famous bears can be found in the Hall of Fame. Fozzie Bear came from the TV series *The Muppets*. The little Paddington appeared in the original television series, which featured a fully articulated, three-dimensional bear with painted backgrounds. The Sooty puppet appeared on television, too, with Harry Corbett in the early fifties.

Winnie-the-Pooh and Rupert each have a case devoted to them. In addition to soft toy versions of the bears, there are books and photographs, including a signed first edition of *Winnie-the-Pooh* and some early Rupert annuals.

Further cases honour some of the major manufacturers of teddy bears, including Germany's Margarete Steiff who many believe created the very first teddy bear (although in those days the name teddy bear had not yet been coined). On display are some very early Steiff bears, with the oldest dating from 1903 and therefore one of the very first teddies ever made. Others date from 1905 and 1906.

There are other German bears, too – by Hermann, for instance – as well as interesting bears from British manufacturers Merrythought and Dean's. The Dean's display includes one of the distinctive black bears designed by Sylvia Wilgoss in the late 1950s, as well as some of the company's first bears made specially for collectors. Among the Merrythoughts are three of their distinctive Cheeky Bears, which first went on sale in 1957.

Some of the most unusual bears, however, will be found downstairs, gathered together in a single display case. They range from a teddy bear muff, made in Germany in 1908, to the winners of a knitting competition organized by the women's magazine *Prima* in 1988. There are early clockwork bears by the renowned German company Schuco, later examples from Russia and Japan, and a modern talking Teddy Ruxpin. A German teddy bear purse dates from 1913, while a bear made entirely from reindeer moss is a much more recent creation.

The museum also puts on special displays from time to time, so there is quite a variety of things to see.

There are many more teddies in the Museum shop, which stocks bears by various manufacturers, including Steiff, Hermann, Merrythought, Dean's and Big Softies, as well as Paddingtons, some souvenir Museum Bears, and various soft toys.

Steiff's Shakesbear, exclusive to the Museum, is also on sale there, as well as the Big Softies version of the museum's Marmaduke. A special Gyles Bear is produced by the House of Nisbet, and there are a number of artist bears, which generally include some made specially for the shop.

As the shop naturally attracts many tourists as well as serious collectors, there are also many gifts on sale, and pocket-money items for children. Many of these carry the museum's logo. There are souvenir mugs, coasters, badges, pencils and rubbers, T-shirts and sweatshirts for humans, and Bear Museum jumpers for bears.

Few bear-loving visitors to Stratford fail to discover the Teddy Bear Museum. In fact, it is the reason that many of them visit the town in the first place. But less well known is that Stratford has a second little museum that also includes teddy bears.

The **Doll & Toy Museum** is close to Shakespeare's birthplace, at the junction of Henley and Windsor Streets. The museum itself is tucked away behind an antique shop, but a small entrance fee gives admittance to the display area which holds a variety of toys. Among them are a good number of bears.

Some are in display cases, and include a number of later bears like Paddington as well as several older teddies. But more old bears are included in a nursery setting, in which there are also dolls, a rocking horse, an old pram and other nursery memorabilia. One or two wooden bears are on display, too, along with a number of Steiff animals and Merrythought's Thumper, the rabbit from the Walt Disney film *Bambi*.

The shop in front sells general antiques, and some modern bears by a local maker.

Bears can also be found at a whole string of other shops in the town. **The Trading Post** gift shop in Bridge Street was once the home of Shakespeare's daughter, Judith. Now its first floor includes quite an extensive range of bears, by manufacturers like Steiff, Hermann, Dean's and the North American Bear Co., as well as the popular cuddlies by Ty, and characters like Paddington and Pooh. They also have a fairly extensive range of dolls and doll's house furniture, and on my last visit I found bear-sized benches as well.

Downstairs are greetings cards and all sorts of smaller gift items, with some of them invariably bearish, like the Colour Box range.

Bakers Toys and Souvenirs, a stone's throw away in Henley Street, is owned by the same people and also has a few collectable bears by leading manufacturers among its soft toys.

There are a few more at the **Leather and Sheepskin Shop** in Sheep Street, alongside all the cuddly toys for children and the souvenir Stratford Bears and Will Shakespeare Beares. Next door, the **History Craft Factory Shop** is also worth a look, as their range of unusual giftware sometimes includes items of interest to bear lovers.

On the other side of the Leather and Sheepskin Shop, there should be some teddy bear designs among all the kits on sale at the **Needlecraft Centre**.

All over Stratford, there are other gift shops and specialist outlets which may have something of interest for the bear lover. One of my own favourites is **Once a Tree** in Bard's Walk. As the name suggests, its speciality is wood, including beautifully crafted wooden toys (trains, planes, etc.) that look so good with teddy bears.

If you fancy something a bit older, the **Antiques Centre** in Ely Street might provide interesting browsing. Or you could try getting up early on a Saturday morning to visit the large weekly car boot sale. At the time of writing, it is being held on the Cattle Market, close to the railway station, but there is talk of a possible move. The tourist office will be able to give you up-to-date information.

In addition, Stratford's **Civic Hall** has also seen a number of teddy bear fairs in recent years, so it might be possible to turn a visit to the town into an even more exhaustive bear hunt (see Events for Bear Lovers, page 343). This would, of course, leave even less time for exploring all the other places of interest in the town.

There are no fewer than five properties with a Shakespeare connection – three of them in the town itself, and two a short distance away.

One is the house where Shakespeare grew up, in Henley Street. It has seen some changes since then, and the original furniture is long gone. But it has been re-furnished in a style reminiscent of that which Shakespeare would have known.

In 1597, Shakespeare bought New Place, on the corner of Chapel Lane and Chapel Street, and it was there that he died in 1616. Sadly, only the foundations remain. The adjoining Nash House is still standing, and was once home to Shakespeare's granddaughter.

Hall's Croft, home to Shakespeare's daughter, can also still be visited. It is situated on Old Town, and houses a splendid collection of Tudor and Jacobean furniture.

Just over a mile outside the town is the picturesque thatched cottage which was home to Anne Hathaway before she became Shakespeare's wife. And four miles away, in Wilmcote, is the Tudor farmstead where Shakespeare's mother, Mary Arden, spent her early years. Glebe Farm, nearby, houses the Shakespeare

Countryside Museum which offers fascinating glimpses of life in rural Warwickshire since the time of Shakespeare himself.

The farmstead is just a short walk from Wilmcote Station, which can be reached by train from Stratford. If you have no car, one of the easiest ways to see all the Shakespeare properties is to take one of the bus tours which allow you to stop off at each for as long as you wish.

Stratford has numerous other interesting buildings, many of them picturesque, half-timbered constructions. So with all those bears to see as well, not to mention the beautiful trips on the river and possibly one or more visits to the theatre, a single day is really not enough to see all that the town has to offer.

There is another very good reason for spending the night, however. It is called the **Eversley Bears Guest House** and, as its name suggests, it is full of bears, many of which are on view to visitors.

When Judy and Clive Thomas first took it over, from an aunt of Clive's, Judy had not yet been bitten by the bear-collecting bug. She did, however, still have her childhood teddy, an adorable Chad Valley bear called Teddy Edward, and she had even worked for Chad Valley for six months when she first left school. She well remembers a visit to the factory by Harry Corbett, whose Sooty Bears were then being made by the company.

Judy's own passion for bears really started to grow soon after they moved into the house, although at first she would hide all the bears away unless she knew that any expected guests were themselves teddy bear lovers. Now, however, the Eversley Bears are very much a permanent fixture, crammed on chairs and shelves, in display cabinets and on floors. The walls are covered with pictures of bears and bears on plates, and there is even a whole collection of chocolate teddies, now long past their sell-by dates.

The range is enormous, because Judy's main criterion when buying a bear is not whether it is valuable or collectable, but whether it has an appealing face. She does make a point of buying all the Steiff limited editions made only for the United Kingdom, and she also occasionally chooses a bear simply because she does not have one of that particular make. But most are brought home simply because she has fallen in love with them.

There are some lovely old English bears, like a magnificent Chiltern Hugmee and a wonderfully soulful Farnell, not to mention several by Chad Valley (the result of her love for Teddy Edward, she believes, rather than her time at the factory). Modern English artist bears are now finding their way into the collection, too, but amongst all these collectables are many equally well-loved cuddlies. So bear lovers feel perfectly at home, whatever their own preference, and however well-hugged any bears that have accompanied them.

One of my own favourites is a teddy called Bingo, found by Judy at a local market. Sensors in his body can be used to activate his large repertoire of questions and comments, which can give quite a shock to the unwary. Give him a hug, for instance, and a loud voice may suddenly demand, 'Why did you hug me?'

He also loves asking people to scratch his chin, or various other parts a bear can't reach, and he has a disconcerting habit of coming out with totally appropriate responses to any remarks of your own.

Judy has a number of such novelties in her collection. She finds that they are useful illustrations when she gives one of her talks about bears, in aid of St John Ambulance.

She loves to talk to other collectors, too, and actually started a club for bear lovers, the Bear Talk Club. They have monthly Sunday afternoon meetings at the **Golden Cross** at nearby Ardens Grafton (near Bidford-on-Avon), where there are also many teddies and dolls on permanent display.

The club has welcomed a number of guest speakers, including

various American artists, and some of their members travel considerable distances to attend the meetings.

Much of the time is spent simply talking with fellow collectors, and there is nothing Judy likes better than talking about bears with her guests as well. Many is the night she has stayed up until the small hours comparing notes with other enthusiasts, especially when large numbers of bear lovers have descended on Stratford for one of the teddy bear fairs.

Rooms for the nights before such events can be fully booked anything up to a year in advance. But when her own six bedrooms are full (each sleeping anything from one to four people), she simply fills up nearby guest houses with bear lovers as well. Many of them then gravitate towards Eversley Bears at some stage, to meet up with other collectors and to see all the bears.

Some of the other guest houses offer evening meals, but Judy herself decided against it. There are so many places to eat in Stratford, and she felt that people would prefer more choice than she could offer. She does, however, send people off with a splendid cooked breakfast – just what you need before a busy day's sightseeing, or before making difficult decisions at one of the teddy bear fairs.

ADDRESSES

Bakers Toys & Souvenirs, 9 Henley Street; tel. 0789 267228
Civic Hall, Rother Street; tel. 0789 269332
The Doll & Toy Museum, 30 Henley Street; tel. 0789 292485
Eversley Bears Guest House, 37 Grove Road; tel. 0789 292334
Stratford Needlecraft Centre, 37 Sheep Street; tel. 0789 414388
The Teddy Bear Museum, 19 Greenhill Street; tel. 0789 293160
The Trading Post, 1 High Street; tel. 0789 267228
Tourist Information Centre, Bridgefoot; tel. 0789 293127

Sudbury

M ost **Museums of Childhood** have some bears in their collections, and that at **Sudbury Hall** in Derbyshire is no exception. Alongside the outstanding Betty Cadbury Collection of toys, dolls and games in the specially designed Toy Box Gallery is a case in which a teddy bears' picnic is underway.

About nine bears are on display at the time of writing. Their ages range from around ninety to a mere fifteen years or so. The earliest, known as the Edward Hall Grey Bear, is of an unknown American make. Another came from Sweden and dates from about 1920. The mother of his original owner sewed pieces on to his feet so that he could stand up on them.

Two more early bears are again of unknown make. But a relatively recent Rupert Bear was made for the museum, as was a modern Paddington. A Winnie-the-Pooh is of similar age.

One of the most interesting exhibits, however, is the much older Lieutenant Teddy Richardson. He wears a flared tunic and puttees, and his original owner told the museum that he was purchased in 1916.

In fact, Teddy Richardson is one of the many 'mascot' bears produced during the First World War.

Before 1914, many of the bears on sale in Britain were imported from Germany, from companies like Steiff. But of course that all changed when war broke out in 1914. Many new English soft toy companies were thus set up at about this time to fill the gap that had been left. One of them was Harwin.

By 1915, Harwin were producing teddy bears, and in 1916 they introduced a new range which they called the Ally-Bears. The bears wore a variety of Allied uniforms, and one was dressed as a Red Cross nurse. Taking centre stage in the company's adverts was a bear dressed in flared tunic and puttees, just like the bear at Sudbury Hall.

Naturally these very patriotic bears proved very popular during the war years. Many were sold by Hamleys toy shop in London. Harwin also produced dolls dressed in the same flared tunics and puttees as the teddies, and a number of animals were dressed in similarly patriotic outfits. The Ally-Bears continued to be made right up to the end of the war, when other mascots soon took over as favourites.

Very few of these bears are to be found today. Even fewer are still dressed in their original clothes, and that in the museum at Sudbury is also in particularly good condition. Keen collectors have been known to travel considerable distances just to see him.

By the time this book appears, the museum also hopes to have a large early Steiff on display, and there is always a large collection of what they call 'handling' bears, for children to play with.

But of course the museum has much more than just bears on view. Most of the toys date from the late nineteenth and early twentieth centuries, although some are earlier, and they range from eighteenth-century wooden dolls to modern Lego. (I'm told that they even have four Teenage Mutant Hero Turtles tucked away in the storeroom!)

Some of the toys are displayed in period room settings, which include a Victorian schoolroom and parlour, and an Edwardian day nursery. The latter contains a host of dolls as well as a doll's house, rocking horse, building bricks and ninepins, and there is a toy cupboard stuffed with other toys – among them marbles, lead soldiers and a model horse and trap.

Books, puzzles, games, clothes and prams are just a few of the many other items on display.

The museum is housed in a lovely Charles II building, well known for its wood carvings and plasterwork. It was once home to the Lords Vernon but is now a National Trust property, with a National Trust shop. On fine days, you can enjoy a picnic in the grounds, but lunches and teas are also available in what was once the coach house.

Sudbury Hall is thirteen miles to the west of Derby and six miles to the east of Uttoxeter, and can be reached by bus from either Uttoxeter or Burton-on-Trent stations. There is an hourly service between the two towns, and the buses pass Sudbury Hall.

It is open between April and October, each afternoon from Wednesday to Sunday (with the exception of Good Friday) and also on Bank Holiday Mondays. For exact times, telephone the number given below.

ADDRESS

Museum of Childhood, Sudbury Hall, Sudbury, Ashbourne, Derby; tel. 0283 585305

Warwick

Warwick probably has no more bears than many places not included in this book. But all the bear-related attractions of Stratford-upon-Avon mean that many collectors find their way to the area, and often take advantage of the opportunity to visit Warwick's medieval castle. It would be a pity if they didn't also seek out any places of bearish interest while they were there.

Naturally, the ancient castle holds little of bearish interest. But the splendid State Rooms include a magnificent Great Hall, built in the fourteenth century, and Madame Tussaud's have reproduced a late-Victorian houseparty, with the future King Edward VII and a young Winston Churchill among the guests.

The castle has many royal connections (it was once owned by Richard III, for instance) and there is much to see, including beautiful gardens landscaped by 'Capability' Brown. But the only bearish interest is the large bear and ragged staff to be found in the Great Hall. The bear and ragged staff were the heraldic badges of the Earls of Warwick. Now they form the Coat of Arms of Warwickshire County Council.

There are also generally some teddy bear gifts in the Castle gift shop, including little souvenir teddies whose sashes confirm that they were found in Warwick Castle.

Of slightly more direct interest than the castle for bear lovers is the **Warwick Doll Museum**, housed in the lovely Oken's House, not far from the castle. As its name implies, the museum's main focus is dolls, but the collection includes some interesting doll's houses, as well as various other toys and games. There is even a well-used games room where children can themselves play a game of hopscotch, or try out some other traditional toys. Bears are unfortunately rather thin on the ground, but a handful are scattered among the exhibits (hidden away in a doll's house, for instance).

The museum shop sells dolls and games as well as some teddy-related gifts, like the Colour Box miniatures and a few books. There are also souvenir teddies in Warwick jumpers, as well as Steiff animals and some postcards of museum exhibits (including one of their teddies).

There are many gift shops in the town, and some of these will also have bears and bear-related items. Many of the teddies will be cuddly soft toys, rather than more collectable bears. But on my last visit, I found some more traditional teddies among the cuddlies at **Present Days** in Swan Street. There were also some bears 'handmade in Cornwall' among the soft toys at **Touchwood** in the High Street although, as the name suggests, its speciality is wooden items.

In addition, Warwick has a number of general antique shops, both in the High Street and scattered around the town. Some may have the odd bear or interesting accessory, so it is worth taking the time to browse around them. The **Warwick Antique**

Centre in the High Street, for instance, gathers together some twenty-five specialist dealers, and the last time I visited them I spotted several bears of various ages.

Interestingly, though, I failed in my quest to find anything carrying the Warwickshire coat of arms, or to find any wooden carvings of the bear and ragged staff on sale. However, I did spot a fine pair on display at the Brethren's Kitchen, part of the medieval Lord Leycester Hospital at the western end of the High Street. This is therefore the ideal place to stop for light refreshments during the summer opening (Easter to October).

A large Alaskan bear with ragged staff can also be found in the entrance to the Warwickshire Museum in the Market Place, which covers the biology, geology and archaeology of the county.

The tombs of various Earls of Warwick incorporate bears, too – either with or without the ragged staff. That of Thomas Beauchamp in St Mary's Church is one. The feet of the effigy are resting on a bear. In the Beauchamp Chapel, the tomb of Richard Beauchamp again features an effigy with one foot resting on a bear. In addition, both the bear and the ragged staff can be seen in the tomb's inscription, as well as on the chapel's stained glass windows and carved into the wooden stalls.

Another bear can be seen on a brass commemorating Thomas Beauchamp's son, also called Thomas.

ADDRESSES

Present Days, 14 Swan Street, Warwick; tel. 0926 494927

Touchwood, 14 High Street, Warwick; tel. 0926 410575

Warwick Antique Centre, 22 High Street (Corner of Swan Street); tel. 0926 495704

Warwick Doll Museum, Oken's House, Castle Street; tel. 0926 412500

Tourist Information Centre, Court House, Jury Street; tel. 0926 492212

Wellingborough

Margaret and Gerry Grey were among the first people to recognize the collectability of new bears. They took new bears by Steiff and the Devon-based Little Folk along to collectors' fairs and swap meets at a time when even older bears were few and far between at such events.

Dolls were much more common. In fact, **Margaret and Gerry Grey** were themselves very much involved in the doll world. But they saw bears beginning to appear on people's stands at doll and toy fairs, and decided that this was something they should pursue.

When they opened their shop in The Old Bakery Gallery in Cambridge Street, Wellingborough, in the mid-eighties, it was filled with both dolls and bears. But it wasn't long before they began to run down the doll side of the business and turn their attention more and more to the bears.

They began selling artist bears by the likes of Nonsuch and the Old Fashioned Teddy Bear Company when such people were known simply as teddy bear makers, rather than artists. In those days, hand-made bears were more often found at craft fairs than at fairs for collectors, and there were few specialist teddy bear shops around.

Margaret and Gerry's tradition of encouraging artists has continued ever since, and their shop is invariably crammed with a wide range of splendid creations, many of which are exclusive to them.

In the early days, however, good British bear artists were relatively thin on the ground. There were plenty of people making teddies for children in their spare time, but there was a shortage of artists designing and making the kind of bears that would appeal to collectors.

In America, however, it was a different story. Long before modern 'artist' bears became so popular in Britain, they were becoming a major part of the teddy bear scene in America. So Margaret and Gerry began to study what was available there. There were still not many books on the subject (although artists were being featured in American teddy bear magazines). But they met some American makers in person at an international toy fair in London. One, Marcia Sibol, is still one of their most popular artists.

Within a year or so, they were the only British outlet for around six American artists. Now they sell the work of more than twenty. Most either sell exclusively through Margaret and Gerry in Britain, or supply them with bears that are not available anywhere else.

The range is inevitably stunning. But English makers have also been catching up fast – partly with the help of some bear-making workshops organized by Margaret and Gerry, and led by top American artists. So the shop also stocks a good number of bears by top British artists, again with many of their creations being made exclusively for the Wellingborough shop.

Needless to say, they also have bears by leading manufacturers, with an emphasis on the limited editions by Steiff, Hermann and Merrythought. What you won't find in large quantities, however, is inexpensive cuddlies. They do have a few (by Ty, for instance). But right from the outset, they decided that they needed to attract the quality end of the market, and that has remained their policy ever since.

They also sell a number of bear-related items like books, ceramic teddies, pictures, jewellery, clothes for bears, Winnie-the-Pooh items and greetings cards.

On Saturdays, collectors can even sit and enjoy tea and home-made cakes in the shop's upstairs tearoom, where some of the bears and dolls in Margaret and Gerry's own collection are also on view.

They also have a thriving business supplying mohair to bear makers in numerous colours and types. Anyone interested in buying can make an appointment to see the range (or can write for samples).

It is supplied in quantities as small as half a metre (or even a quarter of a metre for the very short-pile furs used by makers of miniature bears). So makers can buy sufficient for just a small number of bears and then move on to try something new. It's a far cry from the early days when makers like Nonsuch and the Old Fashioned Teddy Bear Company could only buy their mohair in complete rolls of thirty metres, and had no choice but to make huge numbers of bears from the same cloth.

Other bear-making supplies are also available, including glass eyes, joints and various stuffing materials (like the tiny plastic pellets).

Wellingborough itself has a long history, with evidence of prehistoric and Roman settlements in the area. It was said that it probably had more wells per acre than any other place.

Later, some of its mineral springs would even attract royalty – the young and childless French Queen of Charles I was one of many who came to take the waters (and nine years later she had borne five children).

The town was bombarded during the Civil War and then in 1738 about two hundred houses were destroyed by a fire. But some of the early buildings still remain, among them the Hind Inn (where Cromwell is reputed to have stayed in 1650) and a sixteenth-century yeoman farmer's house, now the Golden Lion Inn.

The best day for a visit is Tuesday, when there is also a busy antique market. It is just the right kind of place for a good rummage for accessories and props for your bears.

On Wednesday, Friday and Saturday there is a more traditional market.

ADDRESSES

Margaret and Gerry Grey, The Old Bakery Gallery, 38 Cambridge Street; tel. 0933 272123/229191
Tourist Information Centre, Wellingborough Library, Pebble Lane; tel. 0933 228101

Wellington

In 1963, a new town (Dawley New Town) was created in Shropshire, linking a number of existing developments into a single community. When, in 1968, the area covered by the new town was increased, it was renamed Telford, after the eighteenth-century engineer, some of whose greatest work was in East Shropshire.

One of the original developments was Wellington. Now it is clearly a suburb of Telford, but it was once a thriving town in its own right. It was also home to two manufacturers of soft toys, Chad Valley and Norah Wellings.

Norah Wellings actually designed toys for Chad Valley before she set up in business on her own in 1926, together with her brother Leonard. He took charge of the administration and marketing, while Norah herself designed all the toys and oversaw their production.

She is best known for her dolls, especially the many sailor dolls sold on the great ocean-going liners. Other Norah Wellings souvenir dolls, like the grass-skirted Caribbean Islanders, were on sale at the ships' ports of call. But she also produced a variety of animals like monkeys, rabbits and elephants and, of course, teddy bears. The latter are rarely seen today, and are much sought after by collectors.

Sadly, the place of Norah Wellings' Victoria Toy Works has now been taken by a petrol station and some private houses.

In the case of **Chad Valley**, however, one of the old factories is still standing, and can even be visited by those who are interested. For it is now home to just the kind of antique market that can provide good hunting for teddy bear lovers.

The Wrekin Toy Works, as they were called, were in operation there by 1920. But the Chad Valley history goes back much further. In fact, the company grew out of a printing and bookbinding business set up by one Anthony Bunn Johnson soon after Napoleon's defeat at Waterloo. The exact date is not known, but an 1850s letterhead claimed that the business had been in existence for 'upwards of 30 years'.

In 1860, two of Johnson's sons set up a similar business of their own, Messrs Johnson Bros. It was the son of one of these two brothers who then moved the business to the nearby village of Harborne. It became known as the Chad Valley Works, because a stream called the Chad ran nearby.

It was a range of cardboard games which started the company's progression from stationery to toys. Initially, they produced many educational toys (even Snakes and Ladders was designed to promote moral values). But the 1915–16 catalogue included a number of soft toys, including teddy bears.

At that time, many of the teddy bears sold in Britain were German imports, but the outbreak of war in 1914 left a gap in the market, which various British manufacturers endeavoured to fill. In fact, by the end of the war, Chad Valley's production of soft toys had increased so much that new premises were needed, and the Wellington factory was acquired. It was also then that the company changed its name to the Chad Valley Co. Ltd, although the Chad Valley trademark had been in use since 1897

The twenties and thirties were good years for Chad Valley, whose range expanded to include everything from card games to model villages. There were whole catalogues devoted to soft toys. A wide range of dolls was introduced, and animals of every description were created, with teddy bears being produced in many different sizes and fabrics. Soon the Wellington factory had to be expanded to cope with the output.

The 1930s, in particular, were a boom time for soft toys, and by 1938 the Chad Valley catalogue included a large number of different teddies. Soft kapok-stuffed bears were made in anything up to fourteen different sizes, from mohair, alpaca, amber plush, and assorted colours of a fabric known as art silk. (Pink, blue and green bears were all to be found.) There were also Cubby bear cubs in a permanently seated position, as well as a family of four dressed teddies and a bears' tea party made up of three bears plus table and chairs. Bears were made as nursery toys, too, and there were little mascot bears.

It was also in 1938 that Chad Valley was granted its Royal Warrant. Labels were added with the information that they were Toymakers to Her Majesty the Queen, the Queen in question being the wife of King George VI. Then, when her daughter became Queen Elizabeth II, the labels were amended to read Toymakers to H.M. Queen Elizabeth the Queen Mother. This change of wording can be very useful when trying to date a bear, since obviously a bear with the latter wording was made after 1952.

During the Second World War, toy making in the Wellington factory ceased. It turned instead to the making of children's clothes. But after the war, Chad Valley soft toys soon began to appear once more. A number of the older designs remained in the range, although some were now made in different fabrics, like the new nylon. But there were also many new creations. One of the best known is Harry Corbett's Sooty puppet, which also appeared as a fully jointed bear in 1954.

Gradually, mohair was supplanted by more and more synthetic fabrics, especially as the demand for washable toys grew. Expensive, traditional, jointed bears gave way to more and more inexpensive cuddlies. Even these, however, are more often sought out by collectors today, as a more affordable means of obtaining a bear with the Chad Valley name.

In 1967, when Chad Valley took over the Chiltern factory in Pontypool, some of their soft toy production was moved from Wellington to Wales. But it was the seventies recession which finally led to the closure of the Wrekin Toy Works, sometime between 1973 and 1975. (The Chad Valley name is now owned by Woolworths, who still sell Chad Valley soft toys, made in the Far East.)

The old Wrekin Toy Works now houses the **Telford Antique Centre**, a general antique market selling all kinds of bric-à-brac, kitchen utensils, pottery and porcelain, books, and a good deal more, including some collectors toys.

As so many of the area's residents once worked for one of the toy factories, or at least had a relative that did so, there is always just a chance of finding an interesting old teddy if your timing happens to be right. Otherwise, maybe one of the other old toys on sale will prove to be the ideal accessory for one of your bears, or you could find an inexpensive bear book or other bear-related item.

With more than eighty stalls, there is certainly plenty to browse around while remembering all the splendid toys that were once made in the building.

ADDRESSES

Telford Antique Centre, High Street; tel. 0952 56450
Tourist Information Centre, Thetford Chase, Telford; tel. 0952 291370.

NORTH

Beverley

Situated just to the north of Hull, Beverley's best-known buildings are the fourteenth-century St Mary's Church and the twin-towered thirteenth-century Minster. There are two market squares, while old narrow streets and a good number of small specialist shops add to the atmosphere of the town.

One of those specialist shops is the **Toy Gallery** in Lairgate. The building is Victorian, so owner Jackie Kendrew has tried to maintain a traditional atmosphere, with well-crafted toys and friendly, personal service. Her specialities are bears, collector dolls and quality wooden toys.

The shop is a Steiff Club Store, so there is a good range of Steiff bears, including limited editions, as well as dolls and animals. They stock Hermann, Clemens, Dean's, Canterbury Bears and Big Softies, too – again with many limited editions – and there are Winnie-the-Poohs from Gabrielle Designs. But you will also find a variety of bears by British artists. Dormouse Designs, Bo-Bear Designs, Bearwood Bears, Mister Bear, Teddies from Bearyland and Wood-U-Like bears are just some of those sold to date, and there have been various shop exclusives. They expect to have over 250 different bears to choose from at any time.

The Toy Gallery also sells some knitted clothes for bears, and has a few fashions for lady bears, too. In addition, there are a limited number of greetings cards and postcards.

The Toy Gallery, 46 Lairgate; tel. **0482 864890**
Tourist Information Centre, The Guildhall, Register Square; tel.
 0482 867430

Blackpool

With its three piers, famous Pleasure Beach and 500-foot
steel Tower, Blackpool is the kind of place you expect to
find lots of cheap and cuddly children's teddies and brightly
coloured souvenirs. But near the Town Hall in Market Street,
there is also a shop catering for the needs of the collector.

Bee-utiful Bears has bears by both British and German
manufacturers, including the Steiff limited editions and other
Steiff collectables. Hermann, Merrythought, Dean's and Canterbury are also there, as is the work of various British and American
artists. The styles are varied, with bears by leading names in the
teddy bear world as well as by some less-experienced local artists.
Redditoy, Bearwood Bears, Teddystyle, Crafty Bears, Mister
Bear, Imagine and Zena Arts are just some of the makers whose
work has been sold there.

A whole series of limited-edition bears with a circus theme
have also been specially created for the shop by various artists.

There are less collectable cuddlies as well, and a good number
of small, bear-related items including ceramic teddies, jewellery
and cards. The shop's logo – a bear with a bucket and spade, of
course! – has been turned into attractive brooches and keyrings,
and it is also being used on T-shirts and sweatshirts.

Elsewhere in the town, gift shops appear to sell only the
kinds of bears found on just about any High Street. Even special
Blackpool souvenir teddies were less prevalent than expected on

my last visit, although there were some among the cuddly teddies at the Pleasure Beach.

Visitors, however, are usually much more interested in all the rides, and the tallest roller-coaster in the world is scheduled to open there in 1994. Intended to dwarf even Nelson's Column, it is definitely to be recommended only for those with an exceptionally strong stomach.

No visit to Blackpool would be complete without a visit to another tall structure, the famous Tower (open daily during the summer but weekends only in the winter). It now combines a whole variety of attractions, from the magnificent Tower Ballroom (whose refurbishment used 6,750 books of gold leaf) to the creepy-crawlies of Bug World. The animal-free Tower Circus is also included in the price of admission, and brave teddies and their owners can send postcards to prove that they made it right to the Tower's top.

ADDRESSES

Bee-utiful Bears, 11 Market Street; tel. 0253 20304 (day), 0253 44932 (evenings)

Tourist Information Centre, 1 Clifton Street; tel. 0253 25212/ 21623

Bowness

Mention the Lakes to bear lovers, and the chances are that a picture of the Lakeland Bears will flash into their heads. A number of these friendly bears in their colourful togs are now available all over the country. But for many years the only place they could be found was Bowness, and that is still the place to go for a large selection of individually dressed bears available nowhere else.

Lakeland Bears were the brainchild of former art teacher Wendy Phillips, who had already built up quite a reputation as a designer of patterns for machine knitters. Her mother had a wool shop filled with beautiful yarns. But it was only when her son was born that Wendy really started to make use of them. She found hand-knitting far too slow, however, and decided to buy a machine.

At the time, picture knitting was very much in vogue, and she started knitting sweaters with pictures on. Soon she was selling her designs and the business grew so much that her husband gave up his teaching job as well, and the whole family moved up to the Lake District in 1986.

It was there that Wendy fell in love with a teddy bear, made by the Devon-based company Little Folk. She soon discovered that he was the ideal model for her designs. Up until then, her children had acted as models, but the novelty had soon worn off. The bear, however, not only stood perfectly still while his photograph was taken. He actually looked as though he was enjoying it as well.

The only trouble was that when people saw his picture in magazines, they wanted to buy him as well.

Wendy decided to ask Little Folk if they would provide her with a special 18-inch bear to sell by mail order, and soon she was having the time of her life creating a number of different characters, suitably dressed for a variety of Lakeland pursuits. One popular design was the fell walker, in warm outdoor clothing and wearing real wooden clogs. He became the Lakeland Bear logo.

Word of these special bears soon spread, helped by a splendid series of postcards photographed by Wendy's husband John. They took the bears climbing near Langdale, gathering litter near Tarn Hows, quarrying above Elterwater and fishing on Rydal Water – each time photographing them against the beautiful Lakeland scenery. In spite of the abundance of other Lakeland viewcards on the market, the new range was a huge success.

Many more cards have since followed. 'Raining again – Ullswater' and 'Another wet day in Borrowdale' are both particularly popular, with the bears brightly dressed in wellies and waterproofs. Others show the bears striding across the fells in their clogs, bee-keeping, shepherding, camping or simply admiring the view.

Needless to say, the success of the cards also increased the demand for the bears, and in 1990 Wendy and John decided to open a shop. Initially it was housed a little off the main tourist track in South Terrace, but in 1992 the bears moved to less spacious but more central premises at 2 Crag Brow.

Back in the nineteenth century, Crag Brow was already the resort's main shopping area, housing drapers, milliners, shoe makers, saddlers and a wide range of food shops. These days, visitors have different requirements, but the work of the old Victorian stonemasons and joiners can still be seen in the shopfronts.

No. 2 is only small, but visitors will find a large number of special Lakeland Bears that are only available here. The bears are factory made but their clothes are constantly changing, so it is impossible to say exactly what will be available at any one time. Those produced so far have included a beekeeper in a bee-covered sweater with honeycomb pattern trousers, leather clogs and a large straw hat. A sheep farmer was given a sheep-patterned sweater, corduroy trousers, tweed cap and clogs, and a baby lamb under his arm. And there have been backpackers carrying everything from map and compass, mintcake, water bottle and first-aid kit to their own sleeping-bags and a bag in which to take their litter home.

There have been a whole variety of other fellwalkers too. Some are dressed in real waxed jackets and Aran sweaters, with Herdwick tweed caps and trousers. Others sport colourful Fair Isle sweaters or sober tweed jackets (or sometimes both together), and there are girl bears wearing sensible jumpers and skirts. All wear the real leather clogs and carry their own walking sticks. Most have rucksacks, too, and may carry climbing ropes. Others could have a pet lamb or even a toy rabbit.

With all the clothes made specially for the bears in top-quality natural fabrics, and with the clogs alone costing as much as many a bear, the Lakeland Bears will obviously be beyond the range of many collectors. But bears are also available without the clothes for anyone who prefers them 'in the fur', or would like to try making the clothes for themselves.

In addition, a range of dressed Lakeland Bears is now being produced by the manufacturers of the bears, for sale at shops all over the country. These are also available from the Bowness shop, alongside all the individually dressed bears.

It is also possible to buy bear-sized rucksacks, and the special Lakeland Bear Country maps carried by most of the fellwalkers.

Naturally, the postcards are on sale in the shop as well, along with some other Lakeland Bear greetings cards. And there is Lakeland Bear fudge, shortbread or humbugs which make excellent gifts for bear-loving friends back home.

Lots of other teddy-related items are packed into the shop, including a whole variety of ceramic teddies as well as teddy tins and boxes, brooches, badges, magnets, rubber stamps, books, pictures and cards.

There are also many more bears. The Steiff limited editions tend to sell as soon as they come in, but they stock other Steiff bears as well – like the Classics range and the Original Bears. There are bears by Merrythought and Dean's, including limited editions, and some bears made not too far away in Carlisle.

Soft, cuddly bears fill some of the other shelves, and there are little souvenir teddies wearing Lakeland Bears backpacks.

On the walls are dozens of photographs of Lakeland Bears now happily settled in new homes. Inspired by John's magnificent postcards, many owners have sent Wendy pictures of their purchases in their new surroundings, or enjoying holidays at home and abroad. They have been used to turn any empty spaces in the shop into a colourful picture gallery.

In the old shop, there was room for some splendid bear displays, too. In the present building, space is at a premium. But they have still managed to include a couple of delightful scenes, with one colourful group of bears busily working away in a well-furnished kitchen and another enjoying a holiday in a gypsy caravan.

Holidaying bears and their owners will find greater comfort at **Bruin Lodge**, however – the former home of the Lakeland Bears, but now converted into a cosy holiday home. Situated in a quiet cul-de-sac, just a few steps away from the main street and a short walk from the current shop, the stone terraced cottage now comfortably sleeps up to four people, and any number of bears.

For humans there are two double bedrooms (one with a double bed and one with two singles), a comfortable dining-room and lounge (with colour TV) and a newly fitted kitchen with electric cooker, fridge/freezer and washer/dryer. There are bear books and magazines to read, and bear pictures on the walls.

What makes Bruin Lodge so different, however, is that the bears have been equally well catered for. In the lounge, they have their own table and chairs for relaxing. There's a bear-sized dining table and chairs, too, while upstairs they have their own comfortable beds – four in all, complete with soft mattresses and pillows. They have their own tea service, and even their own dresser containing bear-sized books and jigsaws to keep them happy on rainy days.

The house can be booked for full weeks throughout the year. Short-stay winter breaks of three days or more are available from November to March (excluding Christmas and New Year).

There is certainly plenty to see and do, whether staying for just a few days or for a full two weeks.

Lake Windermere and the steamer pier are just ten minutes' walk away. From there, boats depart for cruises on the Lake at frequent intervals throughout the season.

Windermere's Steamboat Museum in Rayrigg Road is also just a few minutes' walk away, with its displays of vintage craft and a photographic history of the Lake and the boats. As most of the displays are undercover, the museum is a good wet-weather venue, but when the weather is favourable it is also possible to take a steam launch trip on a vessel now more than ninety years old.

For the more energetic, the local information centre can supply leaflets mapping out a number of walks in the surrounding area, as well as round Bowness itself.

Beatrix Potter fans, however, will no doubt head for the World of Beatrix Potter in the Old Laundry Visitor Centre on Crag Brow. Bear lovers, on the other hand, will find the many gift shops worth investigating.

Past and Presents, opposite Lakeland Bears, have bears by Hermann and Romsey Bears, for instance, as well as the popular Tails and Tales bears by Golden Gifts and Windermere Bears in guernsey-style jumpers.

They stock various teddy ornaments, too, and a number of small accessories that could be just right for a special bear. I found good-sized chairs and some lovely musical instruments, including guitars and violins suitable for a fairly large bear as well as trumpets large and small.

Several other shops have bear-related gifts, while **Unicorn Antiques** at 1 Longlands on Lake Road makes interesting browsing for those looking for small 'props' to enhance their bear displays. It was crammed with interesting little jars and pots on my last visit.

There are more gift and antique shops in nearby Windermere, and **Beech House** in Beech Street also has a number of bears – among them some Steiff Classics, Bunbury Bears, souvenir Windermere Bears and various cuddlies.

ADDRESSES

Bruin Lodge Holidays, PO Box 5, Windermere, Cumbria, LA23 3AN; tel. 05394 45417

Lakeland Bears, 2 Crag Brow; tel. 05394 88479

Past and Presents, Crag Brow; tel. 05394 45417

Beech House, Beech Street, Windermere; tel. 05394 44099

Tourist Information Centre, Glebe Road; tel. 05394 42895 (closed winter)

Tourist Information Centre, Victoria Street, Windermere; tel. 05394 46499 (all year)

Castleton

Situated in the Peak National Park, halfway between Sheffield and Stockport, the village of Castleton (population around 750) is best known for its Norman castle and its various caverns. Thousands of tourists visit each year, and numerous gift shops have opened to cater for them. As is so often the case, where there are gifts, there are also bears.

Roger and Maggie Vincent opened **Causeway House Crafts**

in 1979, in what had once been a farmhouse (now their home), a butcher's shop and a number of outbuildings. Initially they sold only British craft products, with hand-thrown pottery a speciality. But when they doubled the size of the shop a few years ago, they knew they would have to be far more 'commercial'. Nevertheless, they still try to seek out things that are just that bit different.

These days, their stock generally includes around two hundred different bears. Some are from major manufacturers like Steiff, Hermann, Merrythought and Dean's. There are Big Softies, and bears by Gabrielle Designs, too, as well as cuddlies from the Manhattan Toy Company. But there are also individually made bears from various British artists and makers. Names like Barbara-Ann, Bearbury of London, Bearwood, Bocs Teganau, Brenda Brightmore, Chasing Rainbows, Naomi Laight, Little Treasures and Marie Stott are among those that have been stocked to date.

Various bear-related items will also be found, including stationery and cards, brooches, fridge magnets, various ceramic teddies, T-shirts, pictures and books. But of course there are still many other gifts and crafts on sale which have nothing to do with bears at all.

A coffee shop called the Cinnamon Bear is adjacent to the shop.

Of course, you may find bearish items at other gift shops in the village. But there are also various non-bearish attractions.

Peveril Castle, for instance, was built by William Peveril, son of William the Conqueror, soon after the Norman Conquest. And the area is especially well known for its caves. The Great Cave in nearby Peak Cavern is the largest interior cavern open to the public in Britain. (It is reached via a low passage known as Lumbago Walk!) At Speedwell Cavern, half a mile to the west of the village, you can take a boat ride through the workings of an eighteenth-century lead mine. Treak Cliff Cavern's Dream Cave is packed with glinting stalactites and stalagmites, while Blue

John Cavern contains particularly rich veins of the rare and beautiful Blue John stone, found only in Castleton. Jewellery and ornaments made from Blue John can be bought in the village.

Several old customs have also survived in the village. Best known, perhaps, is the Garland Ceremony on Oak Apple Day, 29 May. In addition, a Curfew Bell is rung on winter evenings, and at Christmas, unique Castleton Carols can still be heard at the George Hotel.

For those dependent on public transport, bus 272 runs from Sheffield Station to Castleton.

ADDRESSES

Causeway House Crafts and Cinnamon Bear Coffee Shop is technically in Back Street, but it is easier to find if you remember that it is next door to the school; tel. 0433 620343

Tourist Information Centre, Castle Street; tel. 0433 620679 (closed weekdays in winter)

Tourist Information Centre, The Crescent, Buxton; tel. 0298 25106 (all year)

Chester

The picturesque walled city of Chester is just the kind of place where you would expect to find plenty of interest to bear lovers. It is a browser's paradise, with many small shops of the kind that tend to harbour bear-related items. It also has a number of places of more concentrated bearish interest.

Its teddy bear shop is in Lower Bridge Street, and goes by the name of **Bridgegate Teddy Bears**. Clearly aimed at the tourist as well as the collector, its exclusive offerings have so far included not just inexpensive teddies wearing Bridgegate Bear jumpers, but also a number of specially packaged edibles. Clotted cream caramels, humbugs and fruit drops make unusual bearish souvenirs.

Many of their bears are by manufacturers like Steiff (including the limited editions), Canterbury, Big Softies, Dean's and the North American Bear Co. They stock Paddington, always a favourite with tourists, and the popular cuddly teddies by Ty. But I did find some artist bears there as well.

There were also plenty of greetings cards and bearish gifts, ranging from keyrings to towels and with a variety of Winnie-the-Pooh items.

There are more collectable bears at the large **Toycraft** toy shop in Watergate Street. They generally stock a good range of bears by Steiff, Hermann, Merrythought and Dean's, with both cuddly toys and the limited editions (although the Steiff collectables rarely stay on the shelves for long). You may find a few Canterbury Bears, too, and again the popular Paddingtons.

Also in Watergate Street are some of Chester's many antique shops. But, as is often the case in such popular tourist destinations, these tend to be the rather up-market variety, which are less fertile hunting-grounds for bear lovers.

For those who just want to look there is, however, a shelf of old, and not so old, teddies at the **Chester Toy Museum** on Lower Bridge Street. Lovers of Farnell bears may also be interested to see their 1930s Farnell Alpha soft doll, still in her original dress. Although Farnell bears are now much coveted by collectors, the company was originally much better known for its huge range of dolls.

The museum has more soft dolls, by Norah Wellings, who once designed for the famous Chad Valley toy company. She produced some bears, too, but these are rarely found today.

Less cuddly items make up most of the museum exhibits. The collection of cars includes a whole room devoted to Matchbox Toys, and there are tin toys, farm animals and some pop memorabilia, including a 1954 juke box (one of several still-working coin-in-the-slot machines). A museum shop sells mainly toy cars, with a few inexpensive bears.

The museum is actually situated *above* Lower Bridge Street, in one of the unique covered walkways known as the Rows. Stairways lead up from the street to these galleries, off which is a second tier of shops. It literally adds an extra dimension to your shopping, especially as many of the shops are small specialists. Several of the Watergate antique shops are on the upper level.

In fact, walking round Chester can be very hard on the neck, for above many of the modern shop fronts are the black and white buildings for which the town is famous.

Another will be found close to the river, in Lower Bridge Street, just inside the Bridgegate. It was built in 1664 and was the town house of the Earls of Shrewsbury. Later it became an inn, the Bear and Billet. There are over a thousand panes of glass in its rows of windows.

Some buildings in Lower Bridge Street are even older. In fact, number 29/30, known as the Tudor House, is believed to be the oldest house in Chester, built around 1503.

The city's architecture covers a whole variety of styles. The Castle, which dates back to the days of William the Conqueror, was rebuilt in a Classical style in the late eighteenth and early nineteenth centuries. There are some well-preserved Georgian terraces, while Victorian contributions include a splendid Town Hall with a 48-metre tower. The Victorians also carried out a good deal of restoration work on Chester Cathedral, parts of which date back to the twelfth century.

Around them all, the City Walls form a two-mile circuit, restored and re-fashioned in the early eighteenth century to create an elegant walkway which can still be enjoyed today. The Tourist Information Centre, opposite the Cathedral, sells the ideal souvenir of such a walk – inexpensive little 'Chester' Bears, whose sashes proudly proclaim that they come from England's Walled City.

ADDRESSES

Bridgegate Teddy Bears, 56 Lower Bridge Street; tel. 0244 344600

The Chester Toy Museum, 13a Lower Bridge Street; tel. 0244 346297

Toycraft, 35 Watergate Street; tel. 0244 342706

Tourist Information Centre, Town Hall, Northgate Street; tel. 0244 318356

Clitheroe

Within easy reach of Preston, the Dales and the Lakes, Lancashire's Ribble Valley combines splendid walking country with interesting old towns and such attractions as Sabden Treacle Mines and the wartime nostalgia of Wendy's Memory Lane in the grounds of Whalley Abbey. There you will find a grocer's shop and drapery from the era as well as wartime toys.

The main shopping centre in the area is the market town of Clitheroe, whose many small shops include one selling over forty different kinds of sausage.

In King Street, on the other hand, the **Ribble Valley Bears** are busy trying to take over Suzanne Charles' designer fashion shop. It all started with just a few teds alongside all the clothes. But they sold so well that more joined them, and now the shop has a growing selection of both manufactured and artist-made bears.

There are limited editions by most of the major manufacturers, including Steiff and Merrythought, but the range also includes bears by top artists, several of whom are making exclusives specially for the shop. They carry Ribble Valley Bears labels on their feet, leaving no doubt as to exactly where they came from.

Some of the most popular cuddly teddies are on sale as well, alongside some special Ribble Valley souvenir bears. A number of bear-related gifts and teddy bear greetings cards can be found, too, while the owner's fashion background has resulted in a good selection of jewellery.

On my last visit to Clitheroe, I found more Steiff bears at the **Kaydee Bookshop** in Moor Lane and, of course, any gift shops are another possible source of items of interest to bear lovers.

In addition to all the shops, Clitheroe boasts a Norman castle. There is also a museum which includes reconstructions of cloggers' and printers' workshops, and re-creates life in an Edwardian kitchen.

ADDRESSES

Ribble Valley Bears, 40 King Street; tel. 0200 28909
Kaydee Bookshop, 26–30 Moor Lane; tel. 0200 22698
Tourist Information Centre, 12–14 Market Place; tel. 0200 25566

Cockermouth

The birthplace of poet William Wordsworth has remained relatively unspoilt despite its popularity with visitors to the Lake District. Situated in north-west Cumbria, some twenty-five miles to the south-west of Carlisle, the town's attractions include Wordsworth House, where the poet was born, and the **Cumber-**

land Toy and Model Museum. Most of the museum's few teddies are new ones, but there is a wide range of other toys on display.

Bear lovers, however, will probably find themselves drawn even more to the **Cumbrian Quilt Works**. Situated in Market Place, it is not only the place to go if you are thinking of buying a quilt, or want to have a go at making one yourself. Alongside all the country quilts, the fabrics, threads, cutting boards and other tools of the trade (and books to help you use them), you will also find a growing band of teddy bears.

They estimate that there are usually more than a hundred and fifty on sale at any time. Steiff, Hermann, Big Softies and Canterbury Bears are all represented, with limited editions from all four companies included in the range. America's North American Bear Co. and Gund are there, too, as well as inexpensive bears from the Boyds Collection.

There are some artist bears, too, including the odd shop exclusive. But there are also plenty of bear-related items like stationery, rubber stamps, tins, pictures, greetings cards and postcards. Continuing the craft theme of the rest of the shop, there are bear-making and stitch kits as well, and a range of printed bear fabric – some of which is made up into waistcoats, ties, blouses and so on.

There are even handmade Shaker-style bears, for the shop's other specialities are Americana and country crafts. They sell Shaker-style boxes, pails and peg racks, for instance, in addition to all the quilts, cotton 'throws', cushions and other soft furnishings, and the wide range of plain and printed cotton fabrics. American doll patterns are also available, and dolls can be made up on request.

Look out for the Christmas ornaments, too (generally including some bears). They are on display all year round.

Other places to visit include a Working Museum of Printing, housed in a building which dates back to the sixteenth century, and the Creighton Mineral Museum, which includes a collection of minerals from northern England as well as miners' lamps and tools.

A trial bus service has been running from Penrith to Cockermouth. The Tourist Information Centre will be able to supply up-to-date details.

ADDRESSES

Goose Bearies, Cumbrian Quilt Works, 39 Market Place; tel. 0900 828498

Tourist Information Centre, Town Hall, Market Street; tel. 0900 822634

Douglas, Isle of Man

Just thirty-two miles long and twelve miles wide, the Isle of Man has its own money, its own stamps, and its own unique customs and traditions. Visitors are attracted by the unspoilt countryside and sandy beaches (and, thanks to the warming Gulf Stream, the island's good sunshine record). But above all, they enjoy the gentle pace – the 'time enough' approach to life. Or, as it is known in Manx Gaelic, *Traa dy Liooar*.

Up until quite recently, however, they would have been hard put to find any good, traditional teddy bears on the island.

It was a problem Judith Woods discovered when she began to develop an interest in bears herself, and eventually she decided to do something about it. She opened **BearFootin'** in the island's capital, Douglas, in May 1992.

It is actually just a part of a family-run business in the main shopping area, where they also sell compact discs, videos, T-shirts, and suchlike. But Judith generally manages to keep about a hundred bears in stock, ranging in price from around £30 to £300.

They include bears manufactured by Steiff, Hermann, Merrythought and Big Softies, including limited editions produced by those companies. But there are also individually made bears from Bo-Bear Designs, Naomi Laight, H.M. Bears, Bearaphernalia and various other British makers.

Judith is always on the look-out for new lines to offer her customers. With a resident population of only 70,000 and, being on an island, no surrounding catchment area, she wants people to keep on coming back.

In addition to the bears, she also stocks some bear-related items, like china.

Other attractions in Douglas itself include the House of Keys, home of the Manx Parliament, and the Manx Museum which takes you through 10,000 years of Manx history.

Horse-drawn trams operate on the promenade during the summer months. There is a steam railway, and the Manx Electric Railway still uses original 1890s rolling stock for its run from Douglas to Ramsey, which offers some fine views of the island.

Of course, the island is known as the Road Racing Capital of the World. Annual events include not only the famous Manx Grand Prix and various other motor-cycle race meetings, but also a Kart Racing Grand Prix, car rallies and classic car races, and an International Cycling Week.

ADDRESSES

BearFootin', 69 Strand Street; tel. 0624 629717

Tourist Information Centre, Harris Promenade; tel. 0624 686766

Garstang

It was in 1310 that Edward II authorized the Lord of the Manor of Garstang (in Lancashire) to hold a weekly market there. By the sixteenth century it had disappeared, but it was revived in 1597 and is still held every Thursday. These days, however, it is not confined to the Market Place, but stretches right down the High Street, attracting visitors from many surrounding villages into the small town.

The railway passed Garstang by and, as a result, the old town centre has not been subject to the kind of redevelopment that has marred more accessible towns (although the arrival of the motor car brought it within easy reach of Preston, and there are now frequent buses to both Preston and Blackpool).

There have, however, been some recent changes in Thomas's Wiend, one of several narrow 'wiends' which run back from the High Street to the old Back Lane (now Park Hill Road). Among the small shops and businesses in the new Thomas's Court is one that will instantly attract any bear lovers, **Bearing Gifts**.

As the name suggests, it is as much a gift shop as it is a bear shop. But a large number of the gifts are teddy-related. As so often happens, the bears are making a determined effort to take over.

'Traditional bears with character' – and which are not too expensive – tend to be their best sellers. So although they stock Steiffs, Merrythoughts and Dean's bears, you will not find many limited editions here. Canterbury Bears, Bransgore, Big Softies, Little Folk, Nisbet, Ty and Heirloom are other names that you might find. But it is impossible to say exactly which, as the range is changing all the time. Owner Sue Inman prefers to keep ordering different bears, rather than ones that have been successful in the past.

The bear-related gifts include books, pictures, ceramic teddies, wrapping paper, brooches and magnets, as well as Winnie-the-Pooh and the Rupert merchandise. Little pine stools and chairs – intended for toddlers – can be painted to order with a teddy design, and may be just the right size for a bear.

The shop also sells a range of baby sweaters, machine-knitted and then hand-appliquéd by Sue herself. Again, one of these may suit a bear in your collection, although they are rarely sold for this purpose. (Sue has found a distinct lack of interest in dressed bears in Garstang.)

You may find some inexpensive bear-sized clothes on the market, too, or the occasional bear-related gift in one of the other shops as you take a look round the rest of the small town. Its places of interest include an eighteenth-century Town Hall, and a church and school dating from the same period (the latter now used as an arts centre).

ADDRESSES

Bearing Gifts, 7 Thomas's Wiend, Thomas's Court (off High Street); tel. 0995 604745

Tourist Information Centre, Council Offices, High Street; tel. 0995 602125

Kirkby Lonsdale

The ancient market town of Kirkby Lonsdale in Lancashire has the advantage of being situated right between the Lake District and the Yorkshire Dales, with all the attractions of the two National Parks just a short drive away. It was included in the Domesday Book in 1086 (under the name Cherchebi, or village with a church) and has a school dating from the time of Queen

Elizabeth I. Visitors, however, are more likely to be attracted by the beautiful scenery (described by art critic John Ruskin as some of the loveliest in the whole of Europe) and by welcoming inns which date from the seventeenth and eighteenth centuries.

There are attractive small speciality shops as well, and a market every Thursday. But bear lovers will probably want to head three miles south (on the B6254) to Newton Holme Farm, between Whittington and Arkholme. There they will find the workshop and showroom of traditional wooden toymakers **Tobilane Designs**.

They make all kinds of wooden toys – doll's houses, farms, castles, toy boxes, some rocking sheep known as Woolly Rockers and some spinning Trapeze Teddies. There are toys which swing or tumble, turn or twirl, spin or rock, all made in a converted stone barn and on sale in the adjacent toy shop.

Also in the shop, however, are traditional toys made elsewhere, and these include both soft dolls and a growing number of teddy bears.

At the time of writing they generally have about fifty bears on sale at any one time. But the number is growing by the month and the range, of course, is changing all the time. Included are bears manufactured by Germany's Hermann and Britain's Big Softies. But they are not planning to stock those made by Steiff, preferring instead to concentrate on individually made bears.

Like most new shops, Tobilane Designs found it difficult to build up their stocks of artist bears at first, since so many artists find demand for their work far outstrips their ability to supply. As a result, they tend to build up long waiting lists.

Nevertheless, Tobilane's early acquisitions included shop exclusives from Bearwood, Jay-Bee, Bearaphernalia, Redditoy, Marie Stott, Whisty Bears and Willow Bears, as well as the work of a number of new or little-known makers. More are arriving all the time.

They also receive many visits from owners whose bears are

in need of surgery, and hope to have set up a bear repair service to help them by the time this book appears.

ADDRESSES

Tobilane Designs, Newton Holme Farm, Whittington, Nr Carnforth; tel. 05242 72662

Tourist Information Centre, 24 Main Street, Kirkby Lonsdale; tel. 05242 71437

Liverpool

City centres are rarely good hunting-grounds for teddy bear collectors, and Liverpool is no exception. Many of the shops are those found in every High Street, and although there are some cuddly bears (in Lewis's, for instance) and Winnie-the-Poohs (in the Disney Store), there is relatively little of interest to the serious collector or anyone wanting something a little bit different.

George Henry Lee in Basnett Street, is, however, a branch of John Lewis, and its toy department therefore stocks the Merrythoughts made specially for the John Lewis stores. Its gift department also offers some of the Merrythought limited editions.

Out at Albert Dock, however, things become even better. **Just Teddies & Friends** in the Britannia Pavilion has a wide range of collectables as well as shelves crammed full of cuddly toys.

Steiff, Merrythought, Dean's, Hermann, Big Softies, Canterbury, Nisbet and Bransgore are just a few of the names to be found, with a good number of limited editions among the bears on offer. They are also happy to order Steiff animals for interested collectors, and will gladly obtain any bears that may be missing from the shelves but are still available from the manufacturer.

They offer a repair service for sick and injured teddies, too. But when I visited, they had no artist bears, and no immediate plans to add any to their range. As the Dock attracts a large number of tourists, they find that there is more call for Paddingtons, many of which go to Australia and New Zealand, and for soft and cuddly bears by manufacturers like Ty.

Also on sale are various resin teddies – by Small World, for instance – as well as greetings cards and postcards featuring teddy bear photos and drawings.

The Dock is home to many other small specialist shops and gift shops where you may find something with a teddy bear theme. Present Company, for instance (also in the Britannia Pavilion) has Pooh and Paddington items, including some of the bears, as well as cuddly ranges like those by Andrew Brownsword. There are also various bearish gifts, including Colour Box miniatures.

Many of the Dock's other attractions have nothing to do with bears at all, however. For a start, Albert Dock is the largest group of Grade I listed buildings in Britain, with five massive warehouses built entirely of non-combustible materials – brick, granite and cast iron – and providing a total of 1.3 million square feet of floor space. It closed in 1972, but a £100 million refurbishment has turned it into one of the most popular free tourist attractions in Britain.

It is home to the award-winning Merseyside Maritime Museum, the Tate Gallery Liverpool with its displays of twentieth-century art, the new Museum of Liverpool Life, and Animation World, where original sets, models and drawings help to reveal some of the animators' secrets.

For many, however, Liverpool still means the Beatles, and the Beatles Story is told here by means of films, photographs, recordings, Beatles memorabilia and even a reconstruction of the famous Cavern, where the Beatles were playing when discovered by future manager Brian Epstein.

It was another Liverpool group, Gerry and the Pacemakers, who immortalized the *Ferry Across the Mersey*. Ferries depart from the pierhead near the Dock, and there are hour-long cruises on the mile-wide river.

Liverpool has a total of 2,500 other listed buildings. There are two cathedrals. The Anglican is the largest in the country, while the Roman Catholic cathedral has an ultra-modern design, with the congregation circling the altar. There are two universities, too – one the origin of the term 'redbrick'.

Liverpool also has more Georgian architecture than Bath. The Liver Building's clock face is larger than that of Big Ben. The city's Chinese quarter is the oldest in Europe, with street signs in both English and Cantonese. So there is plenty to hold the interest of bear lovers and non-bear lovers alike.

ADDRESSES

Just Teddies & Friends, Unit 16, Britannia Pavilion, Albert Dock Village; tel. 051 707 0650

George Henry Lee, Basnett Street, tel. 051 709 7070

Tourist Information Centre, Atlantic Pavilion, Albert Dock; tel. 051 708 8854

Lytham St Annes

Just a few miles away from all the brashness of Blackpool is the relative gentility of Lytham St Annes, which attracts large numbers of summer visitors. There are golden sands, pleasant gardens and a good selection of shops, while both Lytham and St Annes also cater in some way for the visitor who loves bears.

First stop for most will be the **Toy and Teddy Museum** in St Annes with its host of childhood memories. A number of old bears have made their home there. There may be little information on identities or origins, but the appealing faces are more than adequate compensation.

The museum also contains over two hundred dolls – wax, china, composition, bisque, celluloid, as well as a number by the well-known soft toy maker Norah Wellings. She originally designed toys for the Chad Valley Company, whose bears are now extremely popular with collectors. But later she set up in business on her own in the same area. Her dolls are especially well known, but she did design a few teddies as well.

Many bear collectors love doll's houses, too, and there are over thirty in the museum. There are also a number of rocking-horses, as well as cars, planes, trains, Meccano construction sets, toy washing-machines and cookers, games, books and all the other things that have delighted children over the years. Keen bear collectors will no doubt notice the clockwork toys made by Schuco, whose Yes/No bears and other novelty teddies are much sought after today.

The museum shop sells bears by various manufacturers and a handful of artists, and there are generally some Steiff limited editions in stock. Postcard collectors, on the other hand, will be especially pleased to find a large number of teddy bear postcards featuring museum residents, and there are various small gift items, too.

Other shops in St Annes have the more soft and cuddly teddies. (I found a good number in **J. R. Taylor**, the Garden Street department store, for instance.) But nearby Lytham also has a gathering of collectables.

Paul Goodlad's **Wellbeing Centre** in Clifton Street is primarily a health food and aromatherapy outlet. But he also sells a variety of gifts and has been expanding this part of his business. Included are quite a few bears. I found some by Steiff (including limited editions), Hermann, Merrythought, Canterbury, Nisbet and Big Softies, as well as one or two artist bears. There were teddy bear miniatures and figurines, original paintings (by a local artist) and prints, and a variety of bearish gifts.

The shop also sells some dolls and doll's house furniture, and the way in which everything is mixed up together helps to create a delightful atmosphere.

Lloyds in Park Street, on the other hand, has some of the popular ranges of more cuddly bears. **Tiggywinkle** in Clifton Street's Shopping Arcade has soft toys, too, including some of the softer Steiffs and Merrythoughts, while some of the Lytham gift shops also have some bear-related items. There is the possibility of an old bear at **Clifton Antiques** in Market Square, too, although the only bears I saw there were some attractive (modern) garden ornaments.

ADDRESSES

Toy and Teddy Museum, 373 Clifton Drive North, St Annes; tel. 0253 713705

The Wellbeing Centre, 36a Clifton Street, Lytham; tel. 0253 794179/752563

Clifton Antiques, 8 Market Square, Lytham; tel. 0253 736356

Tourist Information Centre, St Annes Square; tel. 0253 725610

Manchester

Ironically, the major cities can be poor hunting-grounds for bear lovers. But Manchester is better than some – if you know where to look.

Its specialist teddy bear shop, for instance, is actually under a gift shop, **Harriet and Dee**, situated in Police Street, just off the pedestrianized section of King Street (near Deansgate). Owner Irene Bayliss opened up her basement in 1990, although she had been selling Steiff bears before that. Now she finds she is catering for a wide range of customers – not just collectors, but mothers and grandmothers as well, not to mention all the students who fill the town during term time.

Many collectors go for the Steiffs, of course, and the shop generally has a good number in stock, including the limited editions and a few animals. There are limited-edition Merry-thoughts, too, as well as some of their other bears. Hermann, Dean's and Canterbury Bears are also represented, and they order most of Big Softies' boxed limited editions, in addition to their ever-popular Edward.

At the time of writing, however, the shop has only a very limited number of artist bears, and no plans for any significant increase.

There were, on the other hand, lots of Paddington Bears, which are always popular with the students. So, too, are Winnie-the-Pooh and Rupert, and Irene tries to keep a constant supply of these in stock. Then there are the cuddly teddies, like the Ty bears, which seem to appeal to everyone from the smallest child to many quite serious collectors. And for the tourist there are traditional bears wearing special Manchester Bear jumpers.

In addition, the shop has a good range of bear-related items, such as jewellery, pictures, magnets, greetings cards, wrapping paper, and a particularly wide range of miniatures of various makes. There are also mugs which have been made specially for them, showing a teddy bear in front of Manchester's famous Town Hall.

Upstairs in the gift shop are even more teddy bear ornaments, including those by Colour Box and Lorrie-Mac as well as pewter teddies. Among the rubber stamps are some featuring teddies, and the Squiggles Bear, which can be covered in signatures, is a popular alternative to leaving cards and the like.

Although bears can be found in various other Manchester shops, collectors may find few of interest in many of them. **Kendals** in Deansgate (close to the teddy bear shop) had only a very limited selection of bears on my last visit, for instance, although the range will no doubt increase at Christmas. I found some Steiff Original Bears with a handful of cuddly Petsys and animals. Merrythought were mainly represented by piles of policeman bears, some golfers and a cricketer, and there were cuddly toys from the Far East.

Manchester has a massive shopping area, and its Arndale Centre is one of the largest covered shopping areas in Europe. But even good toy shops seem to be few and far between there. There are some gift shops, however, and these are often a source of the more cuddly teddies as well as the occasional collectable and all sorts of bear-related items. In the Arndale Centre's Voyagers Walks, for instance, I found a single Raikes Bear and one or two traditional Dean's teddies, as well as a host of popular gift ranges.

Nearby, in the Royal Exchange Antique Basement (opposite Marks & Spencer), is something of real interest for collectors of old bears. **Irving Antiques** specializes in old toys and that includes teddies. When I visited, those on display were mainly of English manufacture. But if you are looking for something special, it is worth giving them a call in advance, in case they have something which is not out on view.

Among Manchester's other attractions, of course, are the **Granada Studios** at Castlefield, and there, too, you will find a teddy connection. For it is Granada that makes the Sooty TV shows. A 20-minute Sooty show was among the many attractions when last I visited, and there is a special Sooty & Co. shop as well. On sale are Sooty, Sweep and Soo puppets and soft toys, as well as various videos, games and souvenirs.

A special Granada Bear in checked cap, dungarees and scarf is also available from several other shops on the site.

Coronation Street souvenirs are everywhere, too, and some of them (notebooks, for instance) are small enough to be included in teddy bear displays by collectors who are avid viewers of the series.

The backstage tour, which forms the highlight of any visit, includes an opportunity to walk down the Street itself and see all the famous landmarks. There are also visits to an editing suite and a production control room, a chance to see a whole host of special effects, a look at the work of the make-up and wardrobe departments, and even a chance to be photographed outside No. 10 (a great favourite with children).

With various other shows and attractions, it would be easy to spend a whole day on the site. But it would be a pity to miss all the city's other attractions. The Museum of Science and Technology is nearby, for instance. It stands on the site of the world's first passenger railway station.

Manchester also has a Museum of Transport, and is home to the National Museum of Labour History. There is a Police Museum, too (appointments necessary), and the Manchester United Museum and Tour Centre is a popular attraction. Most of the museums (like the studios) are closed on certain days of the week (especially in winter), so it is advisable to check opening times with the Tourist Information Centre if you are planning a visit.

There is the Cathedral, too, mainly built in the fifteenth century. And a splendid Victorian Gothic Town Hall contains nearly a thousand rooms and two and a half miles of corridors. You can also take a ride on the new electric supertram, which runs from Bury to Altrincham, with several city centre stops. Alternatively, if you simply want to shop 'til you drop, that is always easy in Manchester – even though the bears are thin on the ground in some areas.

ADDRESSES

Granada Studios Tour, Water Street; tel. 061 833 0880
Irving Antiques, Royal Exchange Antique Basement; tel. 061 834 1427 (shop)/061 740 9601 (home)
The Manchester Teddy Shop, Harriet & Dee, 7 Police Street; tel. 061 832 6632
Tourist Information Centre, Town Hall Extension, Lloyd Street; tel. 061 234 3157/8

Ribchester

With its rolling hills, fast-flowing rivers and quiet country lanes, the Ribble Valley to the west of the Yorkshire Dales is just made for walking or cycling – and far less crowded than the Dales themselves, or the Lake District to the north. Its ancient villages are also steeped in history and, what's more, the village of Ribchester – site of a Roman garrison – also has a very definite attraction for teddy bear lovers.

The **Museum of Childhood** includes more than three hundred resident teddies, augmented from time to time by many more temporary visitors taking part in special exhibitions.

Owners Ankie and David Wild particularly like to find bears with interesting backgrounds. So this is not the place to go to find the largest number of rare and expensive Steiffs, although you will certainly find some splendid early examples on display. Alongside them, however, are bears whose age and manufacturer are less important than the stories they have to tell.

Probably the best known is the little six-inch teddy who managed to survive the sinking of the *Titanic*. He belonged to the Italian-born Gaspare Gatti, who sailed as catering manager on the ill-fated ship. Sadly, Gatti himself was one of the hundreds who drowned when the *Titanic* hit an iceberg and sank within three hours on the night of 14 April 1912. Being a member of the crew and a man, he would have been one of the last in line for a place in a lifeboat. When his body was recovered, the little bear was still tucked inside his tobacco pouch, which he kept in the tail pocket of his dinner suit.

The bear had belonged to his small son Vittorio, who gave the toy to his father just before the ship sailed. It was eventually returned to Gatti's widow, Edith, along with her husband's pipe. She kept them with her for the rest of her life.

Later, the bear also survived being bombed out of his home during the Blitz, as well as various less traumatic house moves.

When Edith died, he was handed down to her son, his original owner, and it was Vittorio's widow who decided to offer the bear to the museum in Ribchester. Her grandchildren were arguing about who should inherit the bear, and she decided that this way they would all be able to enjoy it.

He now sits in his own special case, along with a photograph of Gaspare Gatti, his pipe, and some *Titanic* memorabilia. There is also one of the special *Titanic* Bears, based on the small survivor, which were made by the English soft toy makers Merrythought to mark the eightieth anniversary of the sinking of the *Titanic*.

Another resident in the museum is a well-travelled 1905 Steiff, who once belonged to a member of the Debrett family. A whole group of appealing but unidentified bears, on the other hand, all came from a single collection. Ankie Wild's own childhood bear is there, too, and so is a bear that was once a fairground prize, in the 1920s.

There are old bears made of wood, glass and metal, and there are later bears which include modern limited editions and character bears like Paddington and Pooh.

The teddy bears on their own would make a fascinating exhibition, but equally interesting are some of the displays which include no teddy bears at all.

They have one of the largest collections of doll's houses in the North, for instance – some fifty altogether, although they change the display from time to time, so not all will be on show at once. In one house, the pieces of furniture still have all the original price and import tags which were attached when they were imported from Germany into Sweden (where Ankie Wild was born) around 1900.

Ankie has a special interest in doll's houses and doll's house miniatures, which is how the teddy bear collection also came to include fifty minute bears tucked inside a goose egg.

Another stunning display, in the same room as most of the bears, is a splendid working replica of an Edwardian fairground. There are roundabouts, a big wheel, cakewalk, steam yachts and all the other fun of the fair, complete with a barrel-organ and authentic fairground music. It took the model-maker ten years to build – a real labour of love.

Every room in the museum contains still more interesting displays. Cars, trains, lead soldiers, farm animals, card games, money boxes, and relatively new arrivals like Noddy, Snoopy, the Flintstones, and characters from *The Magic Roundabout*. Some of the museum's collection of a thousand costume dolls, from eighty different countries, are also on view, as well as many other dolls and soft toys, and two hundred small hand-embroidered figures, all sewn by their original owner.

Some of the displays have been painstakingly researched by Ankie and David, with folders of their findings available for visitors to read. (Photocopies can be purchased to take home as well.) There is information on 'General' Tom Thumb, for instance, to go with a case of mementoes of the man who grew to be little more than two feet tall.

Punch and Judy is another area they have studied, on account of the museum's Punch and Judy collection, most of which is Victorian. But one of the fattest folders relates to the most unusual exhibit of all, Professor Tomlin's Flea Circus. In addition to the tiny tricycles and roundabout ridden by the fleas, the chariots that they pulled and the swords used in the duels, the museum has gathered all sorts of material about the circus, including a video of a 'Look at Life' film which showed it in action.

Ankie and David wanted to use their museum to show that grandfather's childhood wasn't all bleak. In doing so, they have created something that should appeal to all ages, be they bear lovers or not.

Bear lovers, however, will no doubt be delighted to discover that there is also a well-stocked museum shop. Among the bears for collectors are Steiff and Merrythought limited editions, as well as bears by other manufacturers and by a variety of artists. Some of the artist bears are exclusive to the museum, and include a Museum Bear made by Norbeary. Others have included some unusual Scandinavian bears, made from colourful old ticking for those who want something really different.

There are other toys in the shop, too, including dolls and doll's house miniatures. And there are plenty of little pocket-money items as well. Again, these include a number which are made specially for the museum, like thimbles, bookmarks and pens, and a variety of postcards (including several which feature bears). There are also some inexpensive souvenir teddies, wearing T-shirts or ribbon sashes carrying the name of the Museum.

It comes as no surprise to discover that Ribchester's Museum of Childhood has repeatedly won the Best of the North-West award.

ADDRESSES

Museum of Childhood, Church Street; tel. 0254 878520
Tourist Information Centre, 12–14 Market Place, Clitheroe; tel. 0200 25566

Sheffield

When people think of Britain's fifth largest city, they generally think of its industry. But half of the city is inside the Peak National Park, and its specialist teddy bear shop is just ten minutes by car from the moors.

Basically Bears is actually a short drive or bus ride from the city centre – on Sharrow Vale Road, at Hunters Bar. The street contains many other specialist shops, and is particularly lively on a Saturday.

The range of bears is not huge (it is biggest around Christmas and St Valentine's Day). But they have some by Hermann,

Dean's and Merrythought, Big Softies, Canterbury Bears and Bransgore, and there are generally some limited editions among them.

The range of artist bears changes constantly – Bearwood Bears, Teddystyle, Imagine and Changelings are among those they have stocked, as well as Catherine While's miniatures which are made relatively nearby in Chesterfield.

There are bears by some local bear makers, too, and owner Kath Fells and her husband John also make some themselves, under the Basically Bears label. The fact that they are handmade in Sheffield from Yorkshire mohair has proved to be a great attraction to their customers.

Both Kath and John design the bears, and they work together to complete them – each doing everything from machining, stuffing and jointing to the all-important finishing of the faces.

Like a number of other makers, they carried out bear repairs before they began making bears themselves. It was the first time in years that such a service had been available in Sheffield, and they found themselves in great demand. Bears arrived by post from a wide area as well as being brought in by concerned owners.

They still undertake repairs. But now every spare moment is spent making bears, especially during the summer when the shop is at its quietest.

They sell some inexpensive ranges in the shop, too, like Golden Gifts' Tails and Tales, and teddies by Russ Berrie and the Manhattan Toy Company. There are also some bear-related items, including ceramic miniatures, tins, Winnie-the-Pooh merchandise, postcards and greetings cards (some of which are handmade locally).

What you won't see very often, however, is an old bear for sale. Kath confesses that people do occasionally bring one into the shop to be sold. But being a keen collector herself, she finds she can rarely face parting with them.

Sadly, the city centre itself is less promising as far as bears are concerned. There are shops enough, although the massive new Meadowhall centre has taken much of the business away. But most supply the functional rather than the frivolous, and there is little to interest the bear lover.

Cole Brothers, a John Lewis store, is an exception. Its toy department (in Cambridge Street, a few yards away from the main store) generally has some of the Merrythoughts made specially for John Lewis, as well as other children's bears from this and other manufacturers.

Then, a short walk from the Cathedral in Devonshire Street, is **Clutterbuck's** traditional toy shop. It is a Steiff Club Store, so they have a large range of Steiff bears in stock, including many limited editions as well as the popular Original and Petsy Bears. There are Hermanns, too (again including limited editions), and they usually have a good number of favourite character bears like Pooh, Paddington and Rupert.

You will also find bears out in the large, modern Meadowhall Shopping Centre. **Teddies in the Lanes**, part of Little Treasures, has various makes, for instance. They concentrate mainly on British bears, with Big Softies, Canterbury Bears, Dean's, Bransgore and H.M. Bears among those to be found. But they also have some by Germany's Hermann.

Santoro Graphics, on the other hand, has some of the Steiff collectors bears as well as some inexpensive teddies.

So Sheffield really is a town where you can spend all day shopping. But there is a good deal more to see, especially if you are interested in the city's industrial heritage.

There are many factory tours during the summer months, for instance, when visitors can see the famous cutlery being made, or garden tools, or toy soldiers. There is a bakery making 6,000 loaves, 47,000 doughnuts and 25,000 scones an hour. Another company makes curtains, cushions and duvet covers. One factory turns out boxes for everything from Easter eggs to tuning forks, and another manufactures 45,000 tonnes of toilet paper and tissues each year. All open their doors to visitors on certain dates.

The city also has a number of industrial heritage sites, where you can see craftsmen at work or admire some fine old Sheffield plate and cutlery. In addition, Sheffield is home to the South Yorkshire Fire Museum, the Turner Museum of Glass and the Sheffield Bus Museum, although opening times are very limited in some cases.

Among the historic buildings is the Cathedral Church of St Peter and St Paul, rebuilt in the fifteenth century, and with later additions in the sixteenth, eighteenth and twentieth centuries.

The Tourist Information Centre has full details of tour dates and opening times for the various attractions, and also takes bookings for the factory tours.

ADDRESSES

Basically Bears, 390 Sharrow Vale Road, Hunters Bar; tel. 0742 687183

Clutterbuck's, 112 Devonshire Street; tel. 0742 754889

Santoro Ltd, 53 High Street, Meadowhall Shopping Centre; tel. 0742 568660

Teddies in the Lanes at Little Treasures, 34 The Lanes, Oasis, Meadowhall Shopping Centre; tel. 0742 351645

Tourist Information Centre, Town Hall Extension, Union Street; tel. 0742 734671/2

Skipton

The busy Yorkshire market town of Skipton is known as the Gateway to the Dales. But the town itself has plenty of attractions to prevent visitors from moving on. Not least for bear lovers is **Jack Henry Bears**, situated in Victoria Court, right in the heart of a Conservation Area.

The airy, L-shaped shop is considerably larger than most, which is just as well as it welcomes a constant stream of both browsers and serious collectors. In fact, so many noses are pressed eagerly against the shop's windows that cleaning them has become virtually a daily necessity.

The shop is run by Carol Walmsley, herself a keen bear lover, as is her mother Jenny who assists her in the venture (when not caring for the young Jack Henry, after whom the shop is named). In fact, Jenny has been collecting bears for over ten years, and her knowledge of the bear world has been put to good use.

The shop specializes in artist bears and within a week of opening had the work of some thirty different artists on sale – no mean feat when many bear makers have waiting lists of several months. Alongside bears by some of the country's top artists are creations by others who have yet to make their name, and the range includes many exclusive limited editions, since Carol and Jenny know how much appeal such bears have for collectors.

Among the artist bears on sale to date have been the work of Teddystyle, Heritage Bears, Willow Bears, Fluff and Stuff, Bocs Teganau and Dormouse Designs, while Jan Galleymore of My Old Ted is making a special (unlimited) Jack Henry Bear, dressed in a little waistcoat, like the bear in the shop's logo.

In general, however, the range changes constantly, as both Carol and Jenny continue to look for interesting new bears to offer their customers.

They sell bears by most of the major manufacturers as well, among them Steiff and Merrythought (including both companies' limited editions). There are cuddly bears, too – by Ty, for instance – and less expensive bear-related items, including the Colour Box miniatures. As with the bears themselves they also keep a constant eye open for more unusual items, the main criterion being that everything should be well made. A potter, for instance, is making honey-pots specially for them.

Also on sale are dried flowers and dried flower arrangements, a legacy of mother and daughter's previous careers as florists. Jenny had a thriving business in Blackburn, and Carol's arrangements were a popular feature. Now the bears and flowers have proved to be a popular combination.

Like most towns which attract large numbers of visitors, Skipton also has a number of other shops with something of interest to bear lovers. Some excellent children's clothing shops are worth a visit by anyone looking for something special in the way of bear wear, for instance. **Busy Little Bees** in the Craven Court Shopping Arcade is one shop with an attractive selection.

Next door, **Over the Moon** has a variety of teddy bear ornaments and other teddyish gifts, while a number of other gift shops in the town have cuddly teddies or teddy-related items. One such is **Recollections** in the High Street, a pretty shop whose range includes bears by companies like Ty and Russ Berrie as well as a variety of ornaments and other bearish gifts. When I visited, they had some handmade bears, too.

Bears are not all that Skipton has to offer, however. The town has more than nine hundred years of history behind it (it is in the Domesday Book), and there is still plenty of its past to see.

It has, for instance, a long tradition as a market town. It is known that there was a weekly market at least as far back as 1311, and market stalls still line both sides of the High Street on Mondays, Wednesdays, Fridays and Saturdays.

The High Street and adjacent Sheep Street also contain a number of buildings of historical interest. Some date back to the late eighteenth century although, of course, the shop fronts are of more recent date.

There is a splendidly preserved castle, too – much of it built in the late thirteenth century, although some parts originated in Norman times. The castle was extended in the mid-sixteenth century, and substantially restored some hundred years later. It is open virtually every day, although only in the afternoons on Sundays.

The Leeds–Liverpool Canal reached the town in the eighteenth century. Now visitors can enjoy canal cruises or pleasant towpath walks. For railway buffs, on the other hand, the Embsay Steam Railway offers a nostalgic two-mile ride from nearby Embsay Station to Holywell Halt. And, of course, the Yorkshire Dales are right on the doorstep for those with more time to explore.

ADDRESSES

Jack Henry Bears, Victoria Court, Victoria Street; tel. 0756 799882

Tourist Information Centre, Victoria Square; tel. 0756 292809

Southport

For more than two hundred years, Southport on Merseyside has been attracting holidaymakers and day-trippers eager to escape the noise and bustle of nearby Liverpool. In the nineteenth century it was developed as a high-class resort for the 'well-to-do'. Today, it offers miles of sandy beaches, beautiful gardens, a large shopping centre and Britain's second-longest pier. The latter has its own railway carrying passengers for nearly a mile along its length, and crossing the country's largest man-made lake in the process.

The town's main boulevard, Lord Street, is one of the widest in Britain, lined on its western side by smart shops. Their elegant iron and glass canopies run the full length of the street.

One ornate portico marks the entrance to Wayfarer's Arcade

(originally known as Leyland Arcade) – a splendid piece of Victorian architecture with a domed roof of cast iron and glass. There you'll find both a statue of world-famous steeplechaser Red Rum (a native of Southport) and the town's Steiff Club Store, **Wayfarers Arts**.

This massive gift store sells everything from small gift items to furniture and has a wide range of teddy bear ornaments as well as a good number of teddies.

There are Steiffs, of course, with limited editions, Classics, Original and Petsy Bears, as well as various animals. Hermann are represented, too, and the Merrythought range includes some of their limited editions. But there are also cuddly toys (by the Manhattan Toy Company, for instance, and the ever-popular Paddington and Pooh.

There are more bears at the pretty **Poppins** gift shop, just a short walk away in Market Street, on the opposite side of Lord Street. Many of their teddies are sold for newborn babies rather than collectors (they have a gift service which is well used by the local maternity unit). So most are of the cuddly variety, by companies like Ty. They do have a few Merrythoughts, but again these are mainly the children's toys rather than the collectables.

Other bears are made by the shop's owner Ann Bentley, and include a long-legged Bentley Bear dressed in Highland regalia, complete with sporran. His clothes can be made to order in the tartan required.

She will dress other bears to order as well, researching a uniform, for instance, and then making a bear-sized version of it. But the shop's biggest sellers are bears for christenings.

They used to sell only teddies, but branched out into other gifts at the height of the recession. (A popular line is monogrammed lacy cushions.) They still have a number of bear-related gifts, however, ranging from ceramic miniatures to a few teddy bear books. There are also greetings cards and wrapping paper.

In addition, a teddy repair service is available for those who have seen better days.

The back streets of Southport contain other interesting small shops. Browsing around them is a relaxing way to pass the time in a town where it is still possible to enjoy a more leisurely pace of life.

ADDRESSES

The Wayfarers Arts Ltd, The Wayfarers Arcade, Lord Street; tel. 0704 532514
Poppins, 20 Market Street; tel. 0704 545632
Tourist Information Centre, 112 Lord Street; tel. 0704 533333

Sowerby Bridge

A large warehouse on a busy main road, half a mile from town, is not really the place one would expect to find a splendid selection of collectable teddies. But **Memory Lane**, a ten-minute drive from Junction 24 on the M62, is worth a considerable detour. Upstairs is everything from antique pine furniture to jugs, bowls and cutlery. Downstairs is a room absolutely crammed with dolls and teddies.

Old and new sit happily side by side, and it is one of those shops where you have to keep looking again, because there will always be something you miss. Many people have likened it to a museum. But that implies a certain sterility, which is certainly not the case here. New bears are arriving all the time, so others are constantly being shuffled along to make room for them. And if the result is 'a bit untidy', as Memory Lane's Lynda Robinson puts it, no one minds at all.

Lynda and her husband Keith not only have a large number of bears for sale, they also have a sizeable collection of their own at home. So they know what collectors want, and are happy to put in plenty of effort to ensure that they will find it.

As one of the Club Stores for the German manufacturer Steiff, they naturally have a large number of that company's bears, including limited editions, the Classics and some of the Original Bears, as well as a good selection of other animals. There are more German bears from Hermann, again including limited editions, while the British bears include Merrythoughts, Dean's, Bransgore, Canterbury Bears and Nisbet.

From America, they have some of the distinctive Raikes Bears, with their carved wooden faces, as well as the Gund limited editions, and they also stock the inexpensive Boyds Collection.

But they are always on the look-out for something new and unusual for collectors, and write to makers all over the world trying to find something different. Memory Lane was one of the first British shops to start stocking artist bears from Australia, for instance – not just from one maker, but from several at once.

The range of artist bears naturally changes all the time, with most being made in small editions, but there are invariably a variety of shop exclusives in stock. Lillibet have produced a number of innovative designs specially for them. The Yorkshire-based Imagine Bears, from Bradford, make a special Yorkshire Dales Bear, available only from Memory Lane. There is an exclusive Yorkshire Ted made from Melrose Yorkshire mohair by Mme ZuZu, also based in the county. And offerings from local bear artist Sonia Hall Scott include unique, one-off bears made from fabric she dyes herself to give something just a bit more out of the ordinary.

There are more Yorkshire-made bears, but others come from all over Britain, as well as from other countries.

They always try to have a good number of older bears as well, and these often include some bought in France, which

Lynda and Keith visit regularly. Many, however, are English, of both known and unknown heritage.

Also on sale are old dolls, dogs, cars and other toys, while modern bear-related items like ceramic miniatures are crammed into any remaining small spaces. You'll need to look several times before you can be sure you've seen it all.

It is also worth having a look at all the furniture and other items in the rest of the warehouse. Their speciality is pine furniture, both antique and reproduction, and you can usually watch something being renovated while you are there. (They offer a complete stripping and waxing service.)

Beds, trunks, tables, chests of drawers, chairs and cupboards are just some of the pieces to be found, so if you are looking for pine furniture on which to display some bears you might find just what you want.

All sorts of other bits and pieces are dotted about – pottery, for instance, and cutlery. Or you can ask to see their splendid selection of old linen, which includes a good deal of lace. Again, some of the pieces might enhance a teddy bear display, or might be made of just the fabric you need to make a suitable outfit for an old bear.

From the warehouse, it is just a short drive to the town of Sowerby Bridge itself, where several of the old mills are still standing. But Halifax, too, is just one and a half miles away, with its Piece Hall now home to many craft, antique and other small specialist shops. Adjoining the Piece Hall is the fascinating Calderdale Industrial Museum, whose exhibits include an original Spinning Jenny and Flying Shuttle Loom and other textile and factory machinery, as well as reconstructions of Halifax Streets in the mid-nineteenth century, and much more. At nearby Hebden Bridge, you can explore the World of the Honey Bee. And it is only eight miles to Haworth, one-time home of the Brontë sisters.

ADDRESSES

Memory Lane, 69 Wakefield Road, Sowerby Bridge; tel. 0422 833223

Tourist Information Centre, The Piece Hall, Halifax; tel. 0422 368725

York

It is easy to see why so many visitors return to York again and again. A prosperous medieval city, built over and around a Roman one, it is one of those places which seems to have everything.

Over half the country's medieval stained glass can be found there – much of it in the splendid Minster, built between 1220 and 1472. There are two and three-quarter miles of city walls to walk, savouring the magnificent views of the town within. Fascinating museums delve into the city's colourful past, and the narrow medieval streets and alleyways are a browser's paradise, with countless small shops all vying for the visitor's interest.

Bears are everywhere. Gift shops offer teddies in just about every shape and form. The Minster has its own small teddies, with sashes to say where they were found. And **Famous Names** in Stonegate offers souvenir City of York Bears, as well as Heartbeat Bears for lovers of the television series and bears proclaiming allegiance to football teams from all over the country.

The busy, pedestrianized Stonegate is also home to one of York's more specialist teddy bear shops, which ensure that bear lovers are among those who return to the city. **Stonegate Teddy Bears** opened in May 1990 and welcomes a never-ending stream of both tourists and teddy collectors every day of the week.

It sells bears by many of the major manufacturers. Steiff and

Hermann are well represented, with limited editions from both companies included in the range. Dean's and Merrythought are there, too (including the limited editions), as well as the North American Bear Co.'s Muffy and the Tails and Tales range from Golden Gifts.

A number of artist bears can be found as well. But a distinctive feature of Stonegate Teddy Bears is the large number of bears which are actually made in Yorkshire.

Many are by Big Softies, based in Ilkley, West Yorkshire, and they include some bears that are made specially for the shop – among them the Official City of York Bear, which is a great favourite with visitors.

Various artists have also made bears specially for the shop. Again, a good number are made in Yorkshire. Barnsley's Brenda Brightmore has made a whole family of special Stonegate teddies, for instance.

A few old bears are usually on sale as well, while modern Paddington Bears are a favourite with the tourists, and there are plenty of inexpensive, cuddly teddies for those who prefer them.

A characteristic of the shop, however, is the huge number of bear-related items to be found there. Some, like mugs and keyrings, are specially made with the shop's logo. There are Stonegate Teddy Bears thimbles, and a special little Transit van with 'Teddies in Transit' emblazoned on its sides. But there is also an unusually wide range of other 'bearabilia' guaranteed to appeal to the thousands of visitors who pass by every day.

On my last visit, the list included tea towels, tins, trays, ceramic miniatures, soap, showergel, boxes for the tooth fairy, rubbers, magnets, greetings cards, postcards and chewy bear gums, not to mention a whole variety of items featuring Winnie-the-Pooh. I've also seen money boxes, Christmas decorations, posters, lollipops, chocolate teddies, cookie moulds, locally made dough bears and clocks, book-ends and even tiny, teddy-shaped bath confetti – and the list is far from complete.

They have also had a number of postcards produced specially for them, including one that features the Official City of York Bear.

While Stonegate Teddy Bears bulges with browsers from morning 'til night, there is quite a different atmosphere in the shop of another York teddy specialist, **Mary Shortle**. Situated in Lord Mayor's Walk, just off the main tourist track, her shop enjoys a much more leisurely pace. It is also absolutely crammed full of teddies old and new, not to mention dolls, doll's houses and doll's house miniatures, and a good deal more besides.

It is a wonderfully cluttered shop. Nothing has a special place, but the seemingly haphazard nature of it all really encourages leisurely browsing, and it is easy to spend hours looking at all there is on offer.

Mary and her husband Chris started selling general antiques in the shop in the early eighties. But in 1984 they made the decision to specialize in bears and dolls, and sold everything else at auction. In those days, old bears were much easier to find, and much less expensive, than they are now. There were still large numbers hidden away in attics and cupboards, and no one attached much value to them.

Over the years things have changed. Certain bears have fetched huge sums at auction: the most famous, Happy, went to an American buyer for a staggering £55,000 in 1989, and another American collector parted with £24,000 for a rare black bear the following year. As a result, many more old bears have been brought out of those attics and cupboards to be sold to avid collectors for steadily increasing sums.

The number of old bears still hidden away is thus going down all the time, making it ever more difficult for dealers to find sufficient for their needs. Many have therefore begun to sell more modern collectables as well. Mary Shortle is one of them.

She still, of course, has as many 'oldies' as she can find, so there is generally a good range to choose from. But she also sells a large number of modern bears, from a variety of sources.

They include many Steiffs, ranging from the highly collectable limited editions to the cuddly Petsys often bought for babies and young children. But on my last visit I also found the largest number of Clemens bears I have ever seen. Like Steiff, this company is based in Germany where they have been producing high quality teddy bears since the 1940s.

Some other collectable German bears are made by sigikid. And Mary had replicas by the Austrian company Berg before most shops even knew they existed.

There are some British bears, too (including a number of artist bears), and they also stock North American Bear Co.'s Muffy. But again, Mary and Chris have tried to include plenty of bears that were made in Yorkshire. So you will find more Big Softies here, in addition to the work of some Yorkshire artists.

Favourites with grandmas, however, are the traditional bears by Real Soft Toy, while large Rupert Bears by Lefray are another popular line. The shop also sells many inexpensive bears, of various kinds, to ensure that there is something for everyone. There are small pewter and ceramic teddies as well.

Large numbers of dolls old and new fill further shelves. Many of them are made by top German artists. Mary and Chris visit

Germany themselves to meet the artists and buy their dolls, and at the same time invariably come home with interesting bears.

There are doll's houses and doll's house miniatures, too, and generally quite a few gollies as well, not to mention other toys and games that creep into any empty spaces.

Mary and Chris are always threatening to remove some of the clutter and tidy the shop up. But for collectors that is really part of its charm. You never know what you might find, and even if you come away empty-handed, you'll have had a thoroughly enjoyable time looking.

If you are interested in Steiff bears, however, a shop not to be missed is **Steads** in Goodramgate. A toy and baby shop, it could easily be missed by the unwary collector, but it is also a Steiff Club Store.

Needless to say, it therefore has a particularly good range of the German company's bears, including their limited editions, and also offers a very large number of Steiff animals. In addition, there are bears by British companies like Canterbury Bears and Dean's (although no limited editions when last I visited), and they also sell popular character bears like Winnie-the-Pooh and Paddington.

Their wide range of toddler-sized clothes may also be of interest to collectors looking for something special in which to dress a favourite bear.

It would be very easy to spend all your time in York doing nothing but look for bears. But there are so many other attractions, you could find that the bears hardly get a look in.

One of the most popular with visitors is the famous Jorvik Viking Centre, where visitors can journey back a thousand years to experience the sights, sounds and even the smells of this stage in York's past. Queues for the museum can be very long, however, so a visit early or late in the day might be advisable.

The splendid Castle Museum, situated in two former prisons, is another favourite with visitors. More than 26 *million* people have passed through its doors since it opened in 1938 – 98 per cent of them from outside York. Many return again and again to see its visions of the past, which include a whole street of Victorian shops and businesses (bank, watchmaker, apothecary, general store and post office, spirit and wine merchant, and many more).

Period rooms range from a Jacobean dining room to a nineteenth-century moorland cottage to a 1940s kitchen and a front room at the time of the present Queen's Coronation. There are agricultural implements, household equipment, military memorabilia and ball gowns. And a children's gallery includes dolls and other toys. The only bear I found, however, was on an Ursa Major Star Card, but the dolls included a Chad Valley Snow White from the late thirties and a Steiff doll in the uniform of a 1914–18 French soldier.

I found no teddies in the museum shop, either, but there were some Yorkshire-made, traditional wooden toys of the kind that go well with teddy bear displays.

ADDRESSES

Mary Shortle, 9 Lord Mayor's Walk; tel. 0904 425168/631165
Steads, 74 Goodramgate; tel. 0904 624335
Stonegate Teddy Bears, 54 Stonegate; tel. 0904 641074
Tourist Information Centre, De Grey Rooms, Exhibition Square;
  tel. 0904 621756/620557

SCOTLAND

Cupar, Fife

Teddy bear shops are remarkable by their absence in most of Scotland. But the market town of Cupar in Fife is a rare exception. Just an hour by train from Edinburgh, and even less by car (across the Firth of Forth), Cupar became a Royal Burgh in 1328 and is now the administrative centre of North-East Fife.

Many visitors touring Scotland find their way to the town during the summer months, and there are a number of small gift shops to cater for their needs. The most interesting for readers of this book will be the **Bear Pad** in Bonnygate. Owned by Claire and Tom Oakman, it has a variety of bears as well as a wide range of greetings cards and other bear-related items.

Claire is a real bear lover herself, with a fast-growing collection of her own, and confesses that bears on sale in the shop often manage to find their way home with her. Those that remain are from a number of makers – Steiff, Merrythought, Dean's, Canterbury, Gund and Bransgore, for instance, as well as Scotland's Jay-Bee bears. She tries to keep most of her prices under £50, however, which means that only an occasional Steiff limited edition will find its way on to the shelves.

Souvenir Cupar Teddies (made in the Channel Islands), are naturally popular with visitors.

The shop also sells various teddy-related items, like ceramic miniatures of various makes and a number of teddy bear postcards. A local artist provides a range of teddy bear stationery, and also paints teddy bear portraits.

There is some doll's house furniture on sale, too, and Tom will even make up complete doll's houses from kits for a very reasonable price.

Further down Bonnygate, at No. 93, **Luvains Bottle Shop** usually have some tartan-clad teddies, some of which come with 'the smallest bottle of whisky in the world'. (The whisky is also sold separately.) And Hendry's Giftware back at No. 3 include Colour Box miniatures and other teddy-related items like mugs among their huge range of gifts.

ADDRESSES

The Bear Pad, 37 Bonnygate; tel. 0334 55751 (evenings); closed
  Sundays and Monday mornings
Tourist Information Centre, 78 South Street, St Andrews; tel.
  0334 72021

Edinburgh

To the casual observer, Edinburgh may not seem like a particularly good hunting-ground for teddy bear collectors. The secret is knowing where to look. A large number of bear colonies are scattered throughout the town, and the shops are full of bear-related gifts and tiny accessories. It would be easy to spend a whole weekend seeking them all out, although it would be a pity to miss Edinburgh's many other attractions.

One of the most popular haunts for visitors is the Royal Mile, which stretches from the Castle to the Palace of Holyroodhouse. The mile in question is actually a Scottish mile, which is two hundred yards longer than an English one. But most of the shops of interest to bear lovers are concentrated at the Castle end.

At first glance, they would appear to have nothing to offer

the serious collector, being filled with souvenirs aimed at the typical tourist. But some of the tartan accessories could add a splendid splash of colour to a teddy bear display.

On my last visit, my own haul included tartan baby shoes (just right for one of my bears), a miniature volume of Robert Burns' poems with a tartan cover, and a reel of tartan ribbon 'woven by members of the Scottish Tartans Society'. I also found bear-sized tartan bags and tam-o'-shanters, while some of the child-sized Aran sweaters on sale would fit a larger bear.

If you wanted something extra special you could even have a proper kilt made to fit your bear – at a price. **John Morrison (Highland Outfitters) Ltd** at 461 Lawnmarket said that they would consider such a project during the quieter winter months. But most people would be quite content with one of their more affordable ready-made children's skirts.

Tartan naturally also figures strongly in the many souvenir teddies on sale. Some wear kilts or tam-o'-shanters and tartan sashes, and I came across others seated in tartan armchairs. I found teddies playing bagpipes (one, made of china, was actually a teapot), as well as tiny resin teddies in kilts.

The Royal Mile isn't all shops, however. It is full of historic buildings, interesting museums, closes and courtyards to explore, not to mention Holyrood Palace and the Castle. You would need at least two days to see it all. But even on a short visit you could take a look at a few of the courts and closes that are accessible to the public, and include visits to a museum or two.

Near the Castle, for instance, the Scottish Whisky Heritage Centre tells the history of Scotland's most famous drink. The Scottish Experience at 12 High Street offers the chance to see Scottish crafts in the making, to discover your own clan or tartan if you have Scottish ancestry, to study Highland Dress through the Ages and taste traditional Scottish foods while watching one of the various videos on Scotland. But it is the **Museum of**

Childhood at 42 High Street which will have the greatest appeal for all who love bears.

The bears themselves form only a small part of the massive collection which covers just about every imaginable aspect of childhood, from 'The Baby' to 'Schooldays' and 'Children at Work'.

Not everything is old. The 'Baby' section, for instance, includes a modern bib and disposable nappies. But it is the glimpses of the past that keep visitors to the museum enthralled.

A 'Food and Drink' display, for instance, takes us back to the days of sulphur and treacle or malt and cod liver oil, as well as the rather more pleasant (if ill-advised) sweet cigarettes. A display on clubs and collecting includes beautiful early greetings cards, cigarette cards and the Robertson's gollies, while a variety of old books and comics are used to take a look at reading and writing.

However, it is toys of every shape and form which naturally make up the greater part of the museum's collection. There are toys that move, musical toys, optical toys, farmyard animals, trains, die-cast model vehicles, puppets, toy theatres, board games, outdoor pastimes, pedal cars, dolls and doll's houses, to name just a few. Then, of course, there are the teddy bears.

A brief history of the teddy bear is included in a display of about thirty teddies, but there is little information on the bears themselves. Some are of considerable age, but there is also a more recent Toffee Bear, from Jane Alan's *Lulupet and Toffee* stories broadcast on *Listen with Mother* in the fifties. One of Wendy Boston's washable teddies can also be seen, along with some advertisements of the time.

Modern Pooh and Paddington Bears have been included, and there are also fund-raisers like Pudsey, the mascot of the 'Children in Need' appeal, and Jamie, who was made to support Edinburgh's own 'Help the Sick Kids' appeal.

Other soft toys in the museum include Dean's famous Dismal

Desmond, a Merrythought Jerry mouse (from the *Tom and Jerry* cartoons), and a number of interesting cloth dolls.

Among the cloth dolls by Dean's, for instance, are Lupino Lane (in his 'Lambeth Walk' costume) and one of the famous Betty Oxo dolls, obtained from Oxo in exchange for a number of cube wrappers or bottle caps. Three of Chad Valley's Prime Minister dolls are there (Lloyd George, Ramsay MacDonald and Stanley Baldwin), as well as some of their Bambina dolls and a Norah Wellings Red Riding Hood.

It is easy to while away many hours looking at all there is to see, including a shop which sells a variety of traditional toys and games, and a number of bears. (On my last visit, there were a handful of Steiffs – mainly miniatures – as well as some Muffys by the North American Bear Co. and some souvenir bears in Museum of Childhood T-shirts.)

Other teddy-related items on sale included some of the Winnie-the-Pooh range, as well as tins and postcards.

A rather different, but even better, hunting-ground for teddies and teddy-related items is the modern Waverley Centre in Princes Street, right by Waverley Station. It is full of the kind of speciality shops that encourage browsing, and teddy bears are everywhere.

Again, there are plenty of bears aimed at the tourist, with kilts and tam-o'-shanters very much in evidence. But **The Owl and the Pussycat** will appeal to more serious collectors as well.

Owner Alison is a keen bear collector herself, and is steadily increasing the range of collector bears she has for sale. She stocks Steiffs, including the limited editions when they are available, and has limited editions by Dean's as well as some of the Muffy Bears.

There is also a growing number of artist-made bears. I found some by Norbeary and H.M. Bears when I visited, as well as a number that were Scottish-made: by Dormouse Designs, The Little Workshop, Geraldine (who also has her own shop in Edinburgh) and the West Lothian-based Audrey's Bears. There were plans to increase the range considerably over the coming months.

They also have less expensive bears, and a whole range of teddy bear-related items, including a wide variety of teddy bear ornaments like the Colour Box miniatures and the Cherished Teddies.

Alison has another shop in the Waverley Centre, too. Called **Alison Original Drawings**, it specializes in prints of Alison's own water-colours. Among them are a large number of teddies, some of them given a Scottish flavour.

It is also possible to commission an original water-colour if you prefer. Alison happily draws her bears in all sorts of situations for customers wanting a picture for a special person or to mark a special occasion.

This second shop also stocks a number of other small teddy-related items, and generally has some souvenir teddies as well.

There are more teddy souvenirs throughout the shopping centre, with plenty of teddies in tartan togs as well as bear-sized tartan bags and shoes. I also found teddy teapots and teddy-sized baskets in the **Ross Cookshop**, teddy candles on offer from the candle specialist, and a whole shop devoted to rubber stamps, which included a variety of teddies.

Outside the Waverley Centre, Princes Street contains a number of other shops of interest to the bear lover. Again, any of the gift shops could have something teddy-related on sale. But when it comes to the bears themselves, **Jenners** (the world's oldest independent department store) has more to offer.

A Steiff Club Store, it naturally has a good number of Steiff teddies, among them some limited editions, bears in the Classic range and other collectables, as well as the soft and cuddly. There are Merrythoughts, too (although no limited editions when I visited), and a number of cuddly toys of other makes.

Another source of bears which could easily be missed is **Burberrys** and **The Scotch House**, both of which have bears made for them. The Burberry Bears include a range of Merry-thoughts in two colours and various sizes, sporting Burberry fabric on the paws and bows. They also appear in a special book, written and illustrated by Prue Theobalds. Stocks are largest at Christmas, but they generally have a few bears on sale at other times of the year.

Winnie-the-Pooh fans, on the other hand, will find bears and various other Pooh-related items at the **Disney Store**, also in Princes Street (nearly opposite Waverley Station). And there are more bears in **John Lewis**, which is situated in the new St James Centre, at the eastern end of Princes Street. The toy department in the lower basement sells a range of cuddly soft toys, but John Lewis also have some Merrythought bears made specially for them, which should have particular appeal for collectors.

There are more bears in the ground floor gift department – this time limited editions from various manufacturers. I found Merrythought and Dean's bears, as well as those Steiff bears made specially for the British market. Colour Box miniatures and Cherished Teddies were also on sale.

To the north of Princes Street is a very different Edinburgh from that found in the Old Town to the south. Here, in the eighteenth century, the elegant New Town was created. Orig-inally, it contained three parallel main streets – Princes Street, George Street and Queen Street – crossed by Castle Street, Frederick Street and Hanover Street, with Charlotte Square at the western end and St Andrew Square to the east. But it was soon expanded to the north, and it is here, in Dundas Street (a continuation of Hanover Street) that you will find more bears in **Geraldine's of Edinburgh**.

The airy basement shop sells both dolls and bears, made in their own factory behind the shop. It is not possible to see the bears actually being made, but a variety are on sale. Some have been given a distinctively Scottish touch, with tartan paws and bows or scarves. Others have tapestry pads, and there are hares with huge tartan-lined ears. But there are more conventional teddies, too, like the six- and seven-inch miniatures in either mohair or distressed cotton.

Geraldine has been making and selling her bears for ten years now, and the workshop can produce up to forty bears a day, although they rarely use its full capacity. Many are sent to America, while others go to shops and department stores in Britain.

There is a busy doll's hospital and bear repair service, too, and they are now turning their attention more and more to clothing for bears, in line with current trends. In fact, they will gladly dress a bear to order (either one of the bears on sale, or a collector's own bear). And if an owner wants something in tartan, such as a kilt, they would be happy to oblige.

Just ten minutes' walk away, on the other side of the Royal Circus, is Stockbridge, where you will find **Stockbridge Antiques**. A general antique shop, they sell both dolls and teddy bears, but the number of bears can range from about two to twenty, depending on what is available. They also have bear-sized carts and chairs, and other props that can help to create an interesting display.

ADDRESSES

Burberrys, 39–41 Princes Street; tel. 031 556 1252

Geraldine's of Edinburgh, 35a Dundas Street; tel. 031 556 4295

Jenners, 48 Princes Street; tel. 031 225 2442

John Lewis, 69 St James Centre; tel. 031 556 9121

Museum of Childhood, 42 High Street; tel. 031 225 2424 (closed Sundays)

The Owl and the Pussycat/Alison Original Drawings, Waverley Centre, Princes Street; tel. 031 557 4420

Stockbridge Antiques, 8 Deanhaugh Street, Stockbridge; tel. 031 332 1366

Tourist Information Centre, 3 Princes Street; tel. 031 557 1700

Glasgow

U nlike Edinburgh, where its seems that bears can be found at every turn, in Glasgow they tend to be very well hidden. But they are still there, for those who know where to find them.

Nevertheless, the city centre proved distinctly bleak for collectors when I last visited. **Frasers** department store in Buchanan Street did have some Steiffs and Merrythoughts in the toy department. But apart from one of the Steiff bears made specially for the United Kingdom the previous year, I found mainly soft and cuddly bears (including the Steiff Molly) and some of Merrythought's Heritage Collection, like the policeman and the beefeater.

There were Colour Box miniatures in the gift department, and there were more in the gift department of **Arnotts** in Argyle Street. But the only bears Arnotts could offer were some of those by Andrew Brownsword, which were on sale alongside the greetings cards.

Also in the centre of town, the Virginia Galleries at 31–33 Virginia Street boasts a doll and teddy hospital, and you may just find the odd bear among its craft and antique shops.

Unexpectedly, I found no bears in the modern Princes Square, which combines small specialist shop units with a number of market-style barrows. Dormouse Designs (see Quarrier's Village, page 337) did take one of the barrows for a while, but they are no longer to be found there.

One Princes Square shop which may be of interest to bear lovers is **Once A Tree**, where everything on sale is made of wood. The occasional item will feature a bear, but of possibly greater interest are their splendid wooden trains and other traditional toys which can add just the right touch to a teddy bear display.

Pinocchio's children's wear may include a suitable outfit for a special bear, too, and they also sell the odd cuddly teddy or teddy bear ornament.

Close to the shopping centre's Buchanan Street entrance, **Burberrys** also have some exclusive Merrythought bears. Stocks are biggest at Christmas, but they usually have a few on sale – in two colours and up to three sizes, with paws and bows specially made from Burberrys' own fabric.

It is away from the centre of town, however, that bear collectors will find a specially interesting Glasgow shop. **Acorn Antiques** is in Kelvinbridge – just five minutes by Underground from the town centre, with the shop just two hundred yards from the station.

It is not a shop dealing exclusively in bears. There is a good deal of interesting old china, too. But the shelves also hold various old teddies (although many are not for sale) and a number of modern, mainly artist-made bears.

Owner John Thompson is a great bear lover himself, and understands that collectors want something different. He contacted Scottish bear makers first, and ordered the first of a series of shop exclusives from the local Jay-Bee Bears, as well as some of the Romsey Bears (now designed and finished in Melrose, see page 332) and the distinctive Changelings, made in the Outer Hebrides.

Since then, however, he has been casting his net wider, and hoped to have extended his range considerably by the time this book appears.

Not far away, the **Sentry Box** – a toy shop in Great George Street (off Byres Road) – also has a number of bears, by Canterbury, Merrythought and Dean's for instance, although I saw no limited editions. I also saw some soft Steiff Petsy Bears, as well as various Dormouse Designs' soft toys.

Another source of bears is nearby Johnstone., just twelve miles or so by car from the city centre, or a fifteen-minute journey by train. Just opposite the station is the new **Growlies** shop.

Margaret McLean and Christine Gribbin had a shop in the city centre for a while, and then concentrated mainly on selling their bears at fairs. But so many collectors still found their way to their home that they decided another shop was the best idea.

There they now sell bears old and new, as well as various bear-related items and a few 'friends of bears' as well.

They try to have bears that collectors will find nowhere else, so alongside the Steiff bears are many artist bears exclusive to them – by Waifs and Strays, the Traditional Craft Company, and miniaturists Kathryn Riley and Katherine Rabjohn, for instance. They have bears by a number of American artists, too, like Mac Pohlen, McB Bears, Duck Soup, Susan Coe and Beth Diane Hogan. And there are non-exclusive bears by other British artists as well.

The bear-related items also include some that are available nowhere else, including postcards and pictures, and they are always looking for beautifully crafted items.

Each year Growlies also organize two teddy bear fairs in Glasgow.

Of course, Glasgow has much more than bears to see. There is a magnificent twelfth-century cathedral, and Art Nouveau buildings designed by the city's most famous architect, Charles Rennie Mackintosh. A splendid range of museums and galleries includes the new Museum of Comparative Religion. Or, if you want to get away from it all, there are paddle-steamer trips down the River Clyde.

ADDRESSES

Acorn Antiques, 350 West Princes Street; tel. 041 339 0616
Growlies, 15 Thorn Brae, Johnstone; tel. 0505 337373
The Sentry Box, 175 Great George Street (off Byres Road); tel. 041 334 6070

Greater Glasgow Tourist Board and Convention Bureau, 35 St
Vincent Place; tel. 041 204 4400

Lauder

The Royal and Ancient Burgh of Lauder has had a long and
colourful past. It is known that there were prehistoric
camps on the site, and by the twelfth century Lauder had become a 'Kirk Town'. In 1502 it was given the status of Royal
Burgh.

Several kings, both Scottish and English, have visited the
town during the course of its history, among them Edward I in
1296. The Scottish parliament met there on a number of
occasions, too. But today there is little evidence of its former
status. Its main street is still busy, but these days it is busy with
cars passing straight through,
barely noticing the existence of
a town which once boasted
two markets a week and six
major fairs a year.

Teddy bear lovers are different, especially the many
thousands who are also keen
collectors of **Colour Box Miniatures**, which are made in
Lauder.

The Colour Box range
includes a large number of teddies, each one a faithful copy
of a teddy bear in the Colour
Box Collection. In Lauder, it is
possible to see the miniatures

being made on certain days, while in the Colour Box shop in East End, it is possible to buy the finished pieces.

Sculptor Peter Fagan was one of the tourists who didn't speed through the town. He loved the rolling Borders hills so much that he decided to set up home there, and one Monday morning he stopped to look at Lauder.

He and his family fell in love with the town where time had stood still, and where the welcome was so warm and friendly. They bought a little cottage right on that main street.

For a while, Peter worked in a local factory. But he continued with various artistic projects in his spare time, and eventually began to make clan crests and coats of arms to commission. Then one day he saw some little bronze figurines in a shop and decided that was something he could do too.

Within three years, he had a staff of six working first in his house and then in a nearby barn. Later, some factory units were built in Lauder and the company, called Bronze Age, moved in there, eventually taking over all three.

When interest in the bronze figurines began to fade, Peter started making the tiny resin cats which would become the Home Sweet Home collection, and a new company called Colour Box was born. They added little animal scenes to the range, and some tiny animals and birds – known as Hopscotch Minis because they were sold at pocket-money prices.

Then, in 1986, Peter and his wife Frances made a fateful visit to Bruges, in Belgium. There, in a curio shop, they found four bears and fell instantly in love.

Frances loves to tell the story of how they bought three of them, but decided against the fourth as he was so much more expensive. The result was a sleepless night, and some anxious minutes waiting on the shop's doorstep until opening time the next morning, when they rushed in and rescued the remaining bear.

In 1988, the first of the miniatures appeared in the Colour

Box range. Since then there have been dozens more, and many others are waiting in the wings. Like so many collectors, Frances and Peter are finding that their collection is steadily trying to take over their whole house.

Peter first models each of the bears in Plasticine, working on a small table in an attic bedroom at his Berwick home. Then, back at the factory, a master mould is made.

To do this, a moulding box is fitted round the sculpture, and moulding rubber poured into it. The box is then placed in a vacuum chamber to remove any small air bubbles. It takes about twenty-four hours to cure the mixture. Then the Plasticine can be removed, to leave a finished mould. As every tiny piece of Plasticine must be picked out, this can take up to two days for a large sculpture.

The next step is to produce the first few whiteware pieces from the mould. These are then sent to be painted and, once Peter has approved the final result, full-scale production can begin.

Visitors to the factory are taken through the whole production process.

Obviously, with large quantities of miniatures being produced each day, the single master mould is not sufficient. So more must be produced, and these must be exactly the same as the original mould.

First a special non-shrinking epoxy resin is poured into the mould to create what are known as production masters. Several of these are then placed in a polystyrene box, and liquid rubber is poured in. After the air has again been removed and the rubber allowed to harden, the production masters can be removed to leave a whole block of moulds which will be used to create several miniatures at once.

Many more identical blocks of moulds will be made, with the number depending on the popularity of the piece in question.

To create the miniatures which will be sold, resin (mixed

with a catalyst to help it set) is poured into the blocks of moulds. Any air bubbles are removed, and the filled moulds are then passed through an oven before being left to harden. The resulting whiteware miniatures are those which will eventually go on sale.

First they are removed from the moulds and dipped into an acetone bath. This is to remove any shiny patches which would not hold the paint.

The next stage is the grinding down of the bases, a highly skilled operation where a false move can result in ground hands as well. The grinders use tape to protect their fingers, and a fast worker can smooth down the bases of 7,000 to 8,000 smaller pieces in a day.

The fettlers are next. They use dental tools to remove any imperfections in the whiteware pieces – another highly skilled process, which demands an intimate knowledge of the piece in question.

The resulting dust is then washed off (with acetone again, as it dries more quickly than water) and, after checking, the miniatures are ready to be painted.

A few of the designs are first spray-painted in the factory, and sometimes it is possible to see this being done. But most go straight to one of the hundreds of outworkers who paint each of the miniatures by hand.

Obviously, it is not possible to see this stage of the process during a tour of the factory. But each outworker has to be trained, and visitors are allowed a look at the training department, where there is usually plenty of work in progress.

In addition to the constant training of new painters, this department is where each new master is copied and the work timed to determine a suitable fee for the outworkers. With hundreds of new models being created every year, there will usually be plenty of opportunity to see a painter at work.

Tours of the factory take place on Tuesday and Thursday mornings, by appointment. But the Colour Box shop is open every weekday from 10.00 to 16.00 (15.30 on Fridays). There, collectors can generally find every miniature in the current Colour Box range. There are often some discontinued lines as well, which are welcomed by those with gaps in their collections.

Some of the Colour Box items made under licence by other manufacturers are also on sale, including the postcards published by Perspectives Photographics and some of the full-sized furry replicas of the bears made by Dean's. There is usually a painter on hand if anyone wants a specially personalized piece. And some of the original Colour Box teds are often there, too – happily playing in the old forge, which is one of the oldest buildings in Lauder.

Sadly, there are few other reminders of Lauder's past in today's town. The parish church, however, dates from 1673, and the old Tolbooth (just a few yards from the Colour Box shop) is thought to have made its first appearance in 1318. Unfortunately, it burnt down in 1606 and was rebuilt in 1773, although it is believed that the building standing today is very much like the original.

The Town Council met on the upper floor until 1975, while the ground floor was used as a gaol until 1843. Later, it housed Peter Fagan's first shop, and is still occupied by Colour Box departments today.

Another local landmark is one of the oldest and finest of Scotland's castles, **Thirlestane**, situated on the edge of the town. It has been home to the Maitland family since 1590. Visitors can see the room where Bonnie Prince Charlie slept in 1745. There are magnificent drawing rooms and state rooms. A kitchen, scullery and wet and dry laundries have been left much as they were in the nineteenth century, and there is an exhibition of Border country life.

But toy collectors will be more interested in the nurseries, which now house a large collection of around 3,000 Edwardian, Victorian and Georgian toys. Most are from the collection of

Mrs Marguerite Fawdry, owner of Pollock's Toy Museum in London, and they include about ten teddy bears as well as a hundred dolls.

ADDRESSES

Colour Box Miniatures, Orchard Estate (the shop is in East End); to book a factory tour ring Pat Learmonth on 0578 722725

Thirlestane Castle; tel. 0578 722430 (the castle is closed for several months of the year; at other times it is open on a number of afternoons each week)

Tourist Information Centre, Abbey House (opposite Abbey), Melrose; tel. 089682 2555

Melrose

The Borders town of Melrose is probably best known for its twelfth-century Abbey, founded by King David I, and for the vintage cars and motorcycles of the Melrose Motor Museum. It was also the birthplace of Rugby Sevens (dreamt up by a local butcher in 1883) and still hosts the Melrose Sevens tournament each April. The walled Priorwood Gardens are another popular attraction, and Sir Walter Scott lived three miles away, at Abbotsford, the splendid mansion he designed himself and which still houses his 9,000-volume library and such relics as a lock of Bonnie Prince Charlie's hair.

For teddy lovers, however, Melrose means just one thing – Scotland's Teddy Bear Museum, **Teddy Melrose**.

The museum was the brainchild of Felix Sear, who owned a shop in Jersey before moving to Melrose. His interest in bears began when he went to a toy auction intending to buy a train or a plane and came back with two bears instead. That was also where he realized that his own childhood bear, a Chiltern Hugmee, was something special in the eyes of collectors.

Felix can still remember travelling to Hamleys toy shop in London's Regent Street with his grandfather, who worked as an engineer on the Gold Coast but came back home for a month every Christmas. The bear they found was to be a fourth birthday present, and was promptly christened Hugmee. He has recently been joined by a number of other bears from the same manufacturer, and can be seen with them in the museum.

The museum is only small, and contains far fewer bears than that in, say, Broadway. But a good deal of thought has been given to the displaying of the bears, most of which can be examined very closely by interested visitors. Some background information is also included, so that the museum is not just a source of entertainment but has an educational side as well.

Each of the major British manufacturers has its own display.

There are Chad Valley bears of various ages, for instance, as well as a golly and two toy dogs made by the company, and a few of their other games and toys. The Merrythought display includes some of their Cheeky Bears in various sizes. There is also an earlier button-in-the-ear Merrythought teddy, along with one of their Yogi Bear toys, and the 1990 Jubilee Bear, made to celebrate the company's sixtieth birthday.

There are several early Dean's bears, too, and other Dean's soft toys, like a pair of dancing dolls, an early golly and the delightfully doleful Dismal Desmond (first introduced in the 1920s). Also included is one of the company's famous ragbooks, featuring a polar bear in the story.

Then there are the Chilterns, with Felix's childhood Hugmee joined by other early Chiltern bears as well as some later designs by Pam Howells. Pam is now a popular bear artist with her own Pamela Ann Designs (see Crowland, page 201), but she was once the chief designer at Chiltern's Pontypool factory. The display also includes one of the Teddy Edward books for he, too, was a Chiltern bear.

The House of Nisbet has its place in the museum as well. The company's popular Bully Bears are there – named after the late Peter Bull, who did so much to promote the teddy bear in Britain. So, too, is their Deli-Mascot, a mascot-sized replica of Peter Bull's Delicatessen, who starred as Aloysius in the television series *Brideshead Revisited*.

Other displays are devoted to character toys like Rupert, Paddington and Winnie-the-Pooh. The latter includes three bears made by J. K. Farnell, since it is believed that the original Winnie-the-Pooh was a product of the same company. Another section is devoted to Misha, the mascot of the 1980 Olympic Games in Moscow, and there is also a display of teddy bear cartoons.

A unique aspect of this museum, however, is a number of special panels devoted to some of the people who have played an important role in the recent history of the teddy bear.

Judy Sparrow, for instance, opened the very first Bear Museum, in Petersfield (see page 117), and also makes bears herself. In addition to information about Judy and her work, there is a photograph of the Petersfield museum, and one of her bears is on show.

Popular artist Prue Theobalds is represented by some of her work, and one of the Bo-Bears replicas of a bear called Theo. He features in a number of Prue Theobalds' drawings and is believed to have been made by Farnell.

Bear repairer and maker Brian Beacock is there as well. So, too, are some of the earliest dealers in teddy bears, and Wendy Phillips with her distinctive Lakeland Bears (see Bowness, page 268). Glenn and Irene Jackman, festival organizers and publishers of *The UK Teddy Bear Guide* and *Hugglets Teddy Bear Magazine*, also receive a mention, and there are panels devoted to a number of Scottish bear makers as well as to Colour Box miniatures, whose factory is in nearby Lauder (see page 327).

It is very much a look at British bears and the bear world in Britain – a fitting approach for an area which attracts so many visitors from abroad.

In addition, the museum shop stocks a variety of collectable bears – some from manufacturers like Merrythought, Dean's, Canterbury and Nisbet, others from British artists. In fact, many of the bears are actually made in Scotland, by a number of different Scottish-based artists.

There are various teddy-related items, too, like tins, notebooks, books, cards and Winnie-the-Pooh merchandise. And a tearoom offers teas, coffees and a variety of cakes, as well as a chance to sit and ponder over which bear is going to accompany you home.

Some of the bears on sale are actually made on the premises, and anyone interested in seeing how bears are made can watch maker Sue Nicoll at work in her basement studio.

Sue has been making bears and other soft toys for over twenty years now. In the late eighties, she set up her own Romsey Bears in Romsey, Hampshire. But when the museum in Melrose opened, she was invited to become their 'bear maker in residence'. Being of Scottish ancestry herself (her family comes from Coldstream), she was happy to return to her roots.

Now, a small band of outworkers continues to work on her Romsey Bears down in Hampshire. But all the bears are designed by Sue herself, and she also takes care of all the finishing. She joins heads, arms and legs to the bodies, inserts all the eyes and stitches the noses, as well as checking that all the bears come up to her standards.

Each is made in a limited edition of 500, with the number of each bear embroidered on the foot. (The outworker who cuts out all the bears also has an embroidery business, and can therefore add the numbers at the same time.)

About forty to fifty Romsey Bears are finished each week, and are sold at shops all over the country as well as in Melrose.

Many go abroad, too. They are especially popular in Holland, and increasing numbers are going to Germany as well.

Sue's arrival in Melrose also marked the start of a new phase in her career. Since visitors to the museum wanted to buy bears made on the premises, she introduced a new range of Border Bruins – with only the cutting out and the machining still done in the south, since that is where all the bales of fabric are kept.

Again, most of these bears are made in limited editions of 500, with large numbers sold elsewhere in Britain, and abroad, as well as in the Melrose shop.

Between the Romsey Bears and the Bruins, Sue expects to create some twenty new designs each year. It is not unusual for her to spend seven days a week at her work, often continuing until late at night. But she is still happy to answer visitors' questions, and to let them see how a bear is created.

The large number of visitors to the town also means that Melrose has a number of small gift shops, and invariably some of these will have teddies in some shape or form.

Sugar 'n' Spice in Abbey Street (off Market Street) generally has some souvenir teddies among its soft toys. (I found some sporting tartan togs.) They also sell Colour Box miniatures and other teddy-related gifts.

There are more Colour Box miniatures at **Abbey Crafts**, where I also found some musical teddies playing 'Scotland the Brave'. And the **Melrose Toy Centre** has a number of bears, among them some by Steiff and Merrythought, and the ever-popular Paddington who is such a favourite with tourists.

ADDRESSES

Melrose Toy Centre, High Street; tel. **089682 2424**
Teddy Melrose, High Street; tel. **089682 2464** (closed January)
Tourist Information Centre, Abbey House (opposite Abbey); tel.
  089682 2555

Quarrier's Village

Many bear lovers will be familiar with the name of Quarrier's Village as the home of the popular Dormouse Designs. But few will be aware of the fascinating background to this unique community, founded more than a hundred years ago by wealthy businessman William Quarrier near Bridge of Weir in Renfrewshire.

Quarrier was not born rich. His father was a ship's carpenter, who died of cholera thousands of miles from home, leaving his wife Annie penniless, and with three young children to care for back home in Greenock.

The family moved to Glasgow, where Annie took in sewing work. But she could never earn enough for her family's needs, and at the age of just seven, William himself started work in a local factory.

Even so, the family often went hungry. Annie was determined that her children's futures would be different, and at the age of eight William was apprenticed to a shoemaker.

It was sheer hard work that turned him into a successful businessman. By the early 1850s he had opened a shoe shop of his own, and by the 1870s that single shop had turned into a whole chain. But William never forgot his poor beginnings. His own memories and his strong Christian beliefs made him anxious to do what he could to help the poor children whom he saw on the city streets, and that work culminated in the creation of his own Children's City near Bridge of Weir in Renfrewshire, sixteen miles from the heart of Glasgow.

His aim was to provide some of the city's orphaned and abandoned children with a real home. So, instead of building huge dormitories to house them, he created a whole village of individual cottages – each one different. Each housed a small group of children, looked after by house-mothers and house-fathers.

Thousands of children passed through their care over the years until social changes led to the gradual disappearance of many such institutions, with foster-parents taking over their role. Quarrier's Homes gradually became Quarrier's Village, with some houses being taken over by small businesses, others being turned into craft workshops, and some becoming private dwellings.

Sue Quinn of **Dormouse Designs** moved in in 1983. She had designed and made soft toys since she was a child, and even started selling some while she was still at school. It was only natural that she would continue to do so after her marriage, and the birth of her son. He was just four, and not yet at school, when Sue moved her business to the Old Drapery in Quarrier's Village, once the place where clothes for the children were stored.

In those days, it was the Wildlife range which occupied most of her time, and the demand was so great that she soon started taking on other staff to help her. But she made teddy bears as well, and in 1983 she introduced her first signed and numbered edition for collectors.

Many more collectors bears have followed, some produced in sizeable limited editions, others as exclusive one-offs. But, unlike the Wildlife range, virtually all the work on the bears is carried out by Sue herself. While her helpers turn out up to a hundred animals a week – rabbits, sheep, mice and the like – Sue will produce anything from one to ten of her bears, accepting help only with such minor but time-consuming tasks as turning the pieces the right way out, packing and labelling the bears, or perhaps putting on their clothes.

Certainly, no one else is allowed to touch any of the bears' heads, and you're more likely to find Sue helping out on the Wildlife production line than to find anyone else helping out with the bears. Instead she'll take work home, and spend her evenings inserting eyes and sewing noses in order to keep up.

Luckily she works very fast, since much of her time is taken up with administration, not to mention all the designing of the animals and overseeing the work on them. She has also written books on teddy bears and other soft toys. Yet still she finds time to send bears to shops all over the country. Many others, however, are sold by Sue herself at fairs, as she loves to meet the collectors themselves and hear their reactions to her work.

Both bears and animals are also on sale in her own **Chest of Bears** shop in the Old Drapery itself, although stocks are sometimes limited, due to the constant demands of other shops for more of her work. Collectors planning a visit are therefore advised to telephone in advance, to make sure that an urgent order hasn't removed just the bear they are after. In general, however, the shop contains a variety of Dormouse Designs, as well as a few other bear-related items like brooches and books.

In the adjacent workshop, visible from the shop, visitors can see Sue and her team at work, making and dressing the animals and bears to fulfil the next urgent order.

Downstairs, a craft shop offers a whole range of local crafts – pottery, jewellery, candles and so on. When I was there, none of the items on sale featured bears. But the range is changing all the time.

There are a total of forty-three cottages in the village. It has its own church and restaurant, and everywhere are trees and well-kept lawns. Its tranquillity makes it the perfect setting for a craft-based business, and this unique village is definitely not to be missed if you are in the area.

ADDRESSES

Dormouse Designs, The Old Drapery; tel. 0505 690435
Tourist Information Centre, Town Hall, Abbey Close, Paisley;
tel. 041 889 0711

Traquair House, Innerleithen

Dating back more than a thousand years, **Traquair House** in Innerleithen, Peeblesshire, is one of the oldest inhabited houses in Scotland. It has been visited by at least twenty-seven Scottish monarchs, and has strong associations with Mary, Queen of Scots. But it is a link with Charles Edward Stuart, better known as Bonnie Prince Charlie, which will be of greater interest to bear lovers.

He visited the house in 1745, during a recruiting drive prior to his march south. The Earl of Traquair promised his support and, when his guest departed, he swore that the gates he had passed through would not be opened again until a Stuart King was once more on the throne.

He had expected a wait of just a few months. Two centuries later the gates still remain closed.

It is those gates which will be of interest to bear lovers. For on top of each gatepost is a large stone bear. The gates were built in 1739, and the bears represented the bears that were once hunted in the surrounding forests, in the days when Traquair House was used as a hunting lodge for the Kings and Queens of Scotland.

The stone bears still guard the main avenue leading to the house. Today, however, the house is approached by a second drive, lying alongside the original avenue and known even now as 'the temporary drive'.

Among the house's other attractions are a maze and various craft workshops, including leather working, silk-screen printing, pottery and wood turning. There is also an eighteenth-century working brewery, where the renowned Traquair House Ale is produced as well as a draught ale which can be found in local pubs. Called Bear Ale, it has an alcohol content of 5 per cent and is said to be a strong, Scottish bear-like brew!

The house can be visited during the summer months, but opening times vary. So it would be wise to telephone for exact details before travelling.

In the nearby small town of Innerleithen, it is also possible to see an old printing works in action during the summer months.

ADDRESSES

Traquair House, Innerleithen; tel. 0896 830323
Tourist Information Centre, High Street, Peebles; tel. 0721 720138 (April–October)
Scottish Borders Tourist Board Tourist Information Centre, Murray's Green, Jedburgh; tel. 0835 863435/863688

Part Three

EVENTS FOR BEAR LOVERS

Teddy bear festivals and picnics are now regular occurrences all over the country, but it was not always so. When the first Great Teddy Bear Rally was held at Longleat, the Wiltshire home of the Marquis of Bath, in 1979, *Time* magazine devoted a whole page to the phenomenon, under the heading 'Arctophilia Runs Amok'. Dutch television audiences were treated to extended coverage of the event, too – with astonishment in every frame.

Nearly 10,000 people attended the rally, some travelling from as far afield as America and Australia. Visitors were invited to bring bears dressed as the Marquis of Bath, who himself decided the winner.

This was not, however, the first teddy bear event in Britain. It is possible that that honour goes to the small Norfolk village of Brundhall, which included some teddy bear competitions in a fund-raising carnival in 1970. It attracted some 1,500 teddies and their owners.

Teddy bear competitions were a feature of most of the early rallies and picnics, which were often fund-raising events for various charities. For the payment of a small fee, bears could be entered in such categories as Biggest, Smallest, Oldest, Most Well-Hugged, Most Travelled or Saddest Bear.

Usually, there would be stalls selling bears, bear wear and other teddy-related items. But these events were for all bear lovers, including children, and not just for serious collectors.

Throughout the eighties, more and more organizations started including teddy bear picnics in their programmes of fund-raising activities. Often these were very small events, with perhaps one or two stalls in addition to the competitions. But every so often a major event would bring bear lovers from all over the country, eager to meet others who shared their interest. A Bears' Bank Holiday was held at Longleat in 1981, for instance, and in 1984, an International Teddy Bear Rally took place during the International Garden Festival at Liverpool.

Organized by the International Teddy Bear Club, the two-day programme of events included a Teddy Bear Trade Fair, selling a wide range of 'bear necessities', a teddy bear hospital, teddy portrait painting, book signings, parachuting teddies, puppet shows, readings from *Winnie-the-Pooh*, and the New Vic Theatre Company presenting the Teddy Bear Olympics.

The following year, the International Teddy Bear Club organized a whole Teddy Bear Tour, with picnics at some fifteen different venues, culminating in a two-day International Teddy Bear Reunion at Longleat. One popular feature was the display of celebrity teds – bears of the famous, including Margaret Thatcher's Humphrey and a number of bears of the royal household.

Today, teddy bears' picnics are still enormously popular with fund-raisers. But in January 1986 a new kind of event was held at the London Hilton in Park Lane. Called the International Teddy Bear Club Convention, it brought together a large number of teddy-related stalls in an indoor setting. The picnic image was gone. Although various other attractions were included, this was a fair where serious buying could be done.

It would be more than three years, however, before the first of the annual British Teddy Bear Festivals was organized on August Bank Holiday Monday, 1989, at Kensington Town Hall. More than eighty stands sold bears old and new, large and small. Some of the earliest bear artists were there, while other stands offered a huge range of bear-related items. Bear repairers were on hand. Free valuations were offered, as well as help with identifying and dating bears, and a series of talks offered a chance to relax for a while before returning to the serious business of bear buying.

Since then, the event has grown steadily. So has a Winter

BearFest, introduced the following February in Stratford-upon-Avon and eventually moved to Kensington when it became too big for its original venue. In 1993, the first Festival of Artist Bears was held at Stratford, in response to the massive increase in demand for such individually made bears. A Golden Oldies festival, with the emphasis on older bears, was also held.

By then, however, numerous other specialist teddy bear fairs were on the calendar. For years, bears had been forming an increasing part of many antique doll and toy fairs. Then, more and more specialist teddy bear fairs started to appear. Today, collectors have a wide range of events to choose from in most parts of the country.

There have also been Teddy Bear Conventions, with days of talks and discussions preceding a teddy bear fair. Bear-making workshops are becoming increasingly popular, while Teddy Bear Weekends combine visits to places of interest with various talks and the opportunity to meet and 'talk bears' with other enthusiasts.

Hugglets Teddy Bear Magazine (see Publications, page 353) gives a comprehensive list of bear fairs in each issue, as well as information on many more general fairs at which bears can be found. They publish information on many forthcoming workshops, and also organize Teddy Bear Weekends for their readers.

For information on some of the smaller events (including most of the picnics), however, you will need to check the local papers of places you are visiting. (Tourist Information Centres may have details of some local attractions.)

Below, you will find a list of just some of the organizers of regular events at which bears are on sale. However, with new fairs appearing all the time, at new venues, it cannot be comprehensive.

SPECIALIST BEAR FAIRS

'Bears Only' Fairs, 221 Cherrywood Road, Bordesley Green, Birmingham B9 4XD; tel. 021 7720910

British Bear Fair, Shelley House, 104 High Street, Steyning, West Sussex, BN44 3RD; tel. 0903 815622/816111

Growlies of Glasgow, 11 Springfield Woods, Ravenscourt Park, Johnstone PA5 8JR; tel. 0505 37373

Hugglets, PO Box 290, Brighton, BN2 1DR; tel. 0273 697974

Ironbridge Toy Museum, The Square, Ironbridge, Shropshire TF8 7AQ; tel. 0952 433926

Rochester Teddy Bear Fair, 68 High Street, Rochester, Kent ME1 1JY; tel. 0634 831615

Mary Shortle, 9 Lord Mayor's Walk, York; tel. 0904 425168/ 631165/634045

Town & Country Bear Fairs, Mrs P. Paulett, Hill Cross, Ashford, Bakewell DE45 1QL: tel. 0629 812008

Ursinus Fairs, 39 Foreshore, London SE8 3AQ; tel. 081 692 9797

OTHER FAIRS WHICH INCLUDE TEDDY BEARS

Antique Toy and Doll Shows Ltd, The Old Workhouse, Ducks Hill Road, Ruislip, Middlesex HA4 7TS; tel. 0895 675558

East Midlands Doll Fairs, 1 The Hallards, Eaton Socon, St Neots, Cambridgeshire PE19 3QW; tel. 0480 216372

Granny's Goodies, PO Box 734, Forest Hill, London SE23; tel. 081 693 5432

Leeds Doll, Teddy & Toy Fair/Tyneside Doll & Teddy Fair, 5 Mariners Cottages, South Shields, Tyne & Wear NE33 2NG; tel. 091 455 2463

WORKSHOPS AND BEAR-MAKING COURSES

Margaret and Gerry Grey, The Old Bakery Gallery, 38 Cambridge Street, Wellingborough, Northants NN8 1DW; tel. 0933 229191/272123

Deborah Canham, 2 Whittingham Road, Collaton Park, Yealmpton, Devon PL8 2NF; tel. 0752 872601

Lynda Graves, Higher Knapp Farm, Sidbury, Sidmouth, Devon, EX10 0QG; tel. 0395 597720

Maddie Janes, The Orchard House, Rhiews Bank, Market Drayton, Shropshire TF9 3RQ; tel. 094 876 242

Vanessa Littleboy, 10 Morgan Way, Heritage Park, Telford, Shropshire TF1 4FB; tel. 0952 257868

ORGANIZATIONS

British Teddy Bear Association, PO Box 290, Brighton BN2
  1DR; tel. 0273 697974
Good Bears of the World (UK), c/o Audrey Duck, 256 St
  Margaret's Road, Twickenham, Middlesex TW1 1PR; tel. 081
  891 5746 (evenings) (*Charitable organization distributing bears
  to comfort those in need*)
British Bear Club, Shelley House, 104 High Street, Steyning,
  West Sussex BN44 3RD; tel. 0903 815622

PUBLICATIONS

PERIODICALS

The UK Teddy Bear Guide, published annually by Hugglets, PO Box 290, Brighton BN2 1DR; tel. 0273 697974 (comprehensive list of shops, bear makers, museums, fair organizers, repairers, sources of bear-making supplies and other bear-related businesses)

Hugglets Teddy Bear Magazine, published quarterly by Hugglets, PO Box 290, Brighton BN2 1DR; tel. 0273 697974

Teddy Bear Times, published bi-monthly by Ashdown Publishing, Shelley House, 104 High Street, Steyning, West Sussex BN4 3RD; tel. 0903 815622

BOOKS

The Brilliant Career of Winnie-the-Pooh, Ann Thwaite (Methuen)

British Bear Artists, Margaret McLean and Christine A. C. Gribbin (Growlies of Glasgow, page 325)

Button in Ear: The History of the Teddy Bear and his Friends, Jürgen & Marianne Cieslik (Marianne Cieslik Verlag)

Collecting Teddy Bears, Pam Hebbs (Collins)

Steiff: Sensational Teddy Bears, Animals & Dolls, Rolf and Christel Pistorius (Hobby House Press)

The Teddy Bear Encyclopedia, Pauline Cockrill (Dorling Kindersley)

Teddy Bears, Judy Sparrow (Bison Books)

Teddy Bears & Steiff Animals, Margaret Fox Mandel (Collector Books)

Teddy Bears & Steiff Animals (Second Series), Margaret Fox Mandel (Collector Books)

Teddy Bears, Annalee's & Steiff Animals, Margaret Fox Mandel (Collector Books)

Teddy Bears Past & Present: A Collector's Identification Guide, Linda Mullins (Hobby House Press)

Teddy Bears Past & Present Volume II, Linda Mullins (Hobby House Press)

The Ultimate Teddy Bear Book, Pauline Cockrill (Dorling Kindersley)

A good selection of books on teddy bear collecting is available from the Mulberry Bush in Brighton (page 73), who also have a mail order service.

INDEX

355